SHORT
AND
SWEET

SHORT AND SWEET

The Life and Times of the Lollipop Munchkin

JERRY MAREN

WITH STEVE COX

FOREWORD BY SID KROFFT

CUMBERLAND HOUSE
NASHVILLE, TENNESSEE

For my beautiful sister Rae Allison, who sent me to the Wizard.

And for my lovely wife, Elizabeth Barrington Maren;
she is my angel and my love for life.

SHORT AND SWEET
PUBLISHED BY CUMBERLAND HOUSE PUBLISHING
431 Harding Industrial Drive
Nashville, Tennessee 37211

Cover design: Gore Studio, Inc. | www.gorestudio.com
Book design: Mary Sanford
Cover photos: Turner Entertainment Company; Warner Home Video; author's collection

Library of Congress Cataloging-in-Publication Data
Maren, Jerry, 1920–
  Short and sweet : the life and times of the Lollipop Munchkin / Jerry Maren ; with Steve Cox.
    p. cm.
  Includes index.
  ISBN-13: 978-1-58182-543-5 (pbk. : alk. paper)
  ISBN-10: 1-58182-543-9 (pbk. : alk. paper)
  1. Maren, Jerry, 1920– 2. Actors—United States—Biography. I. Cox, Stephen, 1966– II. Title.

PN2287.M4827A3 2007
791.4302'8092—dc22
[B]

                                                                    2008001236

Printed in China
1 2 3 4 5 6 7—13 12 11 10 09 08 07

CONTENTS

At a reunion for the cast of *H.R. Pufnstuf* at Planet Hollywood: Jack Wild (holding the original golden flute prop), Marty Krofft, Billie Hayes (Witchiepoo), me, and Pufnstuf (Van Snowden inside the costume).

FOREWORD
BY SID KROFFT

I'm absolutely honored to talk about Jerry Maren. He is and always was such a gentleman, and so professional when we produced *H.R. Pufnstuf* and *Lidsville* for television. I distinctly remember the first time I saw Jerry in the movies.

I've always had a love for little people, because my favorite movie of all time is *The Wizard of Oz*. In 1939 when it opened, I was ten years old and my dad took me to see it. We stood in line, actually waited almost all night, in Providence, Rhode Island, where it was playing at the Majestic Theatre. The movie was just mesmerizing to me. The three most amazing movies of all time for me, were *The Wizard of Oz, Gone with the Wind,* and the first *Star Wars.*

Little people have played a big part in my life and career. I'm a fifth generation puppeteer, my father's father and so on. They did a full production with ballets and operas, and then Marty and I did a show called *Les Poupées de Paris* that really put my brother and me on the map. That played in Seattle, the New York World's Fair, off Broadway, and in Las Vegas. It played to nine and a half million people in almost eight years. It was completely a show in marionettes, in the style of the Folies Bergère. You had to be twenty-one to see it. It wasn't vulgar, but there were some adult themes and humor—a lot of T & A, but with very attractive and lifelike puppets. It was a huge production that took three months to install; we had elevators and waterfalls and a swimming pool and an ice rink. It was Walt Disney himself who gave my brother and me the advice of putting our name above everything we created. Sid & Marty Krofft's *Les Poupées de Paris* was absolutely the show that put our name on the map.

Billie Hayes (Witchiepoo) with puppeteer and producer Sid Krofft today.

There's a great story that happened when we opened at the Seattle World's Fair and the show became the hit of the fair. Marty and I owned the show, and *we* couldn't even get our friends in to see it, because it was sponsored by the fair and they didn't sell advance tickets. People got in line first thing in the morning to get tickets. The theatre was so different. You sat in a French garden and the stage was like a turntable. When the show started, the audience started to revolve around to the front, and the girls (the puppets) came out of the ceiling.

It was Billy Graham who made the show famous, because he cut the ribbon at the Seattle World's Fair. Billy Graham was brought in to our theatre to see the show and the whole audience went backstage after the show to see all the girl puppets. Billy Graham that night had a rally of 100,000 people in the coliseum there, and he announced that everybody should go to the fair, and told how beautiful it was and all. But he said don't go see a show called *Les Poupées de Paris*, because the women do not wear bras. Well, it hit *Time, Newsweek,* and *Life,* and Sid and Marty Krofft became a name.

In all of our puppet shows, we always secretly had a little person on strings, in a suit, who was the same size as the marionettes. We had a number where that "puppet"— because the audience assumed it was a marionette—would tear the strings down out of the proscenium or bridge where the puppeteers were working and start walking on his own. It was a very grande noir type of scene, very dark. The puppet walked to the front and over the orchestra pit and an elevator would take him down and he'd walk up the aisle with all the strings dragging behind him and then we'd drop him into a trap door in the middle of the aisle and he would totally disappear. It was the biggest hit in our show. The audience would freak out. Some people thought it was a radio controlled puppet. And when the people would come backstage, there in a box, displayed on a shelf, was a copy of that puppet just laying in there . . . and they were left wondering. It was quite magical. We never released to the press or anyone else that a little person was involved.

The Wizard of Oz has permeated my life in strange ways and intermingled in my career. I toured with Judy Garland as an opening act for a year and a half, and that was a trip. It was an awesome responsibility and experience. I sat down with her many times and asked her about *The Wizard of Oz*. I used to dress in her dressing room, and sometimes I took her to work and brought her home. We became real pals—and Liza, I used to bring her down to the beach. She wouldn't bathe and I used to throw her in the ocean. She was just a kid of ten or twelve years old. That was an interesting family.

When I traveled with the Ringling Bros. circus, I worked with one of Jerry's compatri-

ots in the Lollipop Guild. Harry Doll was a member of the Doll Family, a family of four midgets: Harry and his three sisters. Harry was in the Lollipop Guild, right next to Jerry. His sisters were Gracie, Daisy, and Tiny, and they were all Munchkins too. They toured with Ringling for years, and when I traveled with Ringling, they were my best friends. I was with Ringling for two years as the World's Youngest Puppeteer, at seventy-five bucks a week, which was a lot of money back then. I choreographed a number for them and they performed it for audiences in the sideshow. I also helped design some of their costumes, little top hats and tails. They were wonderful people.

My years and experiences with Ring-

With cast members from the Krofft TV movie *Side Show*.

ling were made into a movie Marty and I produced called *Side Show,* which we made for NBC television in the late '70s. Jerry played a midget sideshow performer in the movie, along with another little person, Patty Maloney. We had the tallest woman in the world, Sandy Allen, in the cast and a legless woman, too. It was a delicate thing to historically depict "freaks," as they were called years ago in sideshows. Naturally, Jerry was such a pro and did so well with his part, just as I'd expected.

In the Saturday morning television shows that Marty and I created and produced, we were inspired greatly by *The Wizard of Oz.* Living Island, Witchiepoo, the talking trees, that's where all of that came from. We had a whole troupe of midgets working on our shows; I don't know how many, but we employed many little people working here in southern California for several years. I also remember Harry Monty, a great midget stunt man who was also a flying monkey in *The Wizard of Oz.* Harry was a brave, strong little guy. We had him on wires dressed as a goofy bat, knocking into walls, in *H.R. Pufnstuf.*

Margaret Hamilton was on episodes of *Sigmund and the Sea Monsters,* and what a thrill it was to work with her; she was a tiny, gentle little lady. Not a midget of course, just much smaller and delicate than you'd think when you met her in person. She was so genuine and unlike the Wicked Witch from the film. I couldn't help but talk with her about Judy and *The Wizard of Oz.* As you can see, *Oz* was always something of an inspiration, and I took it along my own path.

I always say, wherever you go, where most people turn right—then go left. I've always told my friends that. If there's a left-hand turn, take it. I lived in Hawaii for eight years, in Maui, and I learned that everybody went right. And if you went left, you would discover the most incredible things. If there's a left turn—take it.

Way back in 1938, Jerry took that left out of Boston.

ACKNOWLEDGMENTS

There are so many people to thank in one's life, I don't think I can cover them all in a list. So for those friends and acquaintances I have forgotten to mention, please forgive me and know that I am grateful to you. Meantime, I'd like to present one giant lollipop to all of the following folks . . .

I thank my late sister Rae, who always stood by me, and my wife, Elizabeth, who loves me no matter what. I'm grateful to so many of my little friends: Billy Barty, who introduced me to golf; Billy Curtis, who led me to gamble and smoke cigars (I know he sounds like a bad influence, but he was one of my best friends in life and I miss him); and my pals Nels Nelson, Harry Monty, Felix Silla, Frank and Sadie Delfino, George Ministeri, Victor and Edna Wetter, Patty Maloney, and too many more to list. Thanks also to the fellow Munchkins I reunited with in 1989 and have traveled and appeared with for more than fifteen years: Nita Krebs, Meinhardt Raabe, Gus Wayne (and his wife Olive Brasno Wayne), Margaret Pellegrini, Mickey Carroll, Ruth Duccini, Karl Slover, Clarence Swensen, Emil Kranzler, Lewis Croft, Johnny Leal, Tommy Cottonaro, Alta Stevens, Jeanette Fern, Betty Tanner, Jeanie LaBarbra, Hazel Resmondo, and Mary Ellen St. Aubin (wife of Munchkin Pernell St. Aubin). And my old friend Steve Cox, who found all of us Munchkins and put us on the map again fifty years after we made *The Wizard of Oz,* made this book possible.

I want to express gratitude to my friends Andy Williams, Chris Bearde, and Ted Schulz for much employment over the years. I should acknowledge organizations such as

the Oscar Mayer Company and the McDonald's Corporation for lengthy employment in my past. A big Munchkin cheer to all of the *Wizard of Oz* annual festivals (and the organizers, sponsors, and volunteers) who have repeatedly welcomed us Munchkins over the years to their fair cities: Liberal, Kansas; Chittenango, New York (birthplace of L. Frank Baum); Chesterton, Indiana; Grand Rapids, Michigan (hometown of Judy Garland); and Wamego, Kansas.

I know it is not possible to recognize the photographer and contributor of every single image found inside this book; however I want to thank those whose names I have kept track of and those who generously contributed photos and materials from their private collections to make this a better book: Warner Bros Inc., Academy of Motion Picture Arts and Sciences, MGM/UA, 20th Century Fox Film Corporation, Universal Studios, Paramount Pictures, Sony Television, Little People of America, Andy Williams, Ted Turner, Roger Mayer, Ralph Zellum, Sid and Marty Krofft, Craig Sopin, Randal Malone, Mike Malone, Stephen Barrington, Kevin Marhanka, Mike Mikicel, Gary McCarthy, Ed Sweeney, John Fricke, Bob Moore, Vanguard Photography, Daniel Kinske, Fred Hendrickson, Bert Cooper, Robert Corless, Trig Svendsen, Maceo Sheffield, Lee Weinstein, Kats Tyler, Ginny Royston, Willard Carroll, Ray Savage, Larry Barbier, Carla Sellers, Gordon Dean, Bob Satterfield, Elaine Willingham, Tina Cassimatis, Dan Thome, Liza Minelli, Jean Nelson, Dave Butler, Berliner Studio, Bonnie Towman, Eric Daily, Roy Barlow, Delmar Watson, Tod Machin, King Moody, and Peter Ferman.

A great big Munchkin salute to my publisher, Ron Pitkin, and editor/designer Mary Sanford, who both love *The Wizard of Oz* . . . and Toto too. I thank you all "very sweetly for doing it so neatly."

A Short Life and a Merry One

A few years ago, I was sitting in a quiet, darkened theater looking straight ahead at a particularly tense moment in *The Passion of the Christ*. I was taking in this breathtaking movie with Jerry Maren and his wife. We were all caught up in the drama and the emotion of the film, but suddenly Jerry leaned over, nudged me, and said aloud, "Yep, that's a midget!"

I don't think Jerry realized he'd pierced the silence of the theater. But he was right. Mel Gibson had cast a middle-aged European bald midget as Satan (in the guise of a creepy baby/midget type creature) for this motion picture blockbuster. It was a first in film history, I suppose . . . a midget playing the devil.

A lot of people assume the word *midget* is a bad word. I'm here to tell you that's not necessarily so. Of course, it's all in the usage. Semantics and societal correctness has attempted to erase the word *midget* from common use and has substituted the blanket description "little people" in for good measure. Today, it's "vertically challenged." Tomorrow, who knows? Times change and people have become sensitive . . . you know, sticks and stones

One of Jerry's first publicity photos after landing in Hollywood.

and all that. But have we become overly sensitive? Ventriloquists now prefer their dummies to be called "ventriloquial figures." But why must the word *midget* be tainted? I say it shouldn't be. Should only midgets be allowed to utter such a term? Naahhhh, that's not a solution. Besides, midgets are an extreme rarity in society today. You don't hear the word often because you don't come across a midget often.

The term *midget* took root centuries ago and stayed for the long haul; it simply signified any person of normal proportion standing under four feet. The word *midget* has long signified that type of dwarfism where the individual is affected by an underactive pituitary gland so that they are smaller, but perfect in proportion—a miniature human being. *Dwarfism* is an umbrella medical term that includes hundreds of different types, and currently the more populous group of little people—known as achondroplastic dwarfs—have a differing body makeup from that of midgets, mainly due to genetics. History has seen giants and it has seen midgets. And unfortunately, midgets are a dying breed because of advances in the field of hormones. There will come a day when there are fewer than a handful of pituitary midgets in the world.

The actors who portrayed Munchkins in *The Wizard of Oz* were billed as the Singer Midgets. (Not because they sang—although some did. They were named for their manager, "Papa" Leo Singer, the man who formed the troupe of performers.) Singer and MGM Studios in 1938 deliberately preferred proportioned midgets for their miniature denizens of Oz instead of dwarfs. Little did they know that the word *Munchkin* would take on its own mainstream meaning following the film. MGM and Singer blatantly discriminated against dwarfs; unfortunately, that was a common practice in that era of motion picture making. Years ago, the world's population included many more midgets than today. But back then, there were scores of midget performing troupes and midget circus clowns, who toured Europe in the 1800s and into the mid-1900s; it was a novelty act that successfully entered American vaudeville circuits. Members of the surviving American troupe, Hermine's Midgets, worked in television up until the early 1970s. Today, dwarfs are more prevalent in the entertainment industry. (Think of the actors who portrayed the Oompa Loompas in the film *Willy Wonka and the Chocolate Factory,* or actor Verne Troyer as Mini-Me in the *Austin Powers* flicks.)

Inside these pages are the fascinating stories and eye-popping images that comprise the short life (and merry one) of one of the most famous midgets of all time, a man named Gerard Marenghi who came from Boston, moved to Hollywood in his teens, changed his name to Jerry Maren, and lived out the ultimate Tinseltown dream. Jerry's life and show business experience is unlike that of his famous pint-sized predecessor from the 1800s—the legendary General Tom Thumb, one of P. T. Barnum's stars. You see, Jerry's career has been caught in photographs, on film, on tape, and in every other contemporary media,

Jack Carter, Milton Berle, Steve Cox, and Jerry at a St. Patrick's Day party. Jerry came dressed appropriately, of course.

for posterity. It's a thumbprint in history like no other. Today, Jerry is in his eighties, and he reflects on the decades with great pride and a deserving sense of accomplishment within his chosen field. He achieved a lasting fame that few actors ever experience.

I think I'd trade six feet for that, too.

He was, of course, the Lollipop Munchkin who put his dancing lessons to good use right there for Judy Garland's eyes on the immense yellow brick road. This was his first film. As Dorothy Gale from Kansas opened the door to Munchkinland, she was also opening the door on Jerry's career. The rest is a sweet swirl through the decades. Jerry ended up as maybe the most beloved Munchkin of them all. Who hasn't been charmed by that tough little guy with the crooked face who presents Dorothy an oversized treat in maybe the most widely seen motion picture of all time? There are no phrases to catapult *The Wizard of Oz* into a more classic, more revered status than it already possesses. So, for Jerry Maren, *Oz* was not a bad start, huh?

Still with that glint in his eye, Jerry has opened up the personal archive of his life and career and presents it here to each of us. It's some sweet pop culture eye candy, I might add. This amassed scrapbook of rare images is a treat, an unparalleled journey into the world of show business the likes of which you will never see again.

The AMC Theatres put on a big *Wizard of Oz* event in Fort Lauderdale in 1998 and four Munchkins appeared: Karl Slover, Jerry, Margaret Pellegrini, and Clarence Swensen.

I must warn you: Jerry's a man of few words. So you're getting lots of pictures.

It's only fitting. Because of Jerry's size, he has been cornered and caught by cameras all of his life; so he made friends with the lenses. Years ago, he learned early on to accept it and clown in Kodachrome; today, he mugs for megapixels. He's as captivating a figure in pictures as an old gentleman as he was as a teenager bouncing around Stage 27 at MGM made up as a Munchkin.

Unveiled in this extraordinary archive covering the life of midget Jerry Maren are rare photographs dating back to the late 1930s. Jerry takes you behind the scenes of his world. Thankfully, he scrupulously saved an enormous file of photographs throughout his career and together we have carefully culled this collection of notable moments. These are career highlights—and some lowlights—which will give you a peek into an authentic and most unique Hollywood star. He worked with so many greats in the entertainment world: Groucho Marx, Judy Garland, Bob Hope, Lucille Ball, Mel Brooks, Jonathan Winters, Elizabeth Montgomery, Johnny Carson, and Jerry Seinfeld, just to name some biggies. Jerry has never said it himself, but he is a true pioneer in children's television, having worked in the medium from its inception. Take a look inside, you'll see some of the magic.

In his own words, Jerry's unusual perspective on life and a multidimensional career that spanned sixty years is now shared here for the first time in this memoir. He doesn't apologize for using the word "midget." He doesn't have to. Nor does Jerry attempt to offer you some over-dramatic story of courage . . . you know, the story of a downtrodden little guy who rises from the rubble, beating the odds, fighting society's injustices and shutting down stereotypes . His way was to quietly lead a respectable life and along the way he was lucky enough find work that suited him. Raised as a Catholic, Jerry has never professed to be a religious sort, but I suspect he realizes how blessed he was in his life. And as a role model for others, Jerry has been exemplar. Yes, he is a charter member of an incredibly elite group of diminutive humans on this earth right now, and a fitting subject for this beautiful photoretrospective.

From *Oz* to *Seinfeld,* Jerry reminisces about it all with unusual candor and a cache of photography that will illuminate this fascinating man's years in front of the cameras.

At a Munchkin reunion at the Culver City Hotel in the 1990s. Jerry's at the front of the conga line; behind him are Margaret Pellegrini, Mickey Carroll, Ruth Duccini, Clarence Swensen, and Karl Slover. This is the last hurrah, the final group of Munchkins to tour the country at *Oz* events.

We Three Munchkins: Jerry, Margaret Pellegrini, and Harry Monty posed for this picture when they were interviewed for a local Los Angeles television station in 1995.

Jerry's a humble guy by nature, not a loud, boisterous and overcompensating type. I've walked with Jerry through airports and I've seen children's eyes widen when they see this little man and his little wife in tow. When he's introduced as a Munchkin from *The Wizard of Oz* . . . the Lollipop Munchkin, people's daily worries seem to vanish and nostalgia overwhelms anyone in his presence. I've seen it many times.

I first heard about Jerry when I was a kid growing up in St. Louis. One of my dear friends was Mickey Carroll, a Munchkin from *Oz* who was living in my own hometown. (Believe me, the experience of watching *The Wizard of Oz* on television during its annual broadcast with a Munchkin was something quite sweet and memorable . . . almost always surreal.) I'd always asked Mickey who the other Munchkins were and where they were today. Mickey only knew the whereabouts of one other . . . Jerry Maren. They were pals on the set back then, but it'd been years since they'd been in communication. Eventually, I contacted Jerry and put these two pals in touch after nearly five decades.

When I actually met Jerry, I was about fifteen, not that much taller than him and unable to drive a car yet—so my father drove me to the downtown St. Louis area, where Jerry was staying in our gateway city for a St. Patrick's Day promotion with the Anheuser-Busch company. He was making an appearance and doing press at a local pub as a Leprechaun, complete with prosthetic makeup (a special makeup man had been flown in), pointy ears, shoes, and the green custom-fit costume. I remember his high-rise hotel room overlooked the old Busch Stadium, and he marveled at the view that extended over and seemingly into the massive baseball stadium all lit up and offset by the black Midwestern sky. Jerry couldn't have been more hospitable to this inquisitive young fan and his father as we talked *Oz* and took pictures. I was amazed that Jerry came prepared with a few signed photos for me. When we were leaving, he pointed to a complimentary gift basket full of beer and peanuts on the desk which Anheuser-Busch had sent to his room. Since Jerry was never a drinker—beer never appealed to him—he generously sent the package home with my dad.

Jerry and I stayed in touch over the years, through high school and college, and every time I caught a TV appearance of his, I'd call and tell him so. As the fiftieth anniversary of *The Wizard of Oz* approached, as well as my graduation from Park University in Kansas City, I sprung the news on my pal, Mickey: I was going to write a book about the Munchkins and locate all of the surviving actors whom he'd worked with back in 1938. Both Mickey and Jerry were delighted that their work would finally be recognized and supported me in this project around every corner. But I think they were skeptical, much like the rest of the little people from the movie. Who would buy a book written just about the Munchkins?

The year-long celebration surrounding the golden anniversary of *The Wizard of Oz* included the publication of this unique look at Oz: *The Munchkins Remember* (later revised as

On the set of the 1969 movie musical *Hello, Dolly!*

The Munchkins of Oz). Jerry Maren was an integral source and a supportive force who constantly encouraged me during this arduous process. He led me to other Munchkins, such as Nels Nelson, Billy Curtis, and others. It was a rough pathway, but one Munchkin led me to another . . . sort of like following a yellow brick road, I remember thinking. At that time, I discovered just over thirty of the midgets from *Oz* surviving in different areas all over the United States (of the 124 who worked in the movie), and today, there are fewer than ten. Curiously, the book has remained in print all of these years. The great and powerful Oz knows no bounds. And now, I'm so glad Jerry has agreed to finally tell his story.

I toast "Little Jerry" (as he sometimes calls himself) for being a humble man, a devoted husband, a talented sportsman, a pretty good gambler, and a great friend. Jerry gambled on a career and a life in Hollywood. I'd say his odds were pretty good because there's no question that he took home the prize. I'm sure he could teach us all a thing or two.

SHORT
AND
SWEET

1

GOOD THINGS COME IN SMALL PACKAGES

I GUESS IT CAN BE considered the curse of being the baby of the family. I'm the last of twelve children, and the sole survivor in my family. I watched them all go before me. I'm now nearing my nineties and lately I've been reflecting on my own past more and more.

I was born on January 24, 1920, to Raphaela and Emilio Marenghi. My given name is Gerard Marenghi, a true Italian, and I was born at 301 Highland Street, Roxbury, Massachusetts, a slender three-story brick building with a cellar below. Roxbury is a suburb of Boston. I was the last of twelve children, and the only little person. (I used to tell people that when my father got around to me, he ran out of gas.) I was named after my Uncle Gerard, my father's brother, and a few years after I began work in films, I shortened my name to Jerry Maren.

My father was a hardworking shoe-factory employee. He was extremely strict. I rarely

saw any affection shown between my father and mother. I don't think I ever saw them kiss. But there must have been some sort of interaction between them because they ended up having twelve kids. In my family were Fanny, Angela, Raffaella (who we called Rae), Rose Anna, Anita, Johnny, Guy, Emelio, Joseph, and me. One of the babies had died. The rest of my brothers and sisters were of normal height, or let's say average height. Both of my parents came from Naples, Italy. On their honeymoon, they immigrated to America, in search of that better life that they'd heard so much about. They put down roots in Boston in the late 1800s. My father was an experienced shoe worker, so he got a good job at a place called the Plant Shoe Factory. We went to mass every week at All Saints Church in Roxbury, where I was baptized and got first communion and confirmation.

▲ My mom *(center)* with me and my brothers and sisters. Standing are John, Anna, Anita, Helen. Ambrose is on the left and I'm on the right, the baby of the family.

▶ This is my mother and father. I rarely remember my father being affectionate to my mother, so this picture is unusual for our family.

4

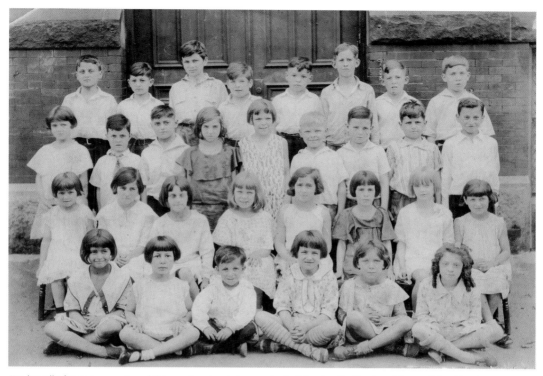

I'm literally front-row center of this grade school class portrait at the Lucille Crocker Primary School in Boston. I'm about ten years old here.

I'd say I was much closer to my mother than to my father. He'd lift his hand like he was going to hit me, but he never did. It was his way of warning me. I'd run around and get under the table and he couldn't get me under there. I think there was something of a communication gap between my father and me. He spoke Italian so much that when he combined it with English, I misunderstood a lot. One time he went to a cowboy movie and in it the cowboys were coming down from the mountain into the valley and yelling "I found gold! I found gold!" My father thought they were saying *va fangul* which in Italian means, "F— you!" He also used to yell at me, "Gerard, I'm gonna breaka yer head!" when telling me not to play ball so close to the street. At home my parents spoke Italian most of the time. Not me; I grew up speaking English. I didn't understand Italian very well, but I could understand the expressions. There were times I had no idea what they were talking about, but I could tell by their tone.

My father hated three things: he hated baseball; I loved baseball. He hated gambling; I loved gambling. He hated the movies; I loved the movies. Anything we didn't make money at, he disliked. He had no use for it. My father was a hard-working man, and he was pretty strict, but he had to be with so many children. For dinner he wanted everyone at the table so we could all be there as a family. As a shoemaker in a factory, he kept a roof over our head, and we always had meals on the table. It got crowded in our house, so a few brothers slept in beds together. I slept with another one of my brothers. Sometimes, when it was really cold, I'd sneak in with my sisters, because they were always warmer.

My mother did not work outside the home. With ten kids, she had to be at home. We were lucky. My mom was always cooking, washing, and keeping the house clean. She was an excellent Italian cook; I remember lots of pastas with thick noodles, sometimes spaghettini, fresh homemade ravio-lis with goat cheese inside of them, sometimes spaghetti with home-made sauces, and it was great to dip some homemade bread into the sauce. At holidays we ate well. Christmas was not a huge thing in our house, but Easter was. We all got new clothes on Easter. My mother was a devout Catholic, but my father was not as religious. We went to church every Sunday. School was more respectful back

This was my childhood home on Highland Avenue in Roxbury, Massachusetts, taken about ten years ago. I think the building might be gone now.

then. We dressed in decent clothes, respected the teachers, and minded them.
We made sure our fingernails were clean. I
was a very good student at school, but I
hated bookkeeping; I loved geography
and history.

When I was about eleven or twelve,
we noticed that I wasn't really growing
much. My parents did some unconven-
tional things to help me grow—nothing
too extreme. My mother used to give me
Scotch Emulsion. It was white stuff in a
little bottle that was supposed to make

With my brothers Joe and Emelio and my sisters Rae and
Anita in the 1970s.

you grow big and healthy. Someone recommended it as a home remedy. I hated the taste
of that stuff. It was terrible. So I took the bottle one
day and I hid it outside by some rocks.

I think I got along being a little person because
I was surrounded by normalcy. I had ten brothers
and sisters, and they didn't let me get too spoiled.
I learned to get along with my size, so it didn't
really bother me that much. If I
wanted a drink, I had to find a
way to get up to the cabinet to
get a drinking glass. If I needed
to use the phone and it was too
high, I found something to help boost me
up.

This is my first publicity
photo, eighteen years
old and dancing in a
vaudeville revue in
Massachusetts. The act
was called "Three Steps
and a Half."

Years later, when I met other little people
on the set of *The Wizard of Oz,* a few little
guys told me stories of their parents doing
some bizarre things to make
them grow. Gus Wayne told me

With my mother in the 1940s when she came to California.

his parents sent him to a treatment center that literally put him on "the rack," where they tried to forcibly stretch you by pulling your arms and legs. Little Karl Slover's parents in Europe tried placing him in a barrel filled with coconut oil and coconut leaves, and immersed him from the neck down, because someone told them that would help him grow.

My parents made the decision to look for a doctor who might help me. Physicians were nothing new to our family. My sister, Rosie, was very ill; she had throat cancer. So my father took her several times to a specialist in New Hampshire and I went on the trips and would sleep in the car on the way home. Those treatments didn't work, and she died. She wasn't even twenty-one. That was the first death in our family, and probably the first big shock of my life. I remember we had her casket inside the house and people came by and visited. That's the way it was done back then.

I was diagnosed as a pituitary dwarf, just a miniature guy with normal body features. My growth hormone was stunted. The most common form of dwarfism is called achondroplastic, and those who have that are noticeably different because of their shorter arms, larger heads, and features that are not really in perfect proportion. Achondroplastic dwarfism is hereditary. Pituitary dwarfism is not; at least most of the time it's not.

Around age fifteen, I was still in school and I was taking injections for a couple of years. It was something from sheep or goats. Twice a week I'd take a bus to the hospital and get that shot. There was no immediate effect, other than I hated going to get the shots and I hated needles. It took time away from playing baseball, something that I dearly loved. When the rest of the kids got older and weren't playing ball anymore, I became the team manager for other teams. I was trying to work around my height as best I could. No, I wasn't the butt of jokes back then. I can't understand it. I can't complain. I didn't have kids picking on me because of my height. I don't know why, but it just didn't happen. Maybe because I had a lot of older, bigger brothers? Who knows. I got into a few fights with other kids, you know—the normal stuff of kids—but it was never about my height.

I asked my doctor, Dr. Aub (at the Collis P. Huntington Hospital), if I could stop getting the treatments. He told me that it might only make me four or five inches taller in the end, so I figured the treatments I'd already had were enough and it wasn't worth the trouble. Nothing was happening. Plus, it was still experimental. I encouraged my mother to cease the injections.

About that time, my mother urged me to put down the baseball glove and take up dancing lessons at a local theatre. My sister Anita and I used to go to the Gertrude Dolan dancing school. My sister Anna was a good dancer and she was in the chorus line. When they had recitals, I went, and it got me interested in going too. I started the dancing lessons with my sister; they were the cheap lessons, you know, with a group. I learned how to dance, tap, and move somewhat gracefully. Eventually they had me do a number on my own, my first song. It was called, "I Like Bananas Because They Have No Bones." I did a little dance with these floppy oversized shoes and it went over well. Later I did a number called "Wa-Hoo," with the group singing behind me, and we were all dressed as cowboys and cowgirls. I was doing recitals every year with the dance class, and I later did an act on my own and traveled.

My first dance teachers were Johnny Mack and Gertrude Dolan. They asked me one time if I'd want to do an act with them one summer, so we toured New England in an act called "Three Steps and a Half." I was the Half. It was my first professional engagement making money. I was getting paid—that was the big thing. Someone saw me in the act and sug-

I don't want to give anyone the idea that I was in the movie *The Terror of Tiny Town*. I wanted to be in that movie, but my father wouldn't let me.

9

In 2002, my wife and I celebrated my sister Rae's ninetieth birthday.

gested that I contact another little guy in Massachusetts named George Ministeri regarding some new movie about to begin production. It was called *The Terror of Tiny Town,* an all-midget musical western. Really! George Ministeri was a little guy who remembered seeing my picture in the newspaper and recommended me.

Later we received word from a producer in Los Angeles named Jed Buell who was producing this all-midget western. This was in early 1937, I think. My dad said, "What, am I gonna pay two hundred dollars to send you out there, no meals, no hotel . . . and then you make fifty dollars a week? Besides, you're in high school and you're not missing any of that." So the whole thing was nixed. I didn't get to do that, but I sure wanted to.

I continued to dance in the act and go to school. My sister Rae, she was my encouragement. She rehearsed with me at home. We had a big piano on the second floor. She wasn't an entertainer or musician really, but she knew what was good and she helped me. She made sure I had my wardrobe. In fact, it was my sister Rae who got me the role in *The Wizard of Oz* and who pushed me on my way to a career in movies. I called her Baby. I did until the day she died in 2006. She was the last surviving member of my family.

Memories from Rae Marenghi Allison

We had a nice neighborhood, mostly Irish, some Italians. We weren't rich, but we never went without. We had a three-story brick building and nine stairs out front. Everyone got along in our neighborhood, and on hot summer nights we had lots of people out on our steps and the neighbors would talk. We'd make sandwiches and watch the kids playing out in the street, playing ball and all those childhood games. There would be guys with carts that came by and sold bananas . . . they couldn't sell during the hot days. We didn't have TV or radio in those days.

My father made wine in the cellar, and the whole family helped out. Trucks would come with the grapes and we'd haul them down into the cellar. Kids would come and my

◄ Not quite twenty and starting my career as an actor in Hollywood. My portraits started reflecting more adult poses by this time, even though I was as small as a ten year old.
▲ Me and my sister Rae. I was just over 3 feet tall then.
▶ This little scrap of paper changed my life: This is the original newspaper clipping which caught my sister's eye and landed me in Oz.

25 pounds in the first 10 days . . . Thyra Samter Winslow and Lawrence Riley oughta make up their minds . . . Darryl Zanuck returns Aug. 9, a week before "Alexander's Ragtime Band" is released . . . Mervyn Leroy needs 100 midgets for "Wizard of Oz," address him at MGM / Music Corporation of America's deal with the Feldman Blum agency calls for M. C. A. to represent them in Europe, New York and Chicago bookings.
* * *

Here is the group of us on our way across country from New York to Hollywood to make *The Wizard of Oz*. I was one of the youngest—and smallest—of the travelers.

father would hand out a bunch of grapes to all the kids who came by.

We all worked as teenagers. My brothers all worked in suit factories. We all pitched in. We went to the same grade school and then Jamaica Plain High. Jerry was always the pet in school. A few times, I took him to his dance classes, and when he got out it would be snowing like crazy outside, foot of snow. I had my snow slippers on, but he didn't bring any snow shoes, so I would put him on my back and he'd ride piggyback all the way home. I loved that.

We used to go to the Rivoli Theatre and the Supreme Theatre nearby, and Jerry's first job was handing out flyers there at the theater and nearby businesses.

MGM had placed an ad in the newspaper that they were looking for little fellows to appear in The Wizard of Oz. *It said to send a photograph and name and address, which I did. Jerry didn't know about it. I didn't have a photograph of Jerry, so I went down to the Roxbury Crossing, to the photographer who had taken pictures of his dance group. I ordered some more pictures. There were four of them, and I mailed them to MGM in Culver City. Later on, we received a telegram from Leo Singer; we were thrilled. We knew it was going to be the opportunity of a lifetime. My father agreed to let Jerry go because they agreed to supply transportation and meals and hotel during the movie and six weeks employment.*

I took Jerry down to the garment district to buy a suit; the pants were too long, so we had to have it custom fit. Jerry met Leo Singer in New York City with all the other little people and they went from there.

✦ ✦ ✦

We got a Western Union telegram from Loews Incorporated/Metro-Goldwyn-Mayer with instructions to meet Leo Singer in New York for the trip out to California. (In those days, you have to remember, when someone got a telegram, it usually meant somebody died. When the telegram arrived I thought, oh God, everyone's going to be miserable tonight. That was what was going through my head.) It said I would be under the supervision of Leo Singer, the great midget impresario who traveled the country with his famous troupe of midget performers.

My offer was supposed to be like $50 a week plus transportation, meals, hotel, etc. Later on, when I was cast as one of the Munchkins with lines, my pay was upped to $75 a week. I think Singer may have actually taken $25 out of that though. I don't remember exactly, but I do recall that he took a piece of it.

I was off to California, but first I had to meet a group of others in New York. I never saw another midget in person until *The Wizard of Oz*. I saw a few in the movies, I think, but not in person. My eyes lit up. I wondered if they walked like me. Did they have a high-pitched voice like me? Do they eat the same things as me?

I took a train to New York and we first stayed at the Park Central Hotel. I wanted to have some food sent up to the room because I'd seen it done in the movies. I picked up the telephone and ordered room service and had them bring up hot chocolate and donuts. I still remember that.

✦ ✦ ✦

I was three-foot-six when I made *The Wizard of Oz,* and I had never laid eyes on another little person. So when I joined the cast of midgets for the movie, I was astonished that several came right from my area, like George Ministeri and one of the Lullabye League, the tiniest one in the middle, Olga Nardone, another Italian midget like me. She's from Boston, too. Little Billy Rhodes was from Massachusetts. Come to think of it, Ray Bolger and Jack Haley were both from the Boston area too, and when we met at MGM we talked about that. I could tell other Bostonians from their accent.

I remember the bus trip from New York City to Los Angeles as being long and not much else. About thirty of us were in the bus, along with a few taller people who worked with Singer and had to help organize this bunch. Most of the midgets were older than me, I remember that. Just a few of us were in our teens.

The Wizard of Oz was one of the greatest contributions to the golden age of Hollywood and fantasy. For me, the Munchkins represent a large part of that iconic period and spectacular time in film history.

—STEVEN SPIELBERG

Singer's people were cheap, and they were kind of pressed for rooms in a few of the cities we stopped at during the trip across country, so we had to double and triple up in rooms. I made friends with two guys named Leon Polinsky (we called him Leo) and Gus Wayne from New York, and we routinely stayed in rooms together on the trip. When we got to Culver City, they doubled and tripled us up in rooms, too, so we all shared a room at the Culver Hotel. The three of us slept in one large bed. The Culver Hotel was not far from the studio.

On the cross-country bus trip, a lot of the midgets warned me about Leo Singer, and there were lots of stories going around about how he cheats his foreign midgets and that he's a "son of a bitch." There were stories that he'd gather these midgets from Europe and then take them to America, where they'd be totally dependent on him from

14

"We wish to welcome you to Munchkinland."

An Oklahoma newspaper photographed us during our brief stop en route to Hollywood.

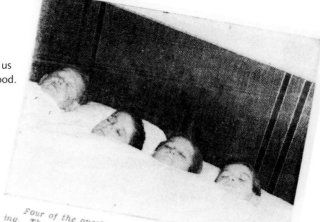

Four of the guests could sleep in one bed without crowding. The sleepers, left to right, are Ike Rogers, 37 years old, 42 inches tall; Jerry Marenghi, 18 years old, 40 inches tall; Gus Wayne, 22 years old, 37½ inches tall, and Prince Leon, 21 years old, 39 inches tall.

This rare behind-the-scenes photo shows a huge group of us Munchkins on MGM's Stage 27 surrounding our producer Mervyn LeRoy, Judy Garland, and director Victor Fleming (holding Toto). Mervyn LeRoy is looking directly at me in the front row.

In Hollywood with the neighbor's dog. You can see I wasn't much taller, standing about 3-foot-six back then.

there on in. My situation was so different that I don't think I was that worried about it, but I listened to all the stories and I was wary of him.

When we arrived in Culver City, it was very early in the morning. Most of us went to bed, and about 9:00 a.m. I heard a huge band playing outside our window, down in the street. It was loud. I got up out of bed and ran to the window to see what it was . . . it was a big parade. I woke up the other guys and said, "Hey look at this, they're welcoming us to Culver City." Then after closer observation, I noticed it was Armistice Day. I thought it was just for us! That was my first morning in California, November 11.

In the movie we had 124 midgets and about a dozen children, little girls, who were kept mostly in the background so as not to ruin the illusion of all Munchkins being midgets. The group of midgets were from all over the country, guys from Texas, New York City, Louisiana, the Midwest, Okalahoma. It floored me that several came from Texas. I thought everybody was big and strong in Texas! Some of the midgets had German accents, mostly the little people from Europe that Singer had brought over with him. You knew who were Singer's midgets from their accents, and most of them lived with him and his wife at their home.

Once we were at the studio and rehearsing, some of us were lined up and sized up to portray specific Munchkins. I was chosen to be one of the little tough guys, as the script called us. On

My first taste of sunny California. I arrived for *Oz* and never left.

either side of me were Harry Earles (sometimes called Harry Doll) and Jackie Gerlich. We were about the same height and the director, Victor Fleming, made us the Lollipop Guild, with me in the middle carrying the lollipop. We had a few weeks for wardrobe testing, some makeup tests, and rehearsals.

As soon as I heard the music around the piano during rehearsals, I loved it. I knew it

was going to be a hit. Harold Arlen was there, and Yip Harburg. I remember seeing them, and some others who played the piano and rehearsed our songs. Script pages were handed out, and we each had these two mimeographed pages. All the songs were lively, you know, "Ding-dong the Witch Is Dead . . ." and "Follow the Yellow Brick Road." While we did sing along on the set and the music played in the background, we found out later that our voices were dubbed by professional singers and the tones were altered to sound high-pitched and cute. Only a few actual midgets' voices were used, recording the lines "We thank you very sweetly, for doing it so neatly." and "You killed her so completely, that we thank you very sweetly."

▼ The camera captures a dance sequence as some of us watch in the foreground. You can see the back of my head right in the center as I watch the action going on.

▲ A group of us Munchkin men on the backlot of MGM during the production of *Oz*. I'm one of the youngest.
◄ Judy Garland and her mom pose in the new portable dressing room the studio presented to her while working on *The Wizard of Oz*. One day, we all streamed in and out of her dressing room, in single file, while Judy signed photos with a fountain pen and gave them to us as gifts. She was a sweetie.
► A rare behind-the-scenes image of a group of us gathered on the Munchkin set.

Judy Garland was just an average teenager. Granted, she was on her way to becoming a huge star in the movies, but she never acted like it. Remember, I grew up with several teenage sisters, so I had something to compare her to, and she was just lovely. We didn't see much of her because she had schoolwork to do. When she arrived in makeup and wardrobe ready to go, she'd wave at all of us and say "Hi, gang!" As soon as she was finished with a scene, they would grab her and bring her back to her school room. We wanted to chat with her, and sometimes during the "down time" on the set she'd sit on the steps and talk with some of us Munchkins. She was a star then. For Christmas, she had all of us stream into her new dressing room on wheels, which was parked on the side of the set. She sat and autographed an 8 x 10 for each one of us, and that was our gift that we took home with us.

My dancing teacher in Boston had some friends named Tommy and Margie

THE LOLLIPOP GUILD: SWEET SAMARITANS OR HALF-PINT HOOLIGANS?

Okay, there's simply no way to candy-coat this theory: Was the Lollipop Guild there to greet Dorothy as the city's goodwill gang, or rather, were they representing the mysterious Munchkin Mafioso? The Shorty Sopranos?

It all fits.

An examination of some of the film's scripts, specifically the two-page mimeographed pages handed to the little actors creating the citizens of Munchkinland, shows clearly that the Lollipop Guild were actually known as the three "Little Tough Guys." Another studio reference has them as the "Little Tough Boys." How ironic, especially considering that earlier that same year, a popular movie starring the famous street gang known as the Dead End Kids (aka the Bowery Boys) was released under the title "Little Tough Guy."

However, this band of inner-city Munchkins didn't wield baseball bats for protection—their weapon of choice was a big swirly lollipop. (No one was gonna lick them.) And consider their threads. Ever wonder why the Lollipop Guild dressed in rag-tag street clothes with torn cutoff shirts and shorts and mismatched garb? Yes, they

were the Munchkin society's underbelly, tiny thugs even. Munchkinland possessed every sector of society; while the Lullabye League represented the city's sweetest, the Lollipop Guild represented the city's meanest.

Not convinced? Watch the scene again: one of them, in the scrappy blue, emerges from a manhole—and smoking, no less! They were rebels, the type Cagney would

MUNCHKIN MAFIA: Harry Doll (sometimes known as Harry Earles), Jackie Gerlich, and I were the Lollipop Guild. (I'm in the center holding the lollipop.) This is a rare wardrobe test photo taken during pre-production in the fall of 1938 at MGM Studios.

have enlisted. There is no question that these were Munchkinland's version of baby-face gangstas, real bad boys barking orders out of their crooked mouths like Edward G. Robinson in "Little Caesar." Yeah, see?

Were they really small-time hoods, there to strong-arm the Wicked Witch if things went south? You decide. But remember, they couldn't have been all bad if they were handing out all-day suckers.

—STEVE COX

Farmer, who came to see me at the hotel after the first week and offered to have me stay with them in Hollywood at their home. I had my own little room, and they treated me pretty good and helped me a lot. Sometimes they drove me to the studio, and sometimes I took a bus back to Hollywood at the end of the day. At the Farmers' I would write home and tell my family how much I missed them. At the same time, I was so excited about working at the studio, the greatest studio of them all—MGM—that it truly erased any homesick

Just before filming, a man would hold out a "lilly" which was used for white balance and proper color coding for the Technicolor cameras rolling at the time. This rare shot on the set has me tickled by the whole thing, for some reason.

feelings. We had to get up early and work hard all day at the studio, so there wasn't a whole lot of time for extra stuff, maybe only on the weekends. And I even remember working on some Saturdays.

Meeting Hedy Lamarr

When we worked on the set of *The Wizard of Oz,* we were told to stay on the set. Victor Fleming, the director, told us, "Don't get lost, because if we have to go get you, it's all day." So I didn't stray much. I understood. But after lunch one day, I had about ten minutes to spare and I wanted to look around the lot and see some things.

I was walking around some soundstages when I saw one of those big heavy doors on the soundstages and I opened it up. Just as I was opening it, somebody was pushing it from the other side. And there stood one of the most gorgeous creatures I had ever seen. I thought, "Oh my . . ." I was speechless. It was Hedy Lamarr. She had a sarong on and she was filming *Lady of the Tropics.* It really was my first sight of a huge star on the lot, outside of Judy Garland, and even Judy wasn't the star with a name that she later became. We eventually had many stars visit our massive Munchkinland set: Spencer Tracy, Wallace Beery, Myrna Loy, Robert Young. So many of the actors wanted to see the sets and they wanted to get a good look at 124 midgets dancing around in our colorful wardrobe. I'm sure it was like a circus.

Little Rumors

So many people ask me about crazy things. There were some drunkards among us; one guy named Kelly started some problems on the set and in the hotels. He was in the middle of a messy divorce, and he got rough with his wife, Jessie, one of the little ladies. Prince Ludwig, a handsome little guy in a suit, had a cane. He was always drinking and always had to go to the toilet. He was a townsperson in the scene. There were two Irish twins named Mike and Ike who

▲ A rare 1939 color Kodachrome of me next to the Rudolph Valentino memorial in De Longpre Park in Hollywood, down the street from where I lived. The statue is still there today, only the park is now overrun by crack addicts and homeless people.
▶ A rare shot without my lollipop.

25

I dressed as Mayor of the Munchkin City at the film's premiere at Grauman's Chinese Theatre in August 1939. Here, fellow Munchkins Billy Curtis, Victor Wetter, and I pose with producer Mervyn LeRoy and actor Wallace Beery and his daughter, Carol Ann.

got drunk pretty often, too, but for the most part we were all well behaved and acted very appropriately.

I was really attracted to one little blond gal named Jeanette Fern. I didn't know how old she really was. In fact, she was still fourteen, but Singer had claimed she was older. She was about my height and probably the first little gal I ever had a crush on. We did an act together a few years after we made the movie, and over the years we kept in touch.

I had to get up so early every morning to drive to the studio, and it was one of the coldest winters ever in L.A. It was rainy some days, miserable. I have to admit, even though I was excited to be working on a motion picture, and everything was still new to me, it didn't temper the fact that the makeup process was a real pain in the ass. We'd go downstairs, below street level, and there was a series of makeup chairs, maybe twenty-five, with a makeup man at each one. They'd group us next to our makeup man. We had to put on a skullcap, makeup, a colorful wig, more makeup, striped tights, etc. I was in more damned scenes, so I was always the first one ready. I wanted to be seen. They had me running everywhere . . . run up the stairs . . . jump up and down at the good witch's bubble (jumping at nothing). I was the first one out in front. They fresh-

At the premiere of *The Wizard of Oz* at Grauman's Chinese Theatre. Munchkin Tommy Cottonaro is on the left, and Nona Cooper and Victor Wetter are also on hand. Here, we are greeting actress Billie Burke, who played Glinda the Good Witch.

ened up our makeup after lunch, and by the time the end of the day rolled around, removing the glue and skullcaps was sometimes painful because it was near the hairline and you were pulling out hair at the same time. Our heads would get sweaty underneath the skullcaps and makeup during the day, so the entire makeup routine was definitely not that pleasant.

Margaret Hamilton was a lovely lady, even in the witch's outfit. Her makeup preparation was done separately and actually took much longer. She didn't scare any of us. To us,

Greeting Chico Marx at the premiere of *Oz*. It was a star-studded night with lights, red carpet, and cameras flashing everywhere. I had already worked with Chico in the Marx Brothers movie, so this was a reunion for us.

Margaret (some called her Maggie) was a sweet lady who would talk with us on the set and sit down and chat even though she was covered in that horrid green paste. One day, that paste nearly took her life. She had an accident on the set where she was burned from the flames when she disappeared in her exit. The trap door didn't work right and she was burning up down below. We didn't really know what was going on at the time, but we found out more of it later on. Her makeup was toxic, and if the makeup man hadn't gotten it removed quickly, she might have died. Her scene was in the can, thank God. That was her last day with the Munchkins.

The rest of us Munchkins worked almost a full two months until some last-minute things in January. During the production, we met the other stars when they'd visit the set. I remember Jack Haley brought his young son to the set, and I think Victor Fleming's children came by too. Mervyn LeRoy, the producer, was on the set occasionally, but I don't recall him being there that often. I remember taking photographs with Fleming, Leo Singer, and Mervyn LeRoy on the Yellow Brick Road for the studio photographer.

When the film opened at the famous Grauman's Chinese Theater on Hollywood Boulevard on August 15, 1939, I was hired with a few other midgets to portray Munchkins out front and entertain the crowds, take photos with the arriving celebrities, and such. The MGM wardrobe department handed me the Mayor's costume, and I had to add some stuffing around my stomach to fill the vest and pants and make it look real. Billy Curtis, Nona Cooper, Tommy Cottonaro, and Victor Wetter all joined me (along with Toto) in posing for photographs outside the theatre that night. It was a huge gala that I'll never forget. The klieg lights were blaring up into the dark sky, and more movie stars than you can imagine showed up. It was magical.

Tribute to Oz Ready

The world premiere of "The Wizard of Oz" will be held tonight at Grauman's Chinese Theater before an audience including innumerable stars of the motion-picture industry.

Hedy Lamarr, Joan Crawford, Wallace Beery, Orson Welles, Harold Lloyd, Pete Smith, Benny Goodman, Eddie Cantor, Virginia Bruce, Eleanor Powell, Frank Morgan, Claudette Colbert, Bert Lahr, Ray Bolger, Margaret Hamilton, Miliza Korjus and Clark Gable are among those who have told the studio—M.G.M.—that they will be present.

Also at the premiere will be Mrs. Baum, widow of the author, who lives in Hollywood, and Fred Stone, who created the Scarecrow character on the musical stage in 1902.

Emphasizing the return of Hollywood to the type of gala premiere which made the city famous, the theater lobby will be decorated with the cornfield of Oz, and tiny midgets, who play Munchkins in the picture, will appear as attendants.

I'VE BEEN DOWN THIS YELLOW BRICK ROAD BEFORE!

I wish I could stay and have a long conversation with each and every fan of *The Wizard of Oz* who has approached me with wide eyes and curious hearts. I'm flattered that I get recognized. I get questions about *Oz* just about everywhere: restaurants, airports, and elevators. Unfortunately, there's just not enough time to answer every question in person, in every situation. I don't recall all of the day-to-day activities of making the movie; remember, it was made seventy years ago. That was a long time ago. It's not that I don't remember it at all, I do: It was the thrill of my life. I made lifelong friends because of *The Wizard of Oz*, too, and the movie probably means more to me today than when it happened.

So in order to handle some of the most common questions I've been asked over the decades, I thought it might be best to offer answers right here for you. I hope you won't mind my doing it this way. Some of these questions you might have already thought of yourself, some might not have

ever entered your mind. I hope this will be sufficient for all you fans who have wondered about
these topics and written me letters. Here goes:

Do you have a favorite memory of making *The Wizard of Oz*?

*I think how wonderful Judy Garland was to all of
us. I think maybe some of us were expecting her
to be a snob because she was just then becoming*

Here is Judy chat-
ting with some of
us Munchkins on the
set. *(left to right)* Fern
Formica, Rae-Nell Lasky
(child Munchkin), Priscilla
Montgomery (child
Munchkin), me, Betty
Ann Bruno (a child
Munchkin whose head is
peeking out behind me),
Judy, and little Olga Nardone.
This is the memory I keep of
Judy, sitting down and talking with
us during the downtime.

a pretty big star. She gave a present to each of us, an autographed photo of herself. That was very sweet. We all filed into her dressing room and she inscribed them to us. But she was terrific and talked to us every chance she had, but remember, she had to go to school every day, too, so her free time was taken up. The studio didn't want her to be socializing, for Pete's sake, that takes up time. So they grabbed her right away and put her back in school. She was just as excited at meeting all of us as we were to meet her. How many times do you see 124 midgets at one time?

Whatever happened to that lollipop?
I don't know. The last time I saw it, I was handing it to Judy Garland. I guess the prop department had it. The lollipop was made of light wood, like balsa wood, painted.

Not too heavy. I sure wish I had it today . . . do you know what that would be worth? If you watch the movie, at one point Judy has the lollipop after I gave it to her, and then the next minute it's gone. What happened to it? Who took it? I don't know. She left it in Munchkinland because she didn't take it with her. Or maybe she got hungry.

Are those your voices singing in Munchkinland?
No. We were given scripts and had to learn the songs for the scene. We sang during the filming, but we later found out that we were dubbed over by some professional singers whose voices were raised to give it that Munchkin sound. Besides, so many of the older midgets were German-born and had to be dubbed. They could speak English, but with a German accent. The gentle-

man who played the Mayor was named Charlie Becker, and he spoke with a thick German accent.

Is there any truth to the rumors about the Munchkins partying and carousing when they made the movie?

No, not really. There were a few little incidents with some of the little guys getting drunk and one even had a weapon. But besides that, they didn't go to late night parties as much as everyone thinks. That's been a Hollywood rumor for years and years. How could we have stayed out till all hours and then make it to the set at 6:00 a.m. to be in makeup and wardrobe the next morning, ready to go? I really didn't hear about much hell-raising and drunken orgies. I wasn't around it in any case, because I didn't stay that long at the Culver Hotel. But I think I would have heard about it the next day. I don't think it happened. Most of those stories were just Hollywood lore. You know, it all makes for a good story and we've had to live this stuff down for years.

Did someone hang themselves in the trees during the movie?

No, that's another myth. Someone started that story, I think, in the 1970s, and it spread. You can't see anybody hanging in the trees in the film. I've looked. I've been asked that so many times. There's no bodies hanging in the forest and no one died during the production of the picture. It just didn't happen. The studio was very careful with things, with the fire and stunts. Even the flying monkeys, well, they didn't use children because that would have been too dangerous to string them up on wires in the haunted forest. They used us little guys and we were all adults.

'Wizard of Oz' Stands Up With 'Snow White'

If Hollywood's human actors have been smarting under the supremacy of animated cartoons in the field of fantasy, they can now sit back and relax. M-G-M's "The Wizard of Oz," previewed to a chosen few yesterday, is an amazing adventure in the world of fairy tales.

The strange creatures that sprang from the imagination of Frank L. Baum magically take life in this picture upon which Mervyn LeRoy, Director Victor Fleming and a host of studio specialists labored for so many months.

The highest compliment you can pay to their efforts is that the film compares favorably to Disney's classic, "Snow White and the Seven Dwarfs."

Its human characters still can't match the quaintness of the best of Disney's pen and ink creations, but Bert Lahr, as the cowardly lion, comes very close indeed. Lahr easily steals the picture, although Jack Haley, as the tin woodman, and Ray Bolger, as the scarecrow, are extraordinarily good.

Judy Garland's Dorothy is very appealing, and Frank Morgan's portrayal of the humbug wizard is in his best manner.

The real triumph of the picture is the fantastic land of Oz through which the characters move. From the moment that Dorothy is deposited out of the sky into the country of the Munchkins, the eye is assailed with surprises, each more beautiful or more impressive in its camera magic than the last.

The technicolor photography of Harold Rosson and his staff is gorgeous, the art direction of Cedric Gibbons is superb, and the special effects of Arnold Gillespie and his assistants are a source of constant wonder.

Never has the screen offered anything like the enchanted forest, the malignant field of poppies. Unique, too, is the Munchkin s e q u e n c e

where the singer's midgets portray the little people. Three tiny actors, names not mentioned in the program, are terrific scene stealers.

Together with all this u n r e a l world, there also is the most realistic cyclone ever filmed. This is in the prologue, which is done in sepia.

If there is any jarring note in the picture, it is in the early reels where there is a tendency to go musical comedy. Too many songs and dances by the characters. The story thereafter becomes straight forward and is vastly more interesting.

Some will wish that the text of Baum's book had been followed more closely, but the picture is faithful in the main idea and in many details.

None will deny that "The Wizard of Oz" is one of the greatest novelties ever offered on the screen.

When you consider this, and the tremendous ready-made audience of Baum readers, it is hard to see how the picture can fail to be a box office hit.

HARRISON CARROLL.

◄ An extraordinary photograph of about half the Munchkin cast posing on the Yellow Brick Road with director Victor Fleming, agent Leo Singer, and assistant director Al Shoenberg.

Reuniting with my Munchkin pals Gus Wayne and Karl Slover in 1989, the fiftieth anniversary of *The Wizard of Oz.*

Did you ever see Judy Garland again after making the movie?

No, I never did. I wish I could have seen her, maybe gone to one of her concerts, but I never did. I think it would have been great to see her years later because I enjoyed her performances on television. I've met all three of her lovely children, Liza Minelli, Lorna Luft, and Joey Luft. And I met her ex-husband Sid Luft at a Wizard of Oz *festival held in her hometown of Grand Rapids, Minnesota. It's just too bad she didn't live longer. The pills and the booze did her in.*

Who were the other members of the Lollipop Guild with you?

The gentleman to my right was Jackie Gerlich. He was from the Barnum and Bailey Circus. Very nice guy. I didn't know him that well, but we were about the same age. The gentleman on my left was Kurt Schneider. He was a German midget, older than me, and he also went by the name of Harry Earles in some films like Freaks *and* The Unholy Three *which was one of Lon Chaney's big movies. He did a bunch of movies at MGM before* The Wizard of Oz. *Later on he* went by the name of Harry Doll, and he had three sisters who were midgets too. The whole family was in The Wizard of Oz. After The Wizard of Oz they moved to Florida and worked with the circus; I think I saw them once or twice in the 1950s, but I didn't stay in too good of touch. Both of the other guys in the Lollipop Guild are gone now.

Have there been Munchkin imposters?
Strangely enough, there are some little people and even some grown people who claim to have been Munchkins in the movie and they really weren't. Lots of them, in fact. I don't know why they do it. I guess the fame and maybe to make some money. There's been more than one guy over the years to claim to be in the Lollipop Guild or claiming to be me and they have writeups in their hometown newspapers and they become these local celebrities until they get caught. Sometimes they do an interview with a local newspaper and they tell the reporter something and the reporter believes it and prints it without checking up on it. Strange how people do that. I guess they think that since we were wearing strange makeup and costumes that nobody would ever know the difference.

Do you like lollipops?
Yes, I love lollipops. But I prefer cigars.

Entertainment Weekly magazine once asked me this question: "What would you want from the Wizard?" Nobody had ever asked me that. I told them, "To tell you the truth, I've got everything I ever wanted. I got lucky. I made smart investments, because we didn't make much doing The Wizard of Oz and none of us Munchkins get any residuals from that film. Guess who made more money than we did? Toto."

I hope I have answered some of your Oz questions.

2

SHORT STORIES

IGHT AFTER THE MUNCHKIN WORK in *The Wizard of Oz,* I was approached by one of the casting people at MGM to get into one of the flying monkey costumes for a scene, and I was going to do it, but they changed their minds and said, "No, wait, we've got something else for you." I went directly into an Our Gang comedy called *Tiny Troubles,* where I played a midget baby thief named "Light-Fingered Lester." The Our Gang short was directed by George Sidney, a great director at the studio, and although he was a young guy back then, he knew how to handle Spanky, Darla, and Alfalfa pretty well. It takes a knack to work so closely with kids.

I enjoyed that job because in the role I was supposed to drink beer and smoke cigars, and I didn't do either of those things in reality. So in the smoking scene, I fumbled around with the big cigar and couldn't produce enough smoke. They wanted more, so they put a

Directly following *The Wizard of Oz*, I was hired to work in an Our Gang comedy at MGM. The original title for this Our Gang comedy was *Baby Blues* but that was changed to *Tiny Troubles*, and the short film was released in February 1939. I played a midget baby thief named "Light-Fingered Lester." This was my second picture, so I thought I was really on my way.

▲ These behind-the-scenes shots show me signing my contract and going over the script with actor Emory Parnell.
▼ Chomping on my first on-screen cigar and other scenes with the Little Rascals.

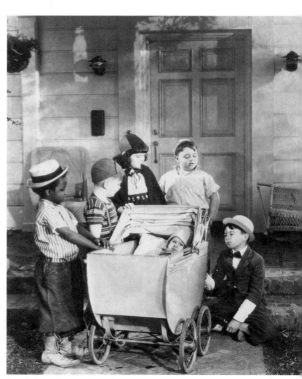

The judge was played by Fred Kelsey.

Years later I met Eugene "Porky" Lee (sometimes called Gordon) at a nostalgia show and we put up our fists again for a picture. I found out that he was a heavy drinker, and he died not long after we reunited.

Spanky McFarland and I met again a golf tournament in the 1980s. He became a very good golfer and loved attending celebrity tournaments around the country.

tube on the side of my mouth that blew out smoke when I pursed my lips. That was my first experience with special effects. A big puff came out.

For the Our Gang short, the makeup man tested out a little mustache on me and they dressed me in a little suit, but sometimes I was in a bonnet like an infant. When the film was released in early 1939, I wanted to see it in the worst way, because it would be the first time I'd really see myself in the movies without the crazy makeup from *Oz*. I had a little mustache, I had some lines. This was a big part for me—something to really write home about and have my family watch. I kept calling the booking agent downtown where they had distributors and I went all the way downtown to a Chinese Theatre where they played the Our Gang short when it first came out. When it was first shown in my hometown, they advertised me as being from Roxbury and starring in the short. My family was very proud.

By that time, I had signed with an agent named Frank Ryan, and his office was located on the Sunset Strip; he got me into a movie called *The Marx Brothers At the Circus*. I was interviewed by Groucho Marx himself in an office at MGM. Without his signature mustache and eyebrows, I wasn't sure it was him. Now remember, I was a lot smaller than I am now; I was a little guy, about three feet tall. Groucho asked me, "Can you get down on your knees?" He was kidding, and I guess I was the right height for the job because he gave it to me. I was eighteen or nineteen then.

I played Professor Atom. This was long before the atom bomb, but it meant the same thing . . . tiny like an atom. I loved the Marx Brothers, and I just couldn't believe

I was going to work with them in one of their films. That was one of my biggest thrills, being featured in a big movie like this. In *The Wizard of Oz,* I was one of many midgets, but here, I was featured. I was still learning my own acting skills, and it was hard for me to keep a straight face during my scenes with them. I kept laughing in the scenes and the director, Eddie Buzzell, kept telling me, "Jerry, stop laughing. You're not supposed to laugh, you're a villain." But I couldn't help myself. If you watch closely, you can still see me smirking, trying to hide my laughs.

There were a lot of midget jokes in the movie. In one scene, they had a little auto-

▲ This was my big scene in the Marx Brothers movie *At the Circus,* where Chico and Groucho try to pry some information out of me about the brand of cigars I smoke. All of the furniture was made to scale and I wanted to take it home after the filming. Someone promised it to me, but I never got it.

▶ This is just a gag shot taken on the miniature Professor Atom set of *At the Circus* with Chico Marx. This never happened in the movie.

An ensemble photo of the cast and some crew of *At the Circus* starring the Marx Brothers, in 1939. I'm next to Groucho and on the other side of him is director Eddie Buzzell.

mobile for me, but some of those scenes got cut out. In Professor Atom's customized miniature house, I wanted to buy the furniture from the studio because it was so perfect for me at my size, but they wouldn't let me. It was just perfect! My little house is on the train traveling with the circus, and Groucho and Chico barge in and they're trying to get evidence from me by seeing what kind of cigars I smoke. They keep hitting their head on the chandelier, tripping over the furniture and small standing lamps, and Chico keeps offering me cigars, which confuses Groucho. Harpo comes in and things really get tangled in the tiny house. At one point, Chico picks me up while I'm lighting my cigar with a lighter. I light his and he literally passes me over to Groucho to light his cigar. Groucho says, "No thanks, bad luck . . . three on a midget!" (Some people might not get that, but

GROUCHO MARX ON *THE DICK CAVETT SHOW*
SEPTEMBER 5, 1969, ABC-TV

In this picture, we had a gorilla. It wasn't actually a gorilla, it was a gorilla skin—with a man inside of it. And he had a manager. This gorilla skin had a manager. This is true, and we engaged him to bring this pelt over to the studio and then we engaged a man to go inside of the gorilla skin. And he also had a manager. So we had two managers there for one gorilla.

And this skin was awfully hot, you know, with all the lights, and it was summertime . . . and we were doing a scene. Then at lunchtime, the fellow who was in the skin went over to the lunch room and he got an ice pick and he bore about forty holes in this gorilla skin, and when he came back he was very comfortable in this skin. But the manager of the skin got wind of this and he was in a rage. He says, "We're not gonna permit this. . . . Gimme my skin and get that guy outta there!" and he threw the pelt over his shoulder and walked out of the studio. Now we had about three more scenes to do with the gorilla but we had no skin. So we had six people from MGM rushing around San Diego and that section of California looking

for another monkey. We needed another gorilla.

But we couldn't find one. We got an orangutan—which is half the size of a gorilla. Did you know that? And then we had to get a midget to go inside this orangutan

skin. And then we got hundreds of letters when the picture came out, from people saying "We don't understand . . . the gorilla was this high, and it was only *this* high in the second half." We never told them we had an orangutan with a midget in it.

years ago, the superstitious thought it was bad luck to light three cigarettes on one match. It was an old showbiz adage, too . . . you never lit three on a match.)

The movie was not what you'd call one of the Marx Brothers' best, but it did well at the box office and it featured Groucho singing one of his signature songs, "Lydia the Tattooed Lady." Today, though, some call it a classic. Who knows? I'm just about the last surviving member of the cast because I was the youngest in the picture.

Making the film was exciting for me, and I watched everything I could, even when I wasn't in the scenes. Chico was always on the telephone; he had no time for anybody. He was too busy placing bets and making deals. Groucho was very kind to me, and he invited me to his home for dinner. I thought, oh my God, I'm going to a movie star's home for dinner!

I told the friends I was living with, Margie and Tommy, and they said, "Sure, sure, go!" But I was nervous. He lived in a huge house on Hillcrest in Beverly Hills and I had Tommy drop me off there that afternoon. Groucho greeted me at the door and was such a kind man. He joked a lot, but he treated me as an equal. He probably knew I was nervous, but he didn't treat me as someone who was new to the business. I remember he had a big Swedish cook and she served chicken and dumplings that night. Dinner was terrific. His son, Arthur, came in and he was holding a tennis racket. Groucho introduced me to his son and we talked a little and then Groucho showed me around his house. We went into his big billiard room. Up the stairway he had pictures of his mother and father, and he showed me a picture of his uncle (his mother's brother) and it was Al Sheen, part of a famous vaudeville act called Gallagher and Sheen. That night was one of my biggest thrills. When it was time for me to go, I called up Tommy and he picked me up. That was a night I'll always remember.

✛ ✛ ✛

As I said, I lived with Tommy Farmer. He was a fight manager, and through him I met all the big fighters and became the mascot of the American Legion Stadium on the corner of El Central and Selma. It was a big fight arena, very famous; all the big stars fought there. Tommy was influential in getting me in the press, posing with fighters like Henry Armstrong, George Latka, and Jackie Jurich. These guys were famous fighters in their day. The great Max Baer was fighting one week, and I met with him and took photos on his lap.

I was under contract to Edgar Bergen on radio and to play the "double" of Charlie McCarthy, his dummy. As it ends up, we only did this in one film, *Here We Go Again,* in 1942, and I was made up to look just like Charlie and also Mortimer Snerd in one scene. You can see me doing all of the running and stunts for Charlie.

I was still very small back then. I grew later on into my thirties, believe it or not. At that time, RKO was looking for somebody small to double for Charlie McCarthy. Edgar Bergen was one of radio's biggest stars, and he and his ventriloquist dummy, Charlie McCarthy, were famous everywhere. They'd made some pictures, too, so everybody knew of them and Charlie was a really popular character. They needed someone to dress and get made up as Charlie. They shaved into my hairline and made me up with some putty. I was in long shots where I danced with girls and did other scenes dressed as Charlie. I was up in a tree in one scene, drove a car in another scene, and we went on location to Lake Arrowhead for some scenes. This was in a movie called *Here We Go Again.* I doubled Mor-

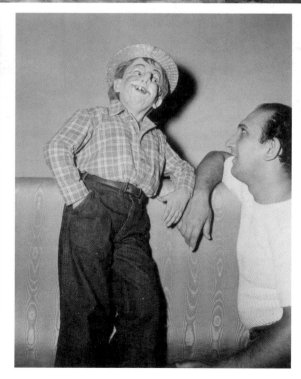

timer Snerd in one scene too, and the makeup for him was a little more extensive.

Edgar Bergen came up to me one day and said, "We'd like to use you on the radio show, Jerry. We have a character named Gopher Puss, Charlie's intellectual friend." I told him I'd love to be on the air, and he put me under his personal contract. I was nervous. I'd never been on radio. As Gopher Puss, they gave me lines that were really complicated. My first line on coast-to-coast radio was, "Due to the phrenological development of the occipital bone. . . ," and I continued. You can bet I practiced that one. I learned later it means I have a pointed head. I was under contract for about eighteen months, and after that I think he had no more use for me and the options ran out. From then I did some more radio on Fanny Brice's show, Ed Gardiner, and *Duffy's Tavern*. I was on *Suspense* and did a commercial for spark plugs.

Little by little, several of my brothers and sisters came out to California. Rae was the first, not long after *The Wizard of Oz*. My father became ill following the war and I went back to see him for what would be

Dressed as Charlie McCarthy in a scene with Edgar Bergen in *Here We Go Again*. Actually, the cameras never got this close in the movie. My scenes were shot from farther away to enhance the illusion of a live Charlie McCarthy.

This was our big dance number in *Here We Go Again,* with me dressed as Charlie McCarthy.

IN ONE WEEK LAST MAY, JERRY MAREN, MIDGET DANCER, DOUBLED FOR A CHIMPANZEE IN ONE PICTURE, AND WAS SIGNED TO DOUBLE FOR CHARLIE MC CARTHY IN ANOTHER!

World heavyweight champion fighter Max Baer sat me on his lap like Charlie McCarthy when I was working with Edgar Bergen.

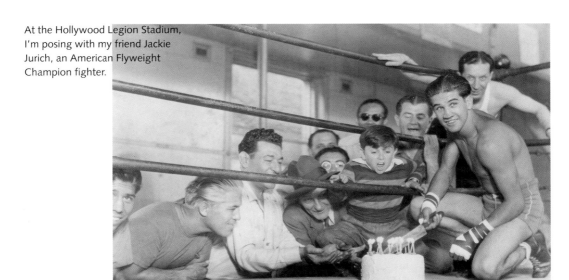

At the Hollywood Legion Stadium, I'm posing with my friend Jackie Jurich, an American Flyweight Champion fighter.

the last time. After he died, my mother moved to Los Angeles to live with my brother Emelio, Rae, and me at a house in Hollywood. Her eyesight had diminished and her health was failing, but I felt good about the fact that we could take care of her in her final years and that she was with family.

◄ In a mock fight appearance for the cameramen with British fighter Tommy Martin in 1940.
▼ I'm keeping the peace in this pose with fighters Sammy Angott and George Latka.

Stunts

My first experience doing a stunt was in a film series of short subjects called *Crime Doesn't Pay* at MGM in 1941. Robert Taylor was in this particular short titled "Coffins on Wheels." I did a stunt for a little boy, a young actor named Darryl Hickman, playing ball in the street. When I went into the street, a car came screaming down, brakes failing, and just missed me. I still remember the name of the driver. It was Bobby Rose, a superb stunt driver at the time.

I remember going to Bobby and asking him, "How are we gonna do this?" Bobby called me "kid." He said, "Listen, kid, I'm gonna put a little mark on the street and when

I was a monkey in this brief scene from the Hope and Crosby picture *Road to Morocco*.

you get to the mark, I want you to trip, like you're chasing the ball but you didn't get to it." It was a dangerous stunt, but it worked perfectly. I was excited doing it, and it ended up being about $35 for two hours' work, which was good money back then. Some stunts can be dangerous, which is why I learned early on not to let them pay me according to size.

Even though I was never a professional stuntman, like my old friend Harry Monty who was trained in doing stunts, I could perform certain things—mostly for children. There was a series called *Red Rider* with "Little Beaver," who was played by Bobby Blake. (Later he went by Robert Blake.) I knew Bobby when he was in the *Our Gang* shorts at MGM, and we were about the same size, we both had dark hair and a similar build, so I could do some stunts for him. When I went to the interview for the *Red Rider* series, they asked me if I could ride. They were talking about horses, of course. They showed me a little pony and I said, "Sure, I can ride him, that's easy."

When I got on the set the next day, the horse was twice as big. Seventeen hands high. They were using a bigger horse to keep up in the chase sequences. I had to ride him bareback, with no saddle, no stirrups, no reigns, nothing. We did the run-through and I had to hold on with all my might. This horse took off and nearly threw me.

I remember Yakima Canutt directed this, and I thought it would be easy, but this chase made me nervous. I was told, "Now Jerry, when the posse comes down the pass, they're going to go right and you go to the left." I told him that I'd do my best, but I wasn't sure I could steer the horse. When the time came, I couldn't get him to move over. I was going so fast I flew off the horse and almost hit the camera. I had no control. I learned from then on to really be careful and plan the stunt out as much as I could.

I worked with some great stuntmen in the movies, guys like Dick Talmage, Joe Aragon. Years later, in the film *The Apple Dumpling Gang*, I was doing a stunt for a little girl, dressed in a nice long white dress with a wig on. (Interestingly enough, while I was doing stunts for the little girl, my wife Elizabeth was doing stunts for the little boy at the studio.) We were on location in Big Bend, Oregon, and we did a lot of chases through the woods. One of the better shots was me in the back of a buckboard wagon that suddenly crashes into a tree.

When I was working in a movie called *The Woman's Face,* with Joan Crawford, we filmed scenes in Sun Valley, Idaho. The second unit director was named Johnnie Waters, and he got me the job. It was wintertime, and the crew had put sandbags in a round area and snow was put over it. I had to jump from a runaway sleigh driven by horses, which was going extremely fast. That one nearly killed me because I landed pretty hard. But I got through it.

I remember one stunt I did in the film *When Worlds Collide.*

We filmed *A Woman's Face* in snowy Sun Valley, Idaho, in 1941. I'm posing with director Johnnie Waters and a stunt woman on the outdoor set.

In this sequence there was a hurricane or a typhoon or something like that. It was torrential weather and downpour with high winds generated by massive fans. In the story, some parents take their son up to the roof and tie him to the chimney so he can be rescued. So I was tied to a chimney until a helicopter came and a guy dropped down on a cable and rescued me. That was a strange one, but it worked out okay.

Some stunts involve groups of little people, like in *Dirty Harry*, where I was with several other little people and we were supposed to be kids riding in a bus. The bus was commandeered by the villain, and the driver had it going sideways and tipping every way around corners. It ends up in a rock quarry and the bus hits some boulders and turns over. I remember we made extra money on that one because it was a location shoot and it rained for several days while we sat and waited out the storm in a hotel.

✦ ✦ ✦

Stand-in work is very important in film and television because the children can only work four hours a day and they have three hours of school time. While the children are in school, they use little people like myself to rehearse under the lights. From a distance, we

◀ Working as a stand-in for the child actors in the Andy Griffith film *Angel in My Pocket* in April 1968.
▼ Here I am relaxing with a cigar waiting for the shot to begin. They had me in drag to do a stunt as a little girl in the Disney film *The Apple Dumpling Gang*.
▶ Actor Greg McClure has me hoisted up above his shoulders in this publicity pose from the set of one of my favorite roles, as Admiral Dot in the 1944 movie *The Great John L.*, in which I sang the song "Kathleen" in a tavern.

◄ In the movie *Johnny Doesn't Live Here Any-more* I played a gremlin. Here I am in costume as the little white creature posing with the producers outside the stages at Monogram Pictures.

▼ Another scene from *The Great John L.*

56

look like children and the arm and leg length matches and such. We can work with the other actors and get the scene set. When the kids get out of class, they are almost ready to go. Anything to save time.

For standing in, you're not really acting, you're just standing in. You're taking directions, moving here, moving there. No lines, no makeup, and sometimes no particular wardrobe. Very easy work, but it has to be done. Many times there's overtime, and then the checks add up, and that's when it's great.

With photo doubling in long shots, it saves time for us to do the scene dressed as the little kid, and from a distance it works. If they need an insert of an arm or a leg and the child is gone, I can do the work. I've done over-the-shoulder and perspective shots (makes it look bigger with midgets in the scene). With kids there's always the chance of an accident, so it saves time to have an adult midget do anything that might be risky on camera, like a chase sequence or something like that. That's the advantage of having a pituitary midget as a stunt person or stand-in. We save a lot of time on the shoot.

This was probably the first–but not the last—time I was dressed as a rabbit for a production. This was called *Rabbit*. I don't recall much about it.

In addition to doing stunts I also stood in for Robert Blake on the *Red Rider* series. That was in the 1940s. Later I stood in for Gary Coleman on *Diff'rent Strokes* for a little while, and I knew he was funny with good timing when that show first hit. I stood in for Jodie Foster, Ron Howard, Butch Patrick, quite a few young actors over the years.

The studios use midgets for perspective shots in films, but rarely on television. I worked on an Alfred Hitchcock film, *Topaz*. I saw Hitchcock there, but the footage was

shot under a second unit director so I had no interaction with the famous director. Although it was supposed to take place in Mexico, we shot it on the back lot at Universal. It was a scene outside of a saloon, and by having midgets far in the background, the perspective is altered and the rest of the set appears larger. I worked a

▲ With my pal Tony Boris in this snapshot taken in November 1943, during WWII.
▶ Talk about a little Nazi. . . . during the war we were all doing Hitler impersonations. Seig Heil!
▼ Believe it or not, I worked at the "Hills U-Drive" in Hollywood as a receptionist to earn some extra money in 1941.

day on the film *The Green Mile,* starring Tom Hanks. I was an old man, dressed in pajamas and robe, walking in the background of a nursing home from one side of the shot to the other. They used me because I'm miniature and it was a perspective shot to make the hallway they were shooting down appear much larger than it was. They ended up cutting the scene.

✛ ✛ ✛

In a scene I did for the movie *Silent Partner* in 1944.

During World War II, Billy Curtis and I did an act, and we played all of the military hospitals and bases around the country for the USO. We worked specifically in hospitals here in the United States. Since we knew we wouldn't be drafted, both Billy and I felt we were doing our part for the war effort. The act was not bad. It was a novelty kind of thing, and two midgets performing on stage for these soldiers was really something different for the men and women in uniform.

I had met Billy during *The Wizard of Oz,* where he played a Munchkin, too. He was a popular little guy and I really looked up to him—a well-dressed and a handsome young man. An Italian like me, his real name was Luigi Curto, and he already knew his way around Hollywood and the studios . . . and the ladies. Billy and I became lifelong friends.

Performing at the hospitals was sometimes scary because we had to visit mental wards at some of the hospitals and one time the nurses had a row of hypodermic needles on a table nearby just in case some of the patients got unruly. The patients who were getting ready to die, well, that was the saddest part. It was hard to try to make them enjoy themselves and they all looked awful, some were yellow and you could just see how sick they were. I remember one time seeing a guy with his hand sewn to his own belly in order to graft skin. I didn't know things like that were done. I was shocked.

When we played on a stage with an audience and a band, Billy would come out and say, "Well fellows, you're now

I appeared with Spike Jones and his crazy gang in the picture *Bring on the Girls* in the early 1940s.

Billy Curtis and I toured in a USO show that we called "Bits o' Fun" and entertained (or tried to) military personnel in hospitals all over the United States. We had a routine all worked out. This was during WWII, and this performance *(below)* was at the San Diego Naval Hospital. *Maybe* our act was awful, but the novelty of us performing together somehow got us through.

looking at the result of rationing," which got a big laugh. Frank Scannell wrote a lot of our material and musical numbers for us, and Billy and I sang and danced our way through a few routines. The money wasn't anything to speak of, but we traveled a lot and we did our part for the war effort. I'm very proud of that fact. We played with Jimmy Durante and a lot of big acts that were traveling too. Jimmy would yell out, "Where are those little cockaroaches?"

Our last stop was in San Bernadino. Right then, Billy and I got word of a movie called *Three Wise Fools* at MGM and we both worked in that. We went right into it from our tour. In one sequence, I played a rock called Sir Boulder. Margaret O'Brien, a cute young actress who'd played in many movies by that time, was the star. Her character sees fairies and she finds it hard to convince the people around her that they are real.

✦ ✦ ✦

The Friars Club called me and Billy and said they wanted us to be in a sketch for their "Friars Frolics of 1945." It was going to be a huge show with Humphrey Bogart and Alan

A bunch of us little people appeared in the fantasy film *Three Wise Fools* with Oscar winner Margaret O'Brien. I was "Sir Boulder" in one scene, where we played fairies who lived in the trees.

At a Friars Club Frolic, Billy Curtis and I dressed as babies armed with tommy guns in 1945. Here Humphrey Bogart and Alan Ladd are posing with us for photographers.

Ladd at the Shrine Auditorium. Al Jolson was in it, George Jessel, Van Johnson, Walter Pidgeon, Fred Astaire, a whole group of huge stars. Billy and I were babies wearing bonnets. I was Humphrey Bogart's little baby and Billy was Alan Ladd's. In the bit, we ride along in carriages pushed by our dads when Bogart and Ladd meet up at a park and strike up a conversation. The big finish is Billy and I getting up out of our strollers at the same time and aiming machine guns at each other and then a blackout. How's that for bizarre?

Then I got a call from an agent named Maxine Lewis, who said they needed me for a job in Las Vegas. Now, all Las Vegas had to offer at that time was the Rancho Vegas and

▲ In Nevada at the Charleston Lodge, I worked as a roulette master, and that's where I learned much of my gambling skills.

▼ A rollicking country band I worked with in Las Vegas at the New Frontier Hotel in the late 1940s. I played "Stuffy Fuddle."

Last Frontier Hotel. It was a lot of open desert and there were no great show palaces or extravagant resorts of any kind. That came later in the early 1950s when it really sprang to life. It was just getting started as a gambling town. They needed someone to dress up as Snuffy Smith, a cartoon strip character . . . only they called me "Stuffy Fuddle." I dressed up like a hillbilly with a jug of moonshine and a shotgun. I was the mascot of the Last Frontier Hotel. They had an annex in Mount Charleston, and I'd go up there where they had casinos. I sang with the band, and they taught me how to deal and play blackjack and learn all the ropes about gambling.

I also worked at the Players Club, where the Desert Inn stands now. It was a small casino with a band, dancing, food. This was my introduction to Sam Boyd, a famous pioneer entrepreneur in Vegas. He taught me so much about gambling. I used to deal blackjack back to back with Sam. I

Jeanette Fern and I are seen briefly in *Flesh and Fantasy,* a long-forgotten film that starred Charles Boyer and Barbara Stanwyck.

even dealt to Howard Hughes, but I didn't know who he was at the time. He was just a friendly gambler, a tall guy who roamed the tables quietly enough. They told me who he was later on.

I worked in television right from the get-go in the late 1940s. As soon as it became popular, I began appearing on television in commercials and local Los Angeles programs taking place in fresh studios that were being built at the time. The television studios were filled with wires everywhere, the microphones were huge, and the cameras were big and bulky. You can imagine the lights were hot and they'd paint you unmercifully with makeup, almost like silent pictures. Your lips would look black.

My first television series was *Magic Lady & Boko.* I was Boko, the elfin assistant to a magician named the Magic Lady. This program was shot on film at the California Studios (now Raleigh Studios) in Hollywood and became a popular kids show right from the beginning. It was a syndicated program, so Telemount Pictures sold it to a lot of burgeoning television stations. Our director was Bill Donovan, and the star was magician Geraldine

Larsen, whose husband and son eventually built the famous Magic Castle in Hollywood, a haven for magicians of all kinds. On our show, Geraldine was a fairy princess performing and teaching magic; a lot of the illusions were accomplished with lights and primitive camera effects at the time, but it worked and it was a cute show. Sometimes my character would screw up the magic and add some comedy effect to the show.

My first commercial was shot at KTLA in Hollywood; I was dressed as an admiral. Just prior to that I had played in the movie *The Great John L,* dressed as a little admiral with a little military outfit and all. We were able to use the same wardrobe, which was perfect because the commercials were for Admiral Televisions and Admiral Refrigerators. I was one of television's first midget spokesmen, right alongside Johnny Roventini, who did most of the on-camera national TV spots for Phillip Morris cigarettes dressed as a page boy yelling, "Call for Philllllip Mooooorrrrrrisssss!" My commercials, in the beginning, were mostly bits for local sponsors and there wasn't much money in it, but it was good experience. Later on, I learned just how wonderfully national spots could pay off.

This is the Follies sketch called "Dan McGrew" in the movie *Show Business,* which was produced by and starred the great Eddie Cantor. They put me on wires and flung me through a door.

I can't count how many times I've played a Christmas elf in advertisements and commercials over the years. This was one of my earlier ones, with Tony Boris as the other elf. This was a Union Pacific Railroad holiday print ad.

◄ I don't remember why I was dressed like a baby for this photo, but I hope the little girl wasn't traumatized for life because of it.
▼ I was "Mr. Twinkles" for an early NBC Christmas show in Los Angeles.

Magic Lady & Boko was a local children's show with magician Geraldine Larsen as the host. I was Boko, her little elfin assistant. Geraldine was one of the first female magicians to appear on television in 1949. Our television show was one of Los Angeles's earliest local kids shows, actually. We performed regular magic, some sleight of hand in closeups, and some illusions on the program. This syndicated show, produced by Telemount Pictures, was shot at Raleigh Studios in Hollywood.

2000 LBS

THIS IS TO CERTIFY THAT
LOS ANGELES CHILDREN'S SHOW
1656 Members Enrolled
Sept. 10 thru Sept. 18, 1949
is a Member in Good Standing of

The Magic Lady and Boko Club
of TELEMOUNT PICTURES, INC.

• Who Has Promised to Keep Secret Any Magic Learned •

Date _____ Age _____ Signed _Magic Lady_
Boko

TELEVISION

"OH, I WISH I WERE AN OSCAR MAYER WIENER"

ONE OF MY FIRST FORAYS into television, when TV was in its infancy, was *Superman,* starring George Reeves in 1951. Originally it wasn't intended to be for television. I was hired along with a few other little guys (Tony Boris, Johnny Bambury, and Billy Curtis) to play subterranean-dwelling mole creatures in a feature film called *Superman and the Mole Men.* Naturally, I knew who Superman was from comic books and the serials, so this was an exciting job. Outside of serials on Saturday afternoons, Superman had never been on the big screen. I was pretty sure this might be something big. In this film, us little guys played these creatures who are angered when an oil company has invaded our space with "the world's deepest well." After the film was completed, a TV series starring the Man of Steel was sold and the first few episodes consisted of this movie chopped up into thirty minute segments.

"You're not going to shoot those little creatures . . . in the first place, they haven't done you any harm. In the second place, they may be radioactive . . ."

—GEORGE "SUPERMAN" REEVES,
SUPERMAN AND THE MOLE MEN

Lippert Films produced the film, and it was low budget. I remember they gave me a prop ray gun that I'm supposed to aim at Superman because we were fearful of him. As molemen, we didn't know what he stood for. Well this ray was made out of a modified vacuum cleaner that had a tin funnel jammed into the end of it. That was supposed to be my ray gun. Special effects was not a strong area with Lippert Films. In fact, I watched George Reeves during a scene where he was strung up on wires and witnessed him fall when a cable broke. He wasn't hurt, but it caused a commotion on the set, and he was understandably angered by the accident. From then on, I think he protested against any wire flying and they shot him soaring through the air lying flat on a table with wind machines making his

In *Superman and the Mole Men*, a movie that was later chopped up into episodes of the television show, a handful of us little guys played the brown creatures from deep within the earth. With me above are Tony Boris, George Reeves as Superman (holding Billy Curtis), and Johnny Bambury. I'm lugging the ray gun. We played aliens who fear humans and attempt to defend themselves from the Man of Steel.

The All-Time
ACE OF ACTION!

in his FIRST Full-Length Feature Adventure!

SUPERMAN
AND THE Mole Men

George REEVES · Phyllis COATES

Jeff Corey · Walter Reed · J. Farrell MacDonald
Stanley Andrews

cape flap around. They used a blue screen effect behind him in all of the episodes that followed.

I didn't socialize much with George Reeves; the producer didn't like it. But from what I could tell, he was a nice, quiet man. When he died several years later, I was

stunned. I didn't know what to make of it. I guess it's still a mystery whether he was killed or it was suicide.

Look for Me in There Too

In the late 1940s and early 1950s I was the famous Buster Brown for a line of shoes and footwear of the same name. The Buster Brown company, one division of the Brown Shoe Company, went back decades and were one of the nation's leading shoemakers, especially for children. The character of Buster Brown can be traced to cartoons in the newspapers around the turn of the century. The little guy was a Little Lord Fauntleroy type of kid with a hat, long hair in a bob (popular in the 1920s on children), and with me was my trusted dog, Tige. As the famous line went, "That's my dog, Tige. He lives in a shoe. I'm Buster Brown. Look for me in there too! Arf! Arf!" I must have delivered that ditty a thousand times.

I got the Buster Brown job by interviewing with Frank Ferrin, the producer of the *Buster Brown Show* on radio in the 1940s. He liked my voice, which was a lot higher-pitched back then. In decades prior, they had other midgets portraying Buster Brown; one of the first—if not the first—was Johnny Clifton, who made personal appearances selling shoes around the country. (Years later, Johnny Clifton's daughter, Myrna Myrle, married Clarence Swensen, one of the Munchkins in *The Wizard of Oz*.) Johnny was maybe one of the first major midget company

▶ "That's my dog Tige. He lives in a shoe. I'm Buster Brown. Look for me in there too." For a few years in the early 1950s I was Buster Brown in print ads and some commercials across the nation. My mug was plastered in ads, on stickers, shoeboxes, store walls, and even on comic books.
◀ This is a favorite of mine, a personal gag shot. Of course, little Buster Brown would never be caught smoking.

mascots, you might say, in the United States. Midget Ed Ansley was another guy who traveled the country as Buster Brown in the early days. By the time I became Buster Brown, midgets in advertising became mainstream and we sold a variety of products in national campaigns, everything from candy bars to hot dogs.

When radio show personality Smiling Ed McConnell came out to the West Coast from Chicago with his show on NBC, I joined the live broadcast, which was a kiddie program on Saturdays at 6:00 a.m. and another live performance several hours later for the West Coast. The sponsors paid almost nothing for radio and I hardly broke even because I had to take cabs twice a day back and forth to the studio, but I stuck with it because I thought it might have some potential and it didn't grab every bit of my time. I could still work in films during the week if I wanted. I wasn't tied down completely. The radio show became successful and I did the role of Buster Brown for their commercial segments for a few years, but I was never shown. I was behind the curtain and a big cardboard cutout of Buster Brown and Tige was hanging in the studio.

The radio show was at NBC on the corner of Sunset and Vine in Hollywood. Every weekend, the studio theater was always filled to capacity with children. The producers thought it would be good to finally show me, so they built a platform in the middle of the stage with a curtain that opened and closed. I sat there with a stuffed bulldog standing in for Tige and recited my lines during the commercials, and then when I pushed a button on cue, the dog would bark and the kids would laugh.

When the show went to television, I put on the hair, the hat, and the costume and smiled big while doing the live commercials and intros as Buster Brown. I made some limited personal appearances in costume for the show as well, but that was rare. But the most amazing part of it all was the print media and exposure from photo layouts and ads featuring my face. I was seen as Buster Brown all over the country, with my face in comic books, on shoeboxes, in newspaper and magazine ads, in giveaway photos, and everything you could imagine. Shoe stores had huge posters of me as Buster Brown in the store windows. The commercials on television amplified all of that exposure.

Then, all of a sudden, someone from the company approached me and said "We don't think we can use you anymore." I wasn't given a good reason, but probably I was getting too old for the role, who knows?

"Wait a minute," I said and then stopped him. "All those years I worked for nothing on radio, then after we're a hit on television, now you want to dump me?" I said okay to it, but I also informed them that they had better take my picture out of every store window and in every store in the country because my mug was splashed everywhere, in store displays, in ads, and on merchandise. The Buster Brown rep said, "We can't do that." So we argued back and forth and finally made a settlement, which was pretty good, something like $25,000 at the time.

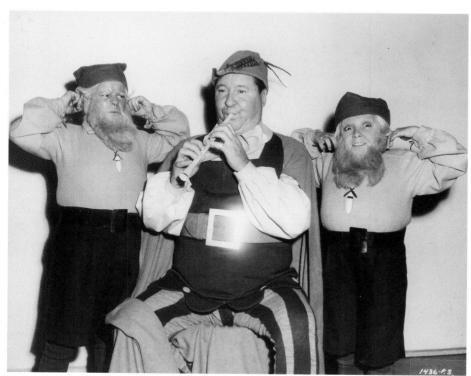

While working in television, I also fit in some film appearances. Billy Curtis and I were sprites in the film *That's the Spirit* with Jack Oakie.

A LITTLE HISTORY OF BUSTER BROWN

(From a vintage Buster Brown press release)

Buster Brown—one of the nation's oldest existing children's shoe trademarks—originated as a character in one of the earliest newspaper cartoon strips. Created in 1902 by Richard Felton Outcault, "Buster" was a mischievous youngster who, with his sister Mary Jane, and his dog, Tige, were as famous in their time as Orphan Annie and Charlie Brown became for succeeding generations. Buster's Lord Fauntleroy clothes and antic behavior were as familiar to those who read the "funnies" at the turn of the century as Annie's blank eyes or Charlie Brown's inability to coach a winning baseball team were later.

The late John A. Bush, who at that time was a rising young sales executive with Brown Shoe Company, saw the value of the Buster Brown name as a juvenile shoe trademark. He persuaded the company to purchase rights to the name from Outcault, and the brand was introduced to the public in 1904 during the St. Louis World's Fair. The company, as a result, won the only Double Grand Prize awarded to a shoe exhibitor at the Fair,

and John Bush went on to become president of the firm in 1915 and chairman of the board in 1948.

Richard Outcault—who patterned his cartoon characters on his own son, daughter, and dog—set up a booth at the St. Louis

World's Fair and sold the trademark rights to Buster Brown to any merchant who came along. The price apparently ranged from $5 to $1,000, depending on the cartoonist's whim and the size of the company involved in the transaction.

The result was a deluge of Buster Brown products ranging from harmonicas to soap and including a soft drink, coffee, wheat flour, and apples. There were at least fifty products under the Buster Brown label at one time, but there are only two surviving: a textile firm and the now famous Buster Brown line of children's shoes.

Brown Shoe Company—which was named for founder George Warren Brown and not for Buster—has consistently promoted the Buster Brown brand on a national scale. A succession of midgets dressed like Buster and accompanied by dogs toured the country between 1904 and 1915. They played to audiences in rented theaters, department stores, and shoe stores.

A national magazine advertising campaign was conducted from 1916 through 1920, and the midgets were employed again between 1921 and 1930 when the company used outdoor billboards. Newspapers and magazines were used throughout the 1930s, and in 1943 Smilin' Ed McConnell and his Buster Brown Gang made their debut on the West Coast NBC radio network, which was composed of 165 stations. In 1951, Smilin' Ed moved to television, where he remained until his death in 1954. Actor Andy Devine replaced Smilin' Ed in 1955 and hosted the program for less than a year.

My friend and fellow Munchkin, Jeanette "Fern" Formica, and I had an act together in the 1940s that we called "Jerry and Jeanette." We traveled around Southern California and played clubs and theatres with our act. We weren't terribly successful, but we had fun.

Relishing the Job

Getting canned from Buster Brown was the best thing that ever happened to me. That job was going nowhere for me. I eventually landed an entirely different job with Oscar Mayer by going in for an interview. I was going to be part of a national campaign with the Oscar Mayer meat company. Little did I know that I'd be surrounded by kids for the next ten years. At this point I was smoking cigars, but never around the kids, and rarely in my white chef's outfit.

As Little Oscar, the company's roving goodwill ambassador and sales promotion representative, I would be chauffeured from appearance to appearance in one of the company's brand-new Wienermobiles. They had just produced a fleet of five or six of these monstrous-looking wieners on wheels, bright orange and about as weird as anything anyone had seen on the road. The first one was made in the mid-1930s, but this new fleet was considerably more customized, with air conditioning and a few more luxuries inside. (I think one of the 1950s models, the earliest model salvaged, is in the Henry Ford automobile Museum on permanent display.)

The Wienermobile, unfortunately, broke down a lot. It was a custom-made vehicle, manufactured by Gerstenslagger, a private organization. I think they were out of Ohio. We'd be driving out in the desert or on the highway and it would break down, and we'd have to wait for a mechanic or a tow truck. We'd have to call the office and ask them what to do. Being a custom auto, it had a fairly common engine, so we could get it fixed easily. One time, though, the axle broke and the giant weenie on wheels was out of commission for a while. When a kid in San Diego asked me what had happened to my Wienermobile, I told him "I put too much mustard on it and it wouldn't start."

There was a big boom for supermarkets in the 1950s all across America. After the war, lots of guys were getting married and having kids, buying houses. So supermarkets were springing up all

across America and we advertised in those. The secret of our success was when we sold a kid, the kid sold the mom, and the mom sold the dad. That's how it worked. That's why they had me on all the kids TV shows, explaining where I was going to be so they could come meet me and see the Wienermobile.

I have always believed in Oscar Mayer products, and that was no joke. I visited the main plant in Madison, Wisconsin, and one in Los Angeles. I never went to the slaughterhouse, nothing I needed to learn there that would

▲ In Southern California, this was a familiar sight at supermarket openings and parades.

▼ This is an official company photo of four Little Oscars in a row: Jerry Maren, George Molchan, Joe White, and Meinhardt Raabe. I was the littlest Oscar.

For twelve years as Little Oscar, I hit all of the local kids shows in southern California that were broadcasting. John Rocvick was "Sheriff John." Tom Hatten was a local Los Angeles kiddie show host known as "Skipper Tom" on the *Pier 5 Club.* I also appeared with Our Gang host Johnny Downs in San Diego and Pinto Colvig as Bozo the Clown in Hollywood. And who could forget *Romper Room*?

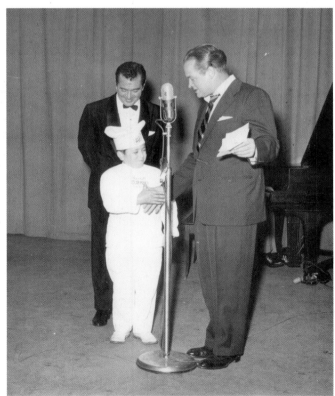

On the air with
Bob Hope.

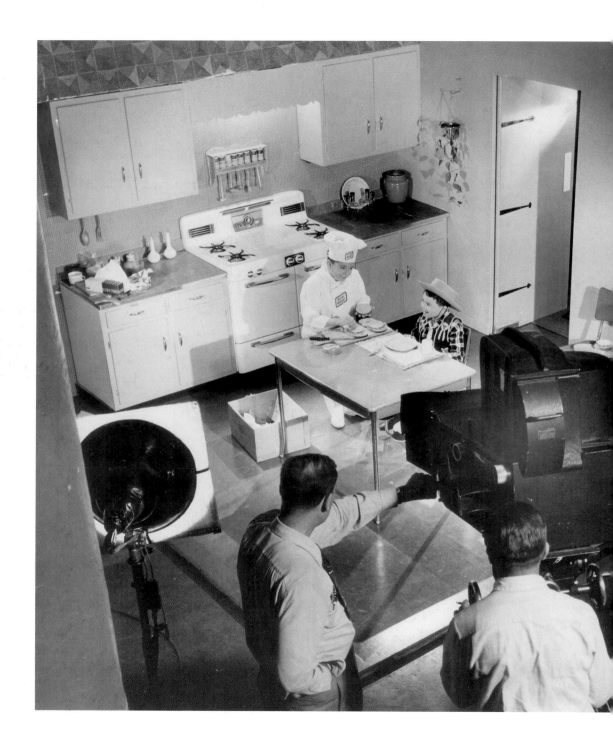

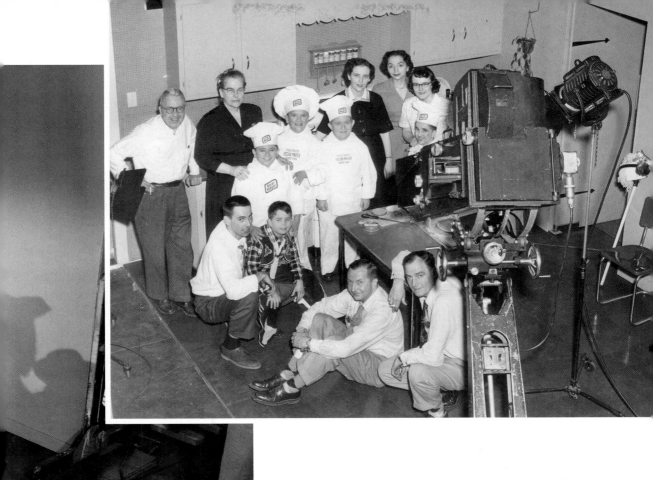

Filming a string of Oscar Mayer commercials on a kitchen set. While the set and studio was rented, the advertising company would film individual commercials with each of us Little Oscars and distribute the spots to television stations in our regions across the country.

Kids Galore! With every city, every supermarket opening, and every parade . . . came kids. They zeroed in on that Wienermobile and when I emerged from the top or the door opened, they cheered for me. It was like playing Santa Claus. I passed out wiener-whistles to everyone! No kid was left without a toy to take home. Of course, with the kids came runny noses and more cases of the flu and cold than I could count. That was the hazard.

help, but a lot was explained to me. We sold mostly hot dogs, but there were other meats. We sold top grade bacon and the company bought the very best hogs that were no less than two hundred pounds. No "buttons" in the bacon, meaning no bones. At one point I remember Oscar Mayer came out with a new product that, to be honest, didn't sound so delicious: peanut butter and bacon spread. It was in a tube, like liverwurst or braunschweiger, and had to be cut and placed on bread. I think that one didn't market as well as their finer meats.

Here I am posing with old man Oscar F. Mayer himself, the German founder of the meat empire. He was in his nineties at the time, but still sharp.

I was one of four midgets who were hired as "Little Oscar" mascots, and in addition to personal appearances we filmed television commercials that aired in local markets and nationally. Meinhardt Raabe (pronounced *MINE-hart robbie*), a German midget, had worked as the first Little Oscar and had been with the company since the late 1930s. I had met Meinhardt on the set of *The Wizard of Oz* when he played the coroner Munchkin in the long robe and hat who pronounces the Wicked Witch dead. He took his job so seriously; I think the other guys and I tended to have more fun with it. The other little guys hired for the job besides us were George Molchan and Joe White. Meinhardt was stationed near the Philadelphia plant and handled most of the East Coast appearances. Joe White was in the

Wisconsin area, and George Molchan worked out of the Chicago plant.

I remember one particular "wine and dine" trip to Chicago where all the bigwigs from the company flew us in and took us to dinner at the famous Pump Room at the Ambassador Hotel; this is where we actually met old man Oscar F. Mayer, the company founder. He was pleasant enough, and certainly old enough. He was about ninety-two at the time, had a little

bit of a hump back, and wore three-piece suits with a pocket watch jangling from his suit. He moved around pretty good for a man of his age. Even though he'd been in America since the 1880s, he still had a thick German accent, and he was quite sharp at the time, all business—a fine gentleman who had started an empire that exists today. We had our picture taken with him in our Little Oscar chef's outfits there at an Oscar

Me and Mr. Peanut working a local fair with announcer Bill Welsh.

◀ Big Frank enjoys a little frank. Little Oscar and Frank Sinatra take a few minutes out to feast on an Oscar Mayer hot dog for the photographer.
▼ At the City of Hope telethon with Abbott and Costello. This was not long before the comedy team broke up, maybe one of their final appearances together, but no one was aware of it.

Mayer promotion in the Windy City. That was my only contact with old man Mayer. Eventually, I dealt more with his son and also local reps from the company. Considering that I was the smallest of the Little Oscars, all advertised as the World's Smallest Chef, I got quite a bit of attention within the company.

I appeared on Sheriff John's kiddie show and Engineer Bill, *Romper Room,* the *Bozo Show* . . . all in the local Los Angeles market. I would plug the Oscar Mayer appearances on all the shows. The Oscar Mayer company loved it, because being out here on the West Coast I was able to hook up with a lot of stars and take pictures with them for publicity, people like Bob Hope, Abbott and Costello, Cliff Arquette, the Lone Ranger, Stan Freberg, Liberace, Jay North (starring as Dennis the Menace on TV then) . . . all kinds of celebrities. There was a TV host in Los Angeles named Chef Milani and I appeared with him on his show to advertise Oscar Mayer meats. I went to a Bob Hope Telethon as Little Oscar and I spotted Frank Sinatra backstage and asked him if he'd mind taking a couple of pictures with me and he said, "Of course not." The photographer got us clowning around with a ham sandwich or something. When these photos got back to the company, they landed in the company newsletter called *The Link.* That was a big plug for me, and I got a nice raise out of that. I sold a lot of meat, let me tell you. The company appreciated it, and the local distributors knew I was doing my job because of the increase in sales within the local supermarkets.

An Average Appearance for Little Oscar

The driver would pick me up at my house in the Wienermobile and I was dressed and ready in my white chef's uniform. I had a couple of uniforms just in case the one I was wearing got soiled with mustard or ketchup when demonstrating for the kids and such. I'd sit in the front passenger seat of the Wienermobile, and when we approached the market, I'd get up in the hatch, open it up, and stand there perched halfway out of the top of the Wienermobile, waving. We had a sound system in the vehicle, and the driver would

There were times when the Wienermobile broke down— in the desert. We had to wait for hours to have a tow truck or repairman come rescue us in the stifling heat.

Getting ready for a parade appearance, poking out of the top of the Wienermobile.

throw the switch, at which point you'd hear a recording of this song blasting out: "Here Comes Little Oscar in his Wienermobile, Little Oscar the World's Smallest Chef. In his tiny tiny kitchen, Oscar Mayer meats he's fixin', Oscar Mayer meats are treats for any meal! So look for the name Oscar Mayer."

Then I'd come down from the hatch, open the door, and there'd be two hundred kids gathered around screaming and waving. We learned our lesson: I'd give out wiener whistles at the END of the event. Once the kids crowded into the store—hundreds of kids with those whistles—they drove the shoppers crazy. All the kids trying to outdo each other. Eventually they stopped giving the whistles because a couple of kids swallowed them. They didn't die, but it became a problem.

Once in the market, I'd demonstrate and sometimes hand out samples of meats, or maybe it was a simple appearance. We'd visit sometimes three, four, and five markets in one day. Then it became six and up to ten or more in one day, and it was almost too much to handle. This was an everyday job, and it was hard to get weekends off. We appeared in parades, at the ballpark, super-

market, mall openings, car dealerships, ribbon cuttings. The company was scheduling us all over the state.

Don't get me wrong, I love kids, but sometimes this job tested my patience. One of the hazards of the job was that you meet so many kids with runny noses, coughing. The ones who were the sickest were the ones who wanted to love you the most. I don't know how many colds I caught during those years, but at times it was miserable. Those bouts with colds and flus tend to stick out in your memory, you know? Kids swarmed around me to take pictures and meet me. They'd want to put my chef's hat on or sneak on board the Wienermobile. I had heard that the other Little Oscars sometimes hit the kids or reprimanded them. I never did that. I just wouldn't do it.

My style was to joke with the kids and ask them their names. Oh, Brian? Brian Barracuda! Oh Jimmy? Jimmy Jellybean! Freddy? Okay, Freddy Freckles, here's your wiener whistle. Do you know the tune?

And then I'd ask them, "Do you know what an angolob sandwich is? You don't? Silly Billy! That's bologna spelled backwards. Have your mom buy some of the Oscar Mayer bologna in the store . . . you'll love it!"

A half an hour and three hundred wiener whistles later I was headed to the next appearance with the hatch secure on the Wienermobile and the air conditioner revved up. Sometimes I brought my own bag lunch and ate it on the way to the next town and scheduled appearance. We got used to the stares on the highway or at the stoplights. People loved looking at the Wienermobile cruising down their

◀ Serving up fine meats from Oscar Mayer to celebrities such
▲ as Hoot Gibson and Charlie Weaver (aka Cliff Arquette).

Appearing everywhere in the white chef's outfit as Little Oscar. I appeared on television, flew from city to city, and hawked hot dogs on radio with Bob Hope. Everywhere I went, kids wanted to meet Little Oscar and ride in the Wienermobile or just take pictures.

neighborhood streets or pulled up to an A&W as we ordered our lunch and ate our burger and fries pulled up curbside outside. One can only eat so many hot dogs, you know.

✦ ✦ ✦

The Wienermobile drivers who escorted us from place to place were young guys; I remember a few of them, one of them named Tony, who was from Costa Rica, drove with me for a while. He was fun to drive around with, and he would tell me about his country and how beautiful it was. A young guy named Earl Evans worked with me for a time, and he was a good driver and assistant. These guys were trained to handle the Wienermobile in all kinds of weather and help handle the crowds of kids. Luckily, we never got involved in any accidents. In almost ten years, no accidents. I was so lucky.

Unfortunately, the hazards of trying to maneuver the huge Wienermobile around crowds of children resulted in one fatality back East. I'm so glad this didn't happen where I was working as Little Oscar, because I'm not sure I could have continued after such a tragedy. Although the company wanted to keep this incident quiet at the time, it naturally hit the newspapers.

This accident involving the Wienermobile occurred in the summer of 1955 in the Chicago area. George Molchan was the Little Oscar working the appearance that day, and in a handwritten letter to me dated September 7, 1955, which I saved in my files, George related the accident. The death of a child in this matter made local news in the Midwest, but it did not affect the overall national Oscar Mayer Wienermobile campaign. For the entire Oscar Mayer company, however, it was a very sad day.

George wrote (in part):

. . . Getting serious for a minute, you probably have heard about the very unfortunate incident that happened to us with the Wienermobile. I'll tell you how it happened if you haven't heard, and if you have, maybe they didn't explain it to you properly but this is what happened.

We were pulling away from the courtesy call [at a store] near the Steel Mills, there were about thirty-five or forty children there. I talked with many of them and passed out whistles to every one then I got in, closed the door, we checked both sides of the Wienermobile and started away from the curb slowly. The store was located next to an alleyway and a car was protruding across the sidewalk and into the street. The driver and myself didn't see the accident, but the witnesses told us what happened. As we pulled away doing about eight miles an hour, this little girl about three and a half years old (I remember patting her on the head), darted out possibly from behind the protruding car, tripped and slid under our wheels.

We didn't know anything happened until we heard the people scream and we stopped. Getting out, we seen what happened and Jerry, I never again want to experience that kind of a feeling as I felt when I saw that little girl lying there in the street. It's really terrible. We had to follow the police and ambulance to the hospital where they pronounced the little girl dead. Well, you know what followed, coroner's inquest and court trials. The driver was exonerated and it was ruled an accident, but I never want to go through anything like it again. It took a while but we got the driver to drive again and he is working with me at present until he goes back to college. . . ."

George Molchan, Meinhardt Raabe, and I were Oscar Mayer's three most popular "Little Oscar" mascots.

It was during the Oscar Mayer years that my mother moved out to Los Angeles and she and my brother Emelio and I all lived in a house in Hollywood. In 1952, I was making an appearance as Little Oscar at a Von's market in Los Angeles down near the airport. I knew my mother was sick. She was a diabetic and she used to hide sweets and donuts, and we had to try to curb that. I think she died of a heart attack. My sister Rae and I had a dear friend name Marie Tuckey, and she called the Oscar Mayer company to track me down and finally got me at the store and someone from the company told me that my mother had died. The driver of the Wienermobile took me home right away and I met Marie at the house with Rae and my brother.

The Lord Don't Play Favorites

One of the biggest television roles of my life was something quite special at NBC. In fact, shows like this were called "spectaculars" back then. It was actually the first color TV spectacular broadcast live from NBC in Burbank, called *The Lord Don't Play Favorites,* and it was part of a series called Producer's Showcase. This was in 1956, and the studio had just been built and wasn't even completed yet.

In this two-hour musical TV special I did everything I wanted to do . . . singing, dancing, and acting, as myself. No elf costumes, no troll outfits. It starred Robert Stack, Kay Starr, and the legendary Louis Armstrong. And it was broadcast in full color, but most homes didn't have color televisions in those days. It was still experimental. Best of all, it was live, which meant lots of rehearsal. I told the Oscar Mayer company that I needed two weeks off, and if they didn't give it to me, I was quitting. That simple. So they gave me the time off. This TV special meant the world to me.

I had a terrific song and dance number called "David," which really went off well. I danced with Robert Stack and sang pretty well, if I do say so myself. It was my first high-salary job in television; I got about three thousand dollars for the job. Since it was live, I never did get to see it back then. But jumping forward several years, I ran into Robert Stack at NBC when I was doing an episode of *Night Court.* We talked about the special, and he told me he had a kinescope of the show at home and that he would dub me a copy. He kept his promise.

In the early 1950s, while I was doing Buster Brown on weekends in Los Angeles, I'd get on a plane or drive to some city and take part in midget wrestling with a couple of other little guys. I was in my early thirties then and in pretty good shape, and most of us little guys had a membership at the YMCA in Hollywood where we could work out and swim and exercise and practice the routines. It was also during this time that I picked up the habit of smoking cigars. I've enjoyed smoking ever since and I still will have one, maybe two cigars a day.

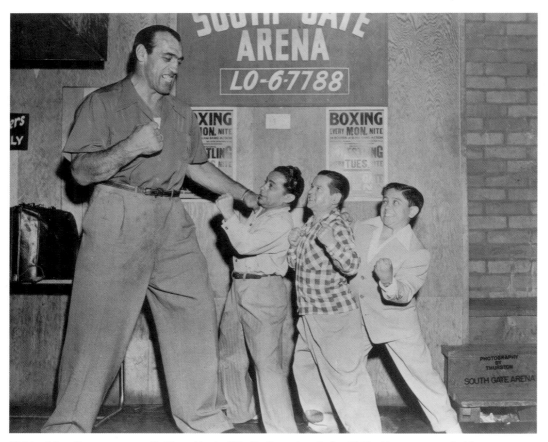

Fighter Primo Carnera poses with Harry Monty, Billy Curtis, and me in the 1940s. He was one really big, scary guy, but such a nice fellow when you got to know him.

A group of us little guys in a 1960s snapshot. *(left to right)* Harry Monty, me, Frank Delfino, Bob Kanter, and Felix Silla.

I've always loved the fights; you know, legitimate boxing. I was always a fan of big fighters over the years. I still am. So I jumped at the chance to get into the ring. The wrestling was mostly an act, although we really did wrestle in the ring and sometimes got hurt, but nothing serious. We'd call each other names, a lot of yelling, and Harry Monty would make his big finish with a bonsai. *Kaboom!* A big jump off the ropes right on top of one of us.

There were four of us in the act: me, Billy Curtis, Harry Monty, and Georgie Spotts. I was the hero a lot because I had the baby face, so my name was Baby Face Maren. Harry was usually the "heavy," because he was Russian and had that mean-looking, antagonistic face. Sometimes we called him "The Mighty Atom." Billy Curtis was "Marvelous Milty." We had two teams and in each state that we traveled to we'd change names. I'd wear red tights and the other guys would wear other colors. We would do a tag team match in the ring and actually throw each other around and jump off the ropes.

Little friends posing in descending height in Phoenix, Arizona, in the 1960s. *(left to right)* Bob Kanter, me, Margaret Pellegrini, and Felix Silla.

Since this was an act, we'd even enter the venue separately to keep up the image, like we were adversaries. We had well-known sponsors, and we were booked into places like the Chicago Stadium, one of our biggest engagements. We had a huge TV audience as well. I remember the night at Chicago Stadium, before the fight, we had interviews on live TV and we met the referee before the fight. He was a big drunken Irishman. He took us aside and told us, "It's gonna be an honest fight tonight, so it better be good." I went to the manager and said, "Look, wrestling is rehearsed; we rely on our tricks. This guy is saying we won't be able to do certain things." We were assured it was okay. It was actually a flop and we looked terrible in the ring.

We wrestled in New Jersey one time, because in New York there was a law that midgets and women could not wrestle. I had to come back to Los Angeles for work, so I asked a little friend of mine, Tommy Cottonaro, to sub for me and wear my tights and use my California license. It was on TV, and he was awful. He was fat and couldn't do the moves. All of my friends thought it was me taking the beating.

✦ ✦ ✦

Billy and me onstage with our act in the late 1940s.

I think I met Billy Barty at an interview for a film. He lived with his mother and father, not very far from where I lived. Billy was part of a showbiz family; they had a musical act that they performed in vaudeville. I was with Billy at his house one day and got a message to call my pal Jaspar, one of the casting guys at MGM. I called in and Jaspar told me that he had a quickie for me: Dave Chasen just called us and Jimmy Stewart is having a bachelor party here for dinner and drinks and they want to have a big surprise. Everybody in Hollywood is going to be there. What they want you to do is make an entrance from a huge platter, dressed in a diaper, and yell "Daddy!" . . . and then pee on him.

With my friend Billy Barty on the course. Together, Billy and I created the Little People of America in 1957. We were the founders. Billy really ran with it and built it into the vital nonprofit organization that it is today.

I said, "What? How am I gonna pee on cue? I can't do that." I convinced them to have Billy do it with me, both of us dressed as babies. So they got us both a syringe and filled it with water and put it right at our crotch. We did it. *Life* magazine covered it with a photo, and other magazines as well. Jimmy Stewart laughed like hell. I'll never

forget it. Later we got dressed and joined them for dinner. I've never been surrounded by so many stars in my life, and I'll never forget the special Russian steak, cooked in salt. It was so tender, it was fantastic.

Billy and I hit it off and quickly became buddies. We did an act together for a while, just after the war. Billy was going to Los Angeles City College to study journalism. He was a few years younger than me. We used to play ball together, and we decided to see if we could do an act with a little singing, dancing, a little of this and that, and try to get booked into some clubs as a real novelty. He did impersonations, like Louis Armstrong and Jimmy Durante. Later he did a great Liberace impression with Spike Jones. My part of the act was to sing "Louise" like Maurice Chevalier. I wrote some lyrics to a song called "Everywhere We Go," and Billy and I did a dance together. The act was never a big hit; we only played a few dates. Come to think of it, our act was probably lousy, but we sure had some fun doing it.

Billy and I worked many times together. I even stood in and doubled him in many films, like *Day of the Locust*. He was a guest star in the movie, and I was with him during the whole film. Billy became a first-rate actor, and Hollywood took notice of him. He was no longer some novelty act who stood on his head or did backflips. We did an episode of *Get Smart* together where he was up on my shoulders the entire time, and in one scene, I peeked my head out of the large trenchcoat we were walking around in.

It was in 1956 or so that Billy and I began talking about gathering us little ones into some sort of an organization, mainly to help each other. That was the prime purpose. Billy and I came up with the concept for the Little People of America, but I will let you in on a secret: the original chosen title for our organization was "Midgets of America." Yes, that's true. That's the title we went with for a while, and eventually Billy thought that Little People might be a more relevant and overall appropriate description, so he adopted that. After all, it is a kinder term.

I've never been crazy about the word *midget*. Over the years, the connotation has changed. The word didn't bother me one way or the other. I am what I am, but I will say this . . . my family never used it in reference to me. But I was raised in a time when it wasn't an unsavory word either. Back then, it wasn't necessarily a derogatory term, just a term. There were midget shows and midget vaudeville troupes, and come to think of it, back then there were more midgets in general. So it was right around the time I began performing onstage in an act and then did *The Wizard of Oz,* I became more acquainted with the word *midget.* After *Wizard of Oz,* I realized just how many little people there were in the world. I wasn't the only one in the neighborhood. Today, the word *midget* has lost

This was a group photo for the 1967 national convention for Little People of America (LPA), held at the Knickerbocker Hotel in Hollywood that year.

This is a group of members from the local chapter of the LPA in Hollywood in the 1970s. Many of us at the time were working actors: In this picture you can spot Billy Curtis, Felix Silla, Frank and Sadie Delfino, Billy Barty, Patty Maloney, and Hervé Villechaize.

its meaning. A lot of dwarfs prefer not to be known by that name, and it was Billy Barty who helped make the phrase "Little People" an accepted alternative. And that has really stuck.

Billy and I both got to work on the project, and in 1957 we had found a place in Reno to host our first convention of little people, the Riverside Hotel. We alerted all of our little friends across the country and urged them to participate if they could. Some of the founding members, our core group, were: Billy Barty, me, Harry Monty, Billy Curtis, Shirley Goldman, Jerry Austin, Gene Austin, Buddy Douglas, Harvey Stone, Frank and Sadie Delfino, Mickey Rosenburg, George Spotts, and Hazel and Buster Resmondo.

I'm not trying to take any credit away from Billy, because he really took the reins and ran with it. I was working quite a lot during these years, and quite frankly I was glad Billy was there to create this fine organization. His organizational skills were better than mine. But I'm proud to say I was there assisting

On the golf course in Azusa, California, in 1973 with Billy Barty, comedian Joe Bingo, and Billy Curtis.

him in laying the groundwork for Little People of America, Incorporated. There were, and there still are, so many more achondroplastic dwarfs like Billy, many more than pituitary midgets, so I urged Billy to become the head of it, even though it was a joint concept that we came up with together. And that's the way it should have been. I feel I was partly responsible, and it was my idea to start a golf tournament every year and Billy kind of ran with it, which was fine. I didn't want the pressure, but I played in many of the tournaments in the beginning.

The constitution for LPA was conceived in Reno, Nevada, in February

▲ Billy Barty and me behind the scenes of our episode of *Get Smart* in which he sat atop my shoulders in all of the scenes.
▶ With a Tattoo on my arm: Me and my pal, Hervé Villechaize, most recognizable from the TV show *Fantasy Island.*

1957. Billy appeared on Art Linkletter's television show that same month to announce the formation and first annual convention of Little People of America. The nonprofit organization was incorporated in the state of Indiana in 1961. Per our original constitution, the object of LPA is

to "provide and maintain, within its resources, an organization dedicated to uniting people of small stature (to be known as little people), in the work of promoting their highest interest, sociability, good friendship, and mutuality on the broadest principles of humanity, on a non-profit, non-political and non-sectarian basis. . . ." The purpose of LPA is to assist its members in adjusting to the social and physical problems of life caused by their small stature. Now more than fifty years old, LPA is still healthy and still going strong.

Eventually Billy and I also started our baseball team, called the Hollywood Shorties. We competed in some charity games against teams of firemen, policemen and such—all of average height. I'd play shortstop or second base, and if there was a big crowd I'd pitch. We always had to tell the competing teams: "No sliding!" If one of those guys came sliding in at us, they'd break our legs. Not that they'd do that, but we had to tell them.

Billy married a little lady, a Mormon from Utah. Billy respected her so much that he never drank at home; away from home, he liked to drink sometimes. But he respected his family. They had two kids, a little girl who was a dwarf and an average-sized boy. Billy introduced me to golf, which was one of the best things that ever happened to me because I ended up playing a lot and I became pretty good. It's been a passion of mine ever since. Billy died a few years ago, and I miss him. He was one of my best friends. I think of him every time I pick up the clubs.

+ + +

The Andy Williams Show

My first appearance on *The Andy Williams Show* was just supposed to be a one-shot thing as a spaceman. I worked really hard on that, and they asked me back to do this Little General character. I was a little German general with a spiked helmet and a colorful uniform dressed with medals. I would hit Andy with my swagger stick and yell German gibberish at him. I started working on some McDonald's hamburgers commercials at the time, and Andy Williams was taped on Saturdays, so it worked out okay.

For a few years, Andy Williams was known pretty much as a straight-as-an-arrow type of host, with musical guests and occasionally a sketch. Eventually, they wanted to compete with Jackie Gleason's show and add some more comedy, so producers Allan Blye and Chris Bearde (who came from *Laugh-In*) were brought in, and the show took on a cra-

A FEW WORDS FROM ANDY WILLIAMS

Jerry was on our show in the 1960s quite often, and he was always quite wonderful. Always great, and terrific to work with. Jerry was the German or Prussian General, and he'd pop up out of nowhere and hit me in the knee with a hammer or a riding crop. One time they had him descend from the top of the studio in a giant balloon, and it made its way center stage and he would bark out orders to me. He was very funny. My daughter Noel, who was little then, she was about five or six, was absolutely crazy about him. She loved this little guy. The sketches and bits Jerry did were very *Laugh-In*. For a couple of years, our show was like a musical *Laugh-In* with some wacky comedy. Some of our writers came right from *Laugh-In*, so our show was evolving and we were having fun with it. There'd be a contortionist who was in a walking suitcase. We had this cookie bear who would knock on doors begging for food, a giant bird, and crazy stuff would go on.

Unfortunately, I've never had the pleasure of playing golf with Jerry, because I understand he's pretty good. Come on down to beautiful Branson, Jerry. We'll hit some and talk about the old days.

◄ And he thinks *he's* tiny. With maybe the oddest guest star on *The Andy Williams Show*, singer Tiny Tim, in April 1970.

▶ The Little General pops out of a mini tank during a sketch.

zier look, with much more comedy and a bigger staff of young writers. I think Steve Martin was on the show once at the beginning of his career, and I had a scene with him, too.

We had an endless stream of new talent, with writers and performers on the show. Tiny Tim was something new back then, after his big appearances on *The Tonight Show*. They wrote sketches and had me in and out on the show in cute musical numbers, sometimes with big stars like Jimmy Durante, Liberace, Flip Wilson, Bob Hope, Jonathan Winters, the Osmond Brothers, all kinds of stars. He had to have sketches to break up the music sequences. They'd have big well-known music groups and guest stars, and once in a while I'd wander up near the dressing rooms and smell marijuana coming out the dressing rooms, especially the musicians'. It was a crazy time to be in television. I never would partake in that stuff, but a lot of writers and musicians did at the time.

Andy had a sequence with a bear that became a huge hit. Andy would be in the middle of a sequence and hear a knock on the door and it would be this talking bear who was looking for cookies. The bear popped up everywhere searching for cookies, and they just called him the Cookie Bear. The bear was played by Janos Prohaska, who had played bears and apes in films for years. A few times they had me in a baby bear costume and I

In a few sketches on *The Andy Williams Show,* I played a little dancing bear, while Janos Prohaska was the larger dancing bear. I wanted cookies! Andy loved to have Jonathan Winters on the show too.

would follow Janos looking for cookies, too. You'd be surprised how many fans sent in boxes of cookies to the show; then the cookie companies began shipping out cases and cases of complimentary goodies, hoping for a plug on the show.

I wish Andy would have used me on one of his Christmas specials during those years. He never did. I could have played an elf, but I guess no one thought of it. I'm not sure

As the Little General in a sketch with the great Jimmy Durante on *The Andy Williams Show* in 1970. The character of the Little General was the most memorable one I did on the show. I would interrupt Andy and yell German commands at him at the wildest times.

TO BOLDLY GO WHERE NO MIDGET HAS GONE BEFORE

BY STEPHEN BARRINGTON

The 1967 *Star Trek* episode "Journey to Babel" was just another job for Jerry Maren. He was not overly familiar with the show. "I had heard of *Star Trek;* I knew it was a space show and they wanted me and my partner Billy Curtis to appear on one of the episodes. The part wasn't much, it was a little thing," he says, intending no pun. "It was a big intergalactic convention and we were guests from one of the planets."

This particular episode featured the first appearance of Spock's parents, Sarek and Amanda. The *Enterprise* is en route to an important Federation conference on a planet. Code name: Babel. Traveling aboard are delegates from a multitude of planets.

Years ago, when *Star Trek* episodes were first released for home usage, two episodes at a time on videocassette, Jerry's scene at the buffet table with Curtis was featured on the box cover.

"The sets were terrific. They were very imaginative," Jerry remembers of his first impression of the Paramount sound stage. The scene was shot over a two-day period. "It was a big scene. A lot of people were in it and some extra makeup for many of them."

The director gave Jerry and Curtis specific instructions for their scene. "The director, Joseph Pevney, said to us, 'You're from another planet, so food is a little different than what you have on your own planet. Be suspicious of what you eat or look at.' Think 'What's that?'"

The food on the table was actually real, with Jerry admonishing his old stage partner, Billy Curtis, not to taste it. "Billy kept eating it. I said, 'Don't eat it! Because it's got to match the next scene. If you take something from the plate, it will look different.' Billy was nibbling at the food, but he was a rabble-rouser anyway."

The scene was a brief one on the television screen, lasting only about thirty seconds. "We were dressed up like Turks," remembers Jerry, made up with heavy gold makeup. Jerry says, "It wasn't very difficult to put on because there were no whiskers or beards to worry about. It took about a half hour to put on. The pay was about $110 a day. We could have insisted on more money, but it was a quickie and we were both working on other jobs, so we took it because the most it would be was two days."

Following that job, Jerry developed a liking for the original *Star Trek* series. "I think the show is still popular because it is

Talk about little men from Mars . . . Billy Curtis and I played visitors from another planet on *Star Trek*.

fascinating and it is different. You never knew what was going to happen and the suspense was wonderful. The people loved the different characters."

"Never in a million years" was Jerry's response when asked if he ever thought *Star Trek* would achieve the fame that it since has. "It was the same thing with *The Wizard of Oz*. But since then, they've both become classics."

More hilarity with Jonathan Winters, cast, crew, and Andy Williams.

Andy was all that crazy about all of the silly stuff on his show, because he was concerned with his image as a singer and the producers were taking his show in some strange directions, but once he let his hair down it all fell together and his show once again gained in the ratings. His holi-

This was one of the few times I was not in costume on *The Andy Williams Show*. This episode had golfer Jack Nicklaus as a guest (and the Cookie Bear on the right, played by Janos Prohaska).

day shows were something the whole country tuned in to; that's why he's done so well in Branson, Missouri, with his own theatre—especially around Christmastime.

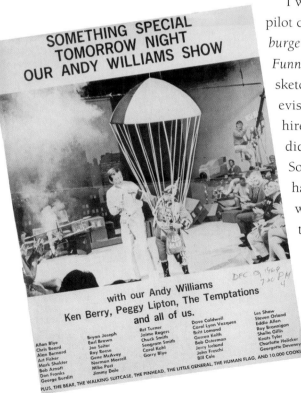

SOMETHING SPECIAL TOMORROW NIGHT
OUR ANDY WILLIAMS SHOW

with our Andy Williams
Ken Berry, Peggy Lipton, The Temptations
and all of us.

Allan Blye
Chris Beard
Alan Bernard
Art Fisher
Mark Shekter
Bob Arnott
Don Franks
George Burditt

Bryan Joseph
Earl Brown
Joe Seiter
Ray Reese
Gene McAvoy
Norman Morrell
Mike Post
Jimmy Dale

Ret Turner
Jaime Rogers
Chuck Smith
Seagram Smith
Carol Kohl
Garry Blye

Dave Caldwell
Carol Lynn Vazquez
Britt Lomond
Gerren Keith
Bob Osterman
Jerry Ireland
John Freschi
Bill Cole

Les Shaw
Steven Orland
Eddie Allen
Ray Brannigan
Sheila Gillis
Keats Tyler
Charlotte Halicker
Georgette Deveney

PLUS, THE BEAR, THE WALKING SUITCASE, THE PINHEAD, THE LITTLE GENERAL, THE HUMAN FLAG, AND 10,000 COOKIES!

I worked a lot with Chris Bearde. We did a pilot called *WOW*. Another one was called *Hamburgers* with Sid Ceasar. And a pilot called *TV Funnies* with Conrad Bain, where I played in a sketch as a little dictator. Chris produced a televised version of the musical *Li'l Abner* and hired several of us little guys. The pilots didn't really sell, but Chris put me in them. Some shows worked and others didn't, but I have him to thank for a lot of television work. He's called me his lucky charm more than once.

Films and television allowed me to meet some of my idols. I was standing in on a movie called *The One and Only Original Family Band* at Walt Disney studios. We had a lot of little people working as

◀ We were called the Williams Weirdos on *The Andy Williams Show*. This episode had guest star Liberace in a sketch with Chris Bearde and Allan Blye.

▼ I've worked several times with Mel Brooks directing, and always the footage was cut. I don't know why. In *Silent Movie* he had several of us little guys playing golf out on a course.

stand-ins for the kids. I saw Jack Nicklaus coming into the stage area with his wife. I couldn't believe it; nobody was making a fuss over him. He was visiting the set. I was so interested in golf, and I knew exactly who he was. I asked the photographer to take our photo together, and eventually we met again several times on *The Andy Williams Show* and we even did a sketch together. He was the golfing champ, and I was the pro out at the miniature golf course.

Lidsville

I thought I'd seen it all on television with the crazy stuff from *The Andy Williams Show,* but producers Sid and Marty Krofft were on the horizon. They produced a movie and Saturday morning kids show called *H.R. Pufnstuf,* which became quite successful. Sid was more on the creative side, very hands-on with the scripts and costumes, designs, and such. His brother Marty was more of the money man, the business side of the shows, keeping the

I played a variety of the wacky hat characters in Sid and Marty Krofft's *Lidsville* on Saturday morning television.

Occasionally I played "Raunchy Rabbit" on *Lidsville*.

productions running. This time, they came back to TV on Saturday morning again with a show about a boy (Butch Patrick) who gets caught up in an amazing world with a crazed green magician named Hoo Doo (Charles Nelson Reilly) and a genie named Weenie (Billie Hayes). The land that they inhabited was overrun with Hat People, and it was all very much like a dream . . . or a nightmare, depending on your tastes. The Kroffts hired all kinds of little people to play these hat characters. They found a troupe that went way back, a group called the Hermine Midgets who started back in the late 1930s and toured Europe and the United States. Some of them were European midgets, and their troupe rivaled Leo Singer's Midgets. I know some of them worked in the Margaret O'Brien film *Three Wise Fools* because I was in that, too. Later on, in the 1950s, Hermine's group was dwindling, but some of them were in the Danny Kaye musical *The Court Jester.* On *Lidsville,* which was around 1970 or so, all that were left were the older midgets, just a few of the last surviving members of the troupe. Some of their last work was as these crazy giant hats.

The show lasted two seasons, from 1971 to 1973. Other midgets who worked with me on *Lidsville* were Buddy Douglas and Felix Silla. This was one of the weirder TV shows I've done. The hats varied: the cowboy hat spoke with a John Wayne voice; the pith helmet had an English

LIDSVILLE IN PERSON

The Torrance Tournament of Roses Association Presents:
IN PERSON: Butch Patrick, Star of the ABC Television Show: *"LIDSVILLE"* and four of the Syd & Marty Kroft Lidsville Characters: **Rah-Rah, Tonsilini, Raunchy Rabbit, The Indian.**

They'll be giving autographs and making merry through our mall Saturday, December 11 and Saturday, December 18 . . . 1 - 5 p.m. Come meet and greet these television "fun" people — stars of the ABC Television show, "Lidsville" — whick may be seen Saturday mornings at 9:30 a.m. on Channel 7.

I also played the football helmet named "Rah Rah" on *Lidsville*.

FANTASYLAND—Sid and Marty Krofft (in background from left) welcome cast of little people who will be featured in new ABC Children's program, Lidsville, airing in the fall. The Kroffts design all of the fantasy costumes for the cast.

Times photo by Harry Chase

accent; the football helmet, which I remember playing fairly often, had a tough voice; the chef's hat had a French accent. You get the picture. From day to day, the midgets changed costumes, so we never really had any set characters to play. The voice actors sat off to the side in a special set-up studio looking at monitors or though the glass, dubbing live as the characters moved on stage. Take after take, and this really became a challenge for Charles Nelson Reilly. He hated the show, but kids loved it. Charlie hated his green makeup and caused delays with the schedule, sometimes not even showing up for work. I think that's why the show didn't last very long.

A FEW WORDS FROM LENNIE WEINRIB
(WRITER AND VOICE ACTOR ON *LIDSVILLE* AND *H.R. PUFNSTUF*)

Like all the other kids on earth, I fell in love with Jerry in *The Wizard of Oz,* so you can imagine my delight to work with him on *H.R. Pufnstuf* and *Lidsville.* I got to see a lot of his work, as we recorded the shows live from a sound booth on the set. We did take after take, live! The voices were performed in sync with the actors and the Hats (Lids) played by Jerry Maren and his little pals. We worked in front of monitors and watched as the Hats ran around, and we did it live over and over along with them. At the end of the day, we couldn't talk anymore, and Jerry and the gang were dead tired. It was hard and hot work for those folks wearing those heavy costumes under the glaring hot lights. Have no fear, though, Jerry came through with flying colors as the pro he has always been.

What a delight for me to watch the little people work. They are so kind and hard-working, and I know it was not easy for them to do all the physical running around, over and over. I've remembered en-joying watching little people since I was a kid, some working in the circus, some in movies. Funny, I never really thought of them as little people. I think they are the grandest and biggest folks I have ever had the pleasure to work with. We have truly been blessed to have the likes of Jerry Maren in our lives, and in our business.

H.R. Pufnstuf and a cast of crazies.

▲ On the set of *Bewitched* in a Halloween episode with Felix Silla, Billy Curtis, and me.
▶ I was also in a Christmas episode of *Bewitched*. Off the set, while we weren't shooting a scene, I'd be in Elizabeth Montgomery's dressing room talking about the races and betting on certain horses with the racing form. She loved betting on the races and knew quite a bit about it. I was impressed by that. What a fun gal to work with.
▼ I worked as a stand-in and stunt double for the little boy (Darby Hinton, with me on the right) in the television show *Daniel Boone* with Fess Parker.

(Clockwise from top left) Making an appearance on TV's bizarre top-rated show *Laugh-In* in 1971 with Dan Rowan and Dick Martin. Billy Curtis and I played little thieves dressed as children (I was Mildred) in *The Lucy Show*. In the groundbreaking 1960s sitcom *Julia*, with Diahann Carroll, I played a little guy in an alien getup. This was the same shiny green Martian wardrobe I used for an episode of *The Beverly Hillbillies* and scared the hell out of Granny Clampett. At right I'm posing with Michael Link and Marc Copage, the kids from *Julia*.

Elizabeth and me in the spring of 1992. This is one of our favorite portraits together.

WITH A LITTLE LUCK

As I SAID, IT WAS Billy Barty who introduced me to golf. He was good at the game, but I beat him all the time. We were competitive about the sport. I'm not bragging, but I've got longer arms and legs. He did much better than a man of his size, but I could still beat him. Later, when his legs got so bad, I'd give him the edge, because I wanted him to still enjoy the game.

After I began playing often, I learned as I went and picked up tips from other people. I used to play with kids' clubs and junior clubs, but later I had custom clubs made.

One of the earliest lessons I learned was following through and keeping your head down. Naturally you want to see where the ball goes. That was hard to break that. Even when you're putting, the head must be still.

I should be the world champion midget golfer—I can beat anybody my size on a

◀ Billy Barty and I competed at the Rio Bravo Country Club in Bakersfield, California, in 1992.

▼ Several of us friends gathered for Ralph Edwards's television show *This Is Your Life* to pay tribute to Billy Barty in 1960. Little Billy Rhodes, Billy Curtis, me, and Ruth Delfino all reminisced about Billy *(far right)* on the episode.

◀ I took part in many of Billy Barty's successful charity golf tournaments over the years.

Comparing swings with my friend, golf champ Jack Nicklaus.

good day. I am confident of that. Depending upon the course now, my handicap is about a 26. For me that's good. I used to be an 18 handicap. I'd say the early 1980s were my best years for golf. I've played in maybe a hundred or more tournaments. I fly out to Vegas and play twice a year in a tournament, and I've been doing that for years. One of my proudest moments was when Jack Nicklaus complimented me on my style and swing. I've never forgotten that.

✦ ✦ ✦

When I left the Oscar Mayer company, I visited the Scripps Clinic in San Diego and had tests and consultations with some endocrinologists there. A doctor there persuaded me to try some new hormonal treatments to promote some growth. I agreed, but I hated the damned shots. It was uncomfortable and sometimes painful. These days they have made strides in synthetic hormones and the treatment of dwarfism. That is why there are so few midgets in the world today.

I had this dream, really more than a dream, that if I could have grown, I might have been the greatest baseball player who ever lived. Joe DiMaggio was my hero, and I've loved the sport since I was a kid in Boston. I was a good little athlete, but I accepted my situation: I wasn't going to be playing pro baseball.

Yes, I played shortstop.

So here I was in my late thirties and doctors were still experimenting with me. Finally, after a year or more, they came to the conclusion that my bones had fused and there was no way of stimulating any new growth. I was, by this time, about four-foot-three. I had been growing, little by little, even into my thirties. What the shots did, however, was thrust me into puberty, which I had not reached at that point. I know that sounds crazy, but the timing of puberty varies widely among pituitary dwarfs. Some reach puberty during their normal teenage stretch; some never reach puberty at all—you can recognize that because of their high-pitched voice and lack of facial hair. In my case, I was forced into puberty by the hormones, and believe me, my life changed drastically. I started growing hair in all kinds of places, and when I was able to grow a nice thick mustache, I loved the look and I've kept it, on and off (mostly on) for years. The sudden alterations in my body had me looking at women like I had never looked before. I was dating much more than I had ever before, and at this time in my life, I was also searching for a mate. I was ready.

✢ ✢ ✢

I was a member of the Hollywood Shorties baseball team for many years. I was the shortstop. No jokes, please—I've heard 'em all.

One of my best friends, Billy Albaugh, a little guy from Florida, was visiting me, and he happened to bring up a monthly LPA newsletter for me to look at and mentioned this gal who was pictured in there who lived in Jacksonville. Their chapter in Florida called themselves the Mini Gators. I inquired about this one little gal in a photo, her name was Elizabeth Barrington. She looked cute and I asked him to get me her address. I wrote her and we wrote back and forth, we corresponded about everything. I'd call her and we'd talk on the phone for long stretches. Then I traveled to see her, and that's how we met.

I was living in a house with my brother on McCadden Place in Hollywood. My brother also owned apartments on Gordon Street, so when Elizabeth came to visit me in Los Angeles, she rented an apartment to stay at while she was visiting me. I think I was ready to get married, too. I was in my mid-fifties, and Elizabeth was in her early thirties. There was a big gap there, but we didn't care. We never really decided whether or not to have children, it just wasn't an issue. It was kind of an unspoken mutual agreement . . . whatever happens, happens. No regrets in that department. As it turns out, we never did have any kids and we have always been content that way.

I was born in 1945, on Christmas day, in Mobile, Alabama. (My mother used to tell me Santa Claus dropped me in her stocking.) I'm the oldest of twelve children. I was very tiny as a kid, and I grew to four-foot-four, which I am now. My parents were both southerners and good providers. We didn't have a lot, but we never went hungry. I helped raise the rest of my brothers and sisters. I attended Catholic schools, and after high school and college I was offered a job in Jacksonville, Florida, as a data processor, and I moved away from home. I worked at the Naval Air Station there until I met Jerry and he kidnapped me and brought me to California.

I'd never dated another little person before, but I was a member of the Florida chapter of LPA (called the Mini Gators). Through LPA I

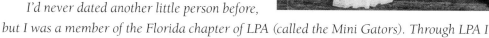

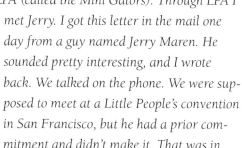

met Jerry. I got this letter in the mail one day from a guy named Jerry Maren. He sounded pretty interesting, and I wrote back. We talked on the phone. We were supposed to meet at a Little People's convention in San Francisco, but he had a prior commitment and didn't make it. That was in

▲ Our wedding in 1975, in Las Vegas, with six-footer Judge James Brennan. I was fifty-five years old and Elizabeth was twenty-eight. At first, when the judge walked in, we thought it was a gag.

◄ Las Vegas mogul Sam Boyd, our good friend, pulled out all the stops and laid out the red carpet for our wedding at the downtown Las Vegas California Hotel and Casino.

With my darling Elizabeth on a cruise aboard the *Dawn Princess*.

1973. He said, "I'll come and see you." At Christmastime of 1974 he came out to see me and we hit it off right away.

At least twice a week he said, "Why don't you come out and visit me here in LA," and so I did a few months later. We did all the touristy stuff, and we also went out to Las Vegas. While I was on that trip, he proposed to me at the Tic Toc restaurant in Los Angeles. So I went back home, quit my job, and came out West. Jerry was living with his brother, Emelio, and I moved in the same apartment complex until we got married and we built our home.

Both Jerry and I were content to be married to each other and have no children. We were both from such big families, we appreciated the privacy, actually. We could have had children, but neither of us wanted children with any great passion. So we have a love story, I think. We're not just lovers, but we're best friends first. He's like my baby now.

When Jerry decided to get married, he called his friend Sam Boyd in Las Vegas and we decided on May 10, 1975, to do this. I shopped for my wedding dress and found a really

nice white dress in a children's store for twenty-five dollars. Jerry went to a tailor and had a
$450 tuxedo custom made. It's usually the other way around. I could have spent more, but
I really liked the dress I'd found.

Jerry Remembers His Wedding

My old friend Sam Boyd said, "What? You're getting married? Stupid!" Of course he was kidding, but he gave me a lot of trouble. I was just asking him about getting a nice room or suite in Vegas when we came out there. He asked me, "When are you coming out here, what plane, what time . . ." I told him the details and flight number. I had no idea what he was going to do, but he arranged a stretch limo to pick us up at the airport. Sam was opening this new place called the California Hotel in downtown. Sam was a big Vegas entrepreneur and hotel owner.

We got to the hotel, and we went up to Sam's office to see him and thank him. We told him we couldn't stay long because we had to get our wedding license. Sam says, "Wait right here. I'm going to take care of everything." He picks up the phone and calls city hall. We then went to city hall, where all the people were waiting. A man came up to us and said, "Are you Mr. Marenghi?" Yes. "Come up here."

Sam arranged the judge for us and our entire wedding in the

Elizabeth and I were appearing at a promotion along with tennis pro Bobby Riggs and actress/ model Mamie Van Doren in October 1976.

honeymoon suite there at the California. At three o'clock, the judge walks in. I looked at him and I said, "Holy shit!" He was about six-foot-six. I thought Sam was trying to pull a stunt to get some publicity, but he wasn't. It was just a coincidence that the guy happened to be so tall, and with him standing next to us it looked like the wedding of Tom Thumb or something. Sam's son used to go to college with the judge, and he came over to do it as a favor.

Sam went all out and had flowers in our room, a bouquet for Elizabeth, everything we could have wanted. And he paid for the entire three-day weekend for our honeymoon. He treated us like royalty, and we were so grateful.

On our wedding night, Elizabeth and I went down to the lobby to eat a nice dinner. We sat down for dinner, and we were sitting in an area where they were playing Keno. Sam was there, and he asked me if I wanted to play. I told him, "No, this is my wedding day, I'm not going to gamble." Well, my usual thing is to bet with six particular numbers. I didn't put in a Kino card and I didn't bet a thing. Well, we were still watching and what comes up? My six numbers exactly. Boom. Boom. Boom. The numbers I always play, there they were. And I didn't bet. I could've won about a hundred thousand dollars. Can you believe that? If I had, I would have given a big portion to Sam, who was responsible for everything on our honeymoon, but that's the way the luck ran.

My brother and I owned this empty lot here in the Hollywood Hills, not far from the Hollywood Bowl, about an acre, and as a wedding gift, he gave me his part of it. We gathered the contractors and landscapers and designed the house with an architect and built the house we live in now, with customized cabinets, countertops, furnishings, all scaled down. The light switches and keyholes are lower. The shower heads are lower. Nothing is extremely low, but they are all reachable for us without making it a hardship to live here. We really wanted a comfortable place for us. We found miniature furniture: couch, dining room table, office desk, and the like. All of my cars have been customized with extensions on the accelerator and brakes and a built-up seat. I used to use pillows in some of my earlier cars, but you slip off the pillows and then you're in trouble. Too temporary.

A Few More Words from Elizabeth

Today, Jerry and I still travel, and he makes personal appearances all across the country. We love to fly. We watch baseball games together, races on TV, and check the horses we've

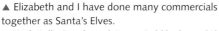
▲ Elizabeth and I have done many commercials together as Santa's Elves.
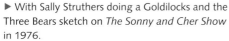
▶ With Sally Struthers doing a Goldilocks and the Three Bears sketch on *The Sonny and Cher Show* in 1976.

bet on. We watch Wheel of Fortune, *and we enjoy spending time with one another. We're private people, and very content. As far as film and TV work, we're both retired mostly. I never intended to work in films until I met Jerry. He got me into the business out here. The first film I worked on was* The Apple Dumpling Gang, *in which I doubled a little boy and did all his stunts. I had no experience. They needed someone who was agile and who could tumble. I worked for Disney a lot in those days, because they had so many children in their movies and TV shows. I am the same size as a little kid, and it's easy to disguise me as a child, so I was able to do it as long as it wasn't anything too dangerous.*

I worked in the movie Freaky Friday, *where I rode in a car that was driving down about four flights of concrete stairs and smashed into something. I did it and got paid pretty* well for a stunt like that. I never had any mishaps.

I've done a lot of doubling. One time I did a commercial for a household cleaner that required a child's handprints on a refrigerator door. They brought me in and dirtied my hands and had me do it. The production company didn't have to hire a child—along with the teacher or welfare worker that might have gone along with the child working on the set.

I did the big-screen version of the musical *Annie* in the early 1980s. There were several little girls on that film, and I stood in for many of them. I did some doubling and stunts for Aileen Quinn, who played Annie. They had me in the red wig and red dress climbing up a steel girder way up in the air. The great John Huston directed that, and it was one of the last things he did. He was sick at the time and had breathing problems.

I have to say, though, that some of the most

Elizabeth and I worked on the pilot for *Wizards and Warriors* wearing some creepy costumes in April 1982.

fun I had was working in television on the McDonald's commericals. They paid well . . . and I got to fly.

Cork Hubbard and I did a funny little bit with Bill Murray in the movie *Where the Buffalo Roam* in 1974. Not one of Murray's best. The movie was based on events in the life of Dr. Hunter S. Thompson.

▶ In the TV show *When Things Were Rotten,* directed by Mel Brooks, Elizabeth and I were dressed in period costumes for a bit that eventually got cut and never made it to air.

▼ This monstrous set was for a Wurlitzer organ commercial in 1973. As elves, we danced out a tune on this gigantic forty-foot-long model of an organ keyboard.

▶ In a series of episodes of the TV show *Mary Hartman, Mary Hartman* in 1977, several of us little actors (including Patty Maloney and Felix Silla) played a mini SWAT team in the town of Fernwood.

▼ In 1965 I played the mayor of Munchkinland in a stage production of *The Wizard of Oz* with Sterling Holloway starring as the Scarecrow. This southern California Valley Music Theatre production was a bright and lively version of the musical with mostly children as the Munchkins.

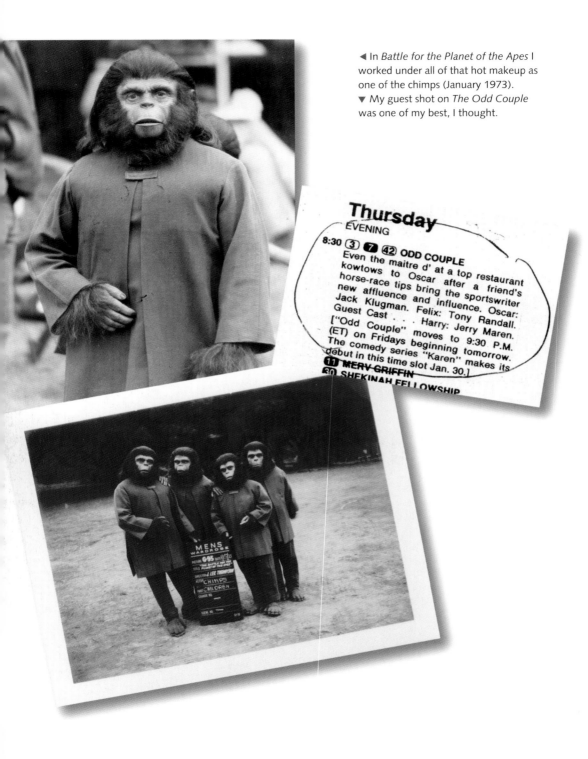

◄ In *Battle for the Planet of the Apes* I worked under all of that hot makeup as one of the chimps (January 1973).

▼ My guest shot on *The Odd Couple* was one of my best, I thought.

Thursday

EVENING

8:30 ③ ⑦ ㊷ **ODD COUPLE**
Even the maitre d' at a top restaurant kowtows to Oscar after a friend's horse-race tips bring the sportswriter new affluence and influence. Oscar: Jack Klugman. Felix: Tony Randall. Guest Cast . . . Harry: Jerry Maren. ["Odd Couple" moves to 9:30 P.M. (ET) on Fridays beginning tomorrow. The comedy series "Karen" makes its debut in this time slot Jan. 30.]

⑪ **MERV GRIFFIN**

㉚ **SHEKINAH FELLOWSHIP**

144

I worked as a stand-in and double for some of the kids in the television show *Bad News Bears* starring Jack Warden.

The mostly midget cast of the low budget action movie *Little Cigars:* Frank Delfino, Felix Silla, Angel Tompkins, Billy Curtis, Jerry Maren, and Emory Souza. *The Little Cigars Mob* (more commonly called just *Little Cigars*) was a funny little movie in 1973 about a gang of midget bank robbers. Blonde beauty Angel Tompkins played the leader of the gang in this action-packed drive-in movie. This was actually a big role for me. I played a character named "Cadillac."

5

FROM MUNCHKINLAND TO McDONALDLAND

*M*aybe one of the luckiest things to happen to me in my career was landing the work in McDonald's commercials for more than ten years. Believe me, Big Mac built my house, which is why I have a little golden arches mounted right on my front door. Anyone who's knocked on my front door knows it's true.

McDonald's hired several little people and a few guys of short stature to get into these huge costumes. Those commercials we made in the 70s were the greatest the company ever did. They created a series of characters with giant heads (very much in the style of Disney's giant-head Mickey Mouse character who wanders Disneyland, or Hanna Barbera's TV show *The Banana Splits,* or Sid & Marty Krofft's *H.R. Pufnstuf* and *Lidsville*). These were very popular at the time, and when McDonald's introduced these colorful characters and integrated them with their Kids Meals, things really took off. I'm quite sure they inspired

I think we made the best commercials McDonald's ever put on television. This rare photograph from the early 1970s shows our director, Lee Marsh, surrounded by the entire McDonaldland cast. Ronald McDonald was portrayed by actor King Moody for many years.

generations of kids, who loved seeing these commercials in between their Saturday morning cartoon shows. We did ten to fifteen commercials a year with McDonald's. Some were more elaborate than others, even with special effects.

Ronald McDonald was hugely popular, and the guy who performed him was named King Moody. King was a stage and television actor, and some might recognize him from the role of "Schtarker," the sidekick of KAOS leader "Siegfried" on the TV show *Get Smart*. I know McDonald's made King a rich man.

King could be strict about his work schedule. He would not work on the weekends. It would have been too expensive, anyway. Elizabeth and I went to several of King's weddings. He always liked his beer on the set. As long as there was a case of ice cold Heineken on hand during the shoot, he was all right. He'd sit in his director's chair and take off that red wig and relax with a beer during the breaks. At the end of the day, he would sometimes be swaying a little bit. I wouldn't say he was drunk, but that's what quenched his thirst while working under that hot makeup each day. Ronald McDonald was a happy clown, believe me. Today, they'd never let the actor do that on the set, and if they did, it would be a closed set. Elizabeth and I knew King fairly well. Sadly, he died suddenly about ten years ago.

Taking a break with the top off. Let me tell you . . . those hamburgers got hot.

✦ ✦ ✦

The storylines in these commercials, if you could call them that, were quite simple: Grimace can't find his french fries and it turns out the Hamburglar has made off with them, shouting "Robble Robble!" Smiling Ronald McDonald jumps to the rescue.

Mostly, we did those McDonald's commercials at what was called California Studios; it's now called Raleigh Studios. That was their first big major set. Then we later moved over to a soundstage at the Columbia Ranch, which is now the Warner Ranch.

Once us little guys were assigned which role we would do, the cast was usually handed a storyboard and a brief script, which was only a few pages for the TV spot. There was some rehearsal, and then we immediately went into shooting. None of us, except Ronald,

supplied our own voices, so we were silent in those costumes. Our voices were dubbed in later by people like Howard Morris and Allan Melvin, and maybe some other cartoon voiceover actors. I'd switch roles off and on, and that made it more fun. Most often, I was Mayor McCheese or Big Mac. When I was Big Mac, my friend Billy Curtis would be Mayor McCheese. We switched off sometimes. One of my favorites was a Western-themed McDonald's commercial, where I was the Hamburglar coming in and out of those swinging barroom doors. Another spot, where I was also the Hamburglar, had me in the zoo standing next to a zebra.

We had fantastic large costumes for Big Mac, Mayor McCheese, the Hamburglar, Grimace, and all the rest. None of us quite knew what Grimace was supposed to be. I don't think we ever found out. He was just some big blob with bulging eyes. The sets were elaborate at times, and always bright with vibrant colors. And the commercials

paid in spades over a period of time, because they were run and rerun over and over.

The main drawback to those commercials was the fatigue. The costumes were hot but bearable. Unfortunately, they were also very heavy. Early on I asked them to build me something where I could just get out of the costume when I needed to. So the prop men build a little corral with wooden posts, where I could walk in between and set the head piece down and get out from under it easily, and then I could get back into it easily without requiring too much assistance.

Sometimes I played Mayor McCheese.

Those character heads rested on a big wire tray that went around our neck. That tray or tracking was connected to a harness that we wore around our waist and chest, which would support the giant headpiece. All of this was strapped in securely. When you're in that giant head for hours, you get a little crazy. The costumes were so heavy, the trick was: when you're not shooting . . . SIT!

You couldn't see very well at all in those heads, so you stared down at the ground to get your placing. When I'd run through it, I'd do it without the headpiece and observe where I'd be going, taking note of what was on the ground and making sure nothing would be in my way. We did the best we could. If we had to go up stairs in those things, we would rehearse it carefully. I never fell

▶ I was Big Mac more often than not.
(*Following pages*) Sample storyboards from several McDonald's commercials we filmed in the 1970s.

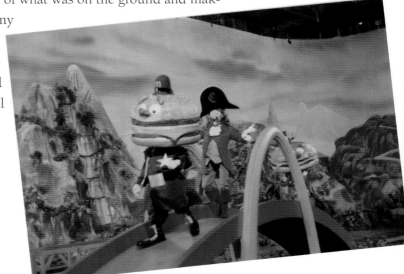

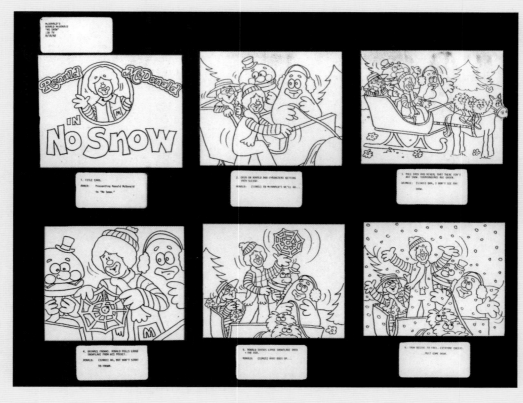

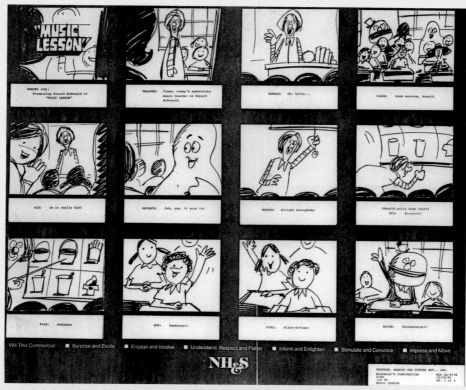

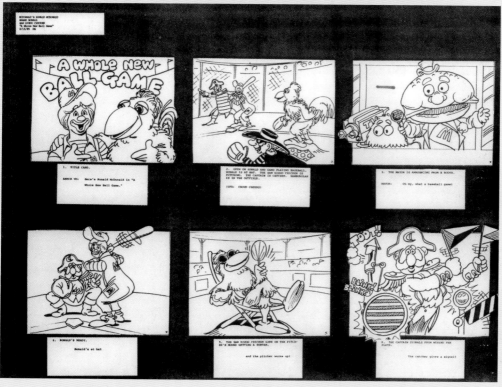

King Moody, the man who played Ronald McDonald in the '60s and '70s.

over in the costume although a few other guys did. It was inevitable to knock into another character or into something else, but I never saw anyone get injured.

They had people help us put these over-sized hamburger costumes on and remove them. The costumes were heavy. At the end of the day, it was a relief. The wardrobe people took those costumes and guarded them because most of the time, they didn't have more than one giant head for Mayor McCheese or Big Mac on hand. No, I didn't take any of them home with me. The earlier giant heads were made of a wood and rubber and fiberglass, painted and glazed, that you could knock on with your knuckles. Inside they were hollow and no ventilation and very little visi-

Help! Billy Curtis, Frank Delfino, and I were dressed as aliens for an appearance at Hollywood's Capitol Records building, and we ran into the Beatles' drummer Ringo Starr.

◄ Behind the scenes with little Angelo Rossitto and Billy Curtis on the McDonald's set.
▼ "Robble Robble" . . . that's all the Hamburglar said!

bility. Later, they made lighter foam-like giant heads and they didn't look as good, but they were lighter to wear.

We never got any product from McDonald's, no free burgers or fries just because I was Mayor McCheese. But one year, when those new gift certificates first came out around Christmas, Elizabeth and I "liberated" a handful of those just like good little Hamburglars. The producer was handing them out one day and left a bunch in the lunch area, so we felt entitled to some freebies, and we gave them out to friends during the holidays.

Elizabeth ended up working on several McDonald's commercials, sometimes as the Hamburglar and other times as a dancing trash can or something like that. She loved the work too, and proved valuable for the production. I'll let her tell you about it.

A McNugget from Elizabeth

Frankie Delfino was usually the Hamburglar, and he was very nervous about heights. He would not do anything if he had to get off the ground. Since Frankie and I were about the same size, I always did the wire work for him; I know Jerry was very nervous watching me forty feet up in the air hanging there on wires.

I did one commercial where I doubled the Hamburglar, and Jerry was in it also as another Hamburglar. Like twin Hamburglars! They had us both in the big hat and striped prison outfit, and we were both sitting on a teeter totter or something like that, with Jerry on one side and me on the other. We worked maybe a few hours and with pay and residuals, I ended up making about fifteen thousand dollars after a year or so when the commercial kept playing and residuals kept adding up. . . . for just a few hours work. How's that? It doesn't happen like that all the time, but once in a while you get a goody like that.

On my busiest day, I'll never forget my frantic schedule. Work stacked up on me, I wasn't sure I could handle it; I had to flee from one job to the next in a panic. This one particular day, I started out working on the *Daniel Boone* television series, where I was standing in for the little boy. I asked them to let me go as soon as possible because I had to do a McDonald's commercial. I called Billy Curtis and he said, "Don't worry, I'll jump in your costume if I need to." Fortunately I got through early with *Daniel Boone* at 20th Century-Fox studios. I made it to the other studio, now called Raleigh Studios near Paramount, and did our McDonald's stuff. I was lucky. I was Big Mac for a few hours as needed. Then I rushed over to NBC for rehearsals for *The Andy Williams Show*. Later that night I had to appear as

▶ I played a Munchkin (that's me on the right) on a Barry Manilow TV special.

▼ Bob Towers (Captain Crook), Frank Delfino (Hamburglar), me (Big Mac), and the director on the McDonald's set.

a Leprechaun, so I brought my wardrobe with me to *The Andy Williams Show.* Knowing those rehearsals might get out late, I dressed as the Leprechaun at NBC, jumped in the car, and drove to Casey's Bar at Sixth and Grand . . . I was their resident leprechaun. I made it down there and did my stuff, and I also had to judge some kind of contest that night. I rushed home at night, and there I was on television because they'd had local news cameras at the bar that night. That was the finish of that day. . . . one helluva day.

I continued to work in commercials and used some of my time off during television hiatuses to do some theater work. Anyone who knows me knows that I'm not much for big stage roles because it's a chore for me to remember long stretches of dialogue. It's just

one of those things. But if the part is right, I'll grab it. I was invited by a theatre company in Los Angeles one year to play the Mayor of Munchkinland in a Valley Music Theatre production of *The Wizard of Oz*. Only one other little guy, Frank Delfino, worked in the show, and the rest of the Munchkins were handled by a talented group of kids. I remember Sterling Holloway was the Scarecrow in this production, and he was a hit in the show.

One summer I traveled out to the Midwest to do a stage musical with several other little guys. It was an elaborate production of *Snow White and the Seven Dwarfs,* a massive new musical adaptation of the Walt Disney animated film. Carmine Coppola (father of film director Francis Ford Coppola) was the music director. The entire production was done under the strict supervision of Walt Disney studios. The play had bright-colored costumes and sets with special effects around every corner. The massive outdoor stage in St. Louis at the Municipal Opera Theatre in Forest Park was so big it was like playing to the Hollywood Bowl. When you're singing, you'd see the bugs flying around in the lights and you had to worry about whether a moth was going to fly into your mouth. The theatre com-

▶ While performing as the Dwarfs in a stage version of *Snow White and the Seven Dwarfs* in St. Louis in 1972, we were greeted by Liza Minelli backstage. She was in town rehearsing her own stage show. I played Sleepy the Dwarf (second from right).

◀ Several of us little guys worked in a television special version of the musical *Li'l Abner* in 1971.

The cast of *Snow White and the Seven Dwarfs* at the massive outdoor St. Louis Municipal Opera. This was the second time we performed *Snow White* on stage at the Municipal Opera, the first being in 1969. This production starred Leslie Easterbrook as Snow White and Walter Willison as Prince Charming.

plex and backstage area was so extensive, like a little city, you could get lost in the maze of scenery back there. This was all outdoors, mind you. If it rained, the show could have been called off. I don't remember that occurring during our run.

All of us Dwarfs had to put on our own makeup, and the costume involved some padding. I played Sleepy, and it was a nice, funny role. Not too many lines, which is the way I like it. As we were playing our week of shows, Liza Minelli was rehearsing on the same stage during the day because she was appearing at the theatre in the next week's show. I talked with her for a while and we spoke of her mom. A photographer saw us and

▲ Yes, I've played the White House . . . in a frog costume. In the early 1970s, the characters from the kids show *New Zoo Revue* played a benefit in the East Room for a group of diplomat's children. Shown here is first lady Pat Nixon and onstage is Henrietta Hippo and Charlie the Owl. I was in the Freddie the Frog costume, but I'm just out of view in this photo.

◄ As Sleepy the Dwarf in the stage version of *Snow White and the Seven Dwarfs.*

While in St. Louis doing *Snow White* in July 1972, I ran into Judy Garland's daughter, Liza Minelli. We talked about her mother, who had recently died, and I told her how much I loved working with her in *Wizard of Oz.* A photographer asked us to pose and do a few dance steps together.

put two and two together and asked if we'd pose together, and that shot ended up in the newspaper the next day.

Snow White was a huge success, and most of the same cast returned a couple of years later for another successful run of the musical. We all had hopes that the production might spark a tour or take the play somewhere like New York, but it never happened.

I'm getting makeup applied for a unique commercial where I was the arms of a planet and actor Hal Smith was the face, in this rare soda pop TV spot.

ELIZABETH MAREN TAKES YOU BACKSTAGE AT *THE GONG SHOW*

Jerry was a regular on *The Gong Show* for three years. The pilot was shot up in San Francisco at an ABC station. I don't know why it was done up there. Gary Owens was the original host, but Chuck Barris, the show's creator and producer, decided to host himself once the show got going. The show featured Milton DeLugg and his Band with a Thug. Adrienne Barbeau was one of the panelists in the pilot.

After Jerry did it, I wasn't sure that it was going to go, but it became a huge hit. When we went to San Francisco for Jerry to do the pilot, nobody thought the show would become anything. I looked at Jerry and Jerry looked at me. We both agreed that this thing will last six shows and it'll be gone. Shows what we know. It took off.

Jerry was happy to be a regular on the show, and that was one of my

favorite shows he did because I got to work on that sometimes too. I went in with Jerry every weekend whether I was in it or not because I liked being around everybody and I would help Jerry with his wardrobe in the dressing room. We taped five shows on Saturday and five shows on Sunday, all at NBC Studios in Burbank. Jerry was the "winner greeter," dressed in top hat and tux with tails, who would come out at the finale of each show and throw confetti up in the air and dance around.

Most of the contestants didn't really care if they got gonged. They just wanted to be on television. Backstage, these people were lined up, ready to do their act. On each show, the winner got a *Gong Show* trophy and a check for $595. These were, for the most part, real live contestants. Then they'd fill with novelty numbers and stupid acts.

"Gene Gene the Dancing Machine" was a prop man at NBC, and Chuck Barris threw him into sketches and little music bits at the end of some shows. I think the Unknown Comic (under the paper bag over his head he was Murray Langston) was originally a contestant, and they brought him back as a gag over and over. Sometimes Jerry would come out in the middle of the

The Gong Show was a terrific experience for me and Elizabeth. I was the little guy who came out at the end of each show in a tuxedo and top hat and threw confetti up into the air and danced around the contestants. Elizabeth participated in several gag bits on stage in some episodes. Chuck Barris was the host most of the time until the show added a night-time version and Gary Owens, shown here, became host.

show dressed as a hospital attendant, holding a giant butterfly net, and would catch the person performing on stage and escort them off the stage.

Some of the acts were hilarious, and I'd sit backstage and talk with some of them. Chuck Barris was always very nice, and one time he got the idea to use me on the show. The one I did that I really liked, he had me come out on the stage and sing a song called "There's a Small Hotel." He told me to sing it off-key, and a man with a trash can and a broom came up and whisked me up and put me in the trash can. He put the lid on, but I didn't pay any attention to him

and kept right on singing. The audience was really laughing at that one. One time they did that same bit, only they used a barrel, and Jerry was already in the barrel. They were about to put me in the barrel and Jerry popped out and said, "Sorry, no room!"

When Jerry had to go to Canada for a few weeks for another job, Chuck Barris let me take his place and throw the confetti out at the end of the show. I loved doing that.

All of the panelists were terrific to work with, like Rip Taylor, Patty Andrews, Phyllis Diller, Rex Reed, Jamie Farr, Arte Johnson, Steve Garvey, Pat McCormick, Paul Williams, and Ken Norton. Sometimes it

NBC Studios

3000 W. Alameda Ave., Burbank, California

NBC Television Network
Presents
''The Gong Show''
With Your Host
Chuck Barris
A Musical Variety With Guest Celebrities
Children under 12 will not be admitted
Ticket distribution is in excess of studio capacity

Studio 3

Saturday
January

15

1977

Show time
7:00 pm

Guests
must arrive
6:00 pm

wasn't just the contestants who were caught up in the craziness. Jaye P. Morgan, well, she was unusual. She had a filthy mouth and could be very funny, but she was very bawdy while the cameras weren't rolling. Sometimes it was while the cameras *were* rolling, which upset Chuck Barris because it took time to reshoot segments. She opened her blouse and flashed the audience a couple of times, and Chuck told her to knock it off. He warned her that if she did it again, she'd be off the show. Well, she did it again and that was the last of Jaye P. Morgan. She got gonged.

One show I remember, there were seven acts on the show and the panel gonged every single act. There were no winners. So Jerry comes out with his basket full of confetti, he's running around Chuck Barris, and he takes a fist full of confetti and throws it right into Chuck's mouth. He gasped and spit it out. Jerry didn't mean it, but it happened, and Chuck was trying to spit it out and keep from laughing.

▲ Billy Curtis and I attended a tribute to *The Wizard of Oz* in 1983 with producer Mervyn LeRoy.
▶ Getting together with fellow *Oz* alumni Jack Haley and Hazel Resmondo (a Munchkin villager).

OZ REVISITED

Under the Rainbow

In the early 1980s, both Elizabeth and I worked on a film called *Under the Rainbow,* which starred Chevy Chase, Carrie Fisher, Billy Barty, Eve Arden, Pat McCormick, and a group of more than a hundred little people. I was once again playing a Munchkin in Oz. The film really exaggerated and exploited the goings-on involving the midgets way back in 1938 when we made *The Wizard of Oz* in Culver City.

For decades, crazy rumors kept haunting all of us who worked in the original film, stories that we wreaked havoc at the hotel, held wild orgies, and partied most of the time during production. People used to say that the police were called every night and murders happened—all kinds of crazy stuff. I'm here to tell you it's all a bunch of crap. Even Judy Garland herself got in on the act and told television host Jack Paar some stories that we were all drunks. That was unfair, even though she was kidding. People thought she must have been telling it like it was because she was there. Judy was actually telling it according to her pills and booze that day. I think when she hit the sauce, she liked to tell some whoppers just for laughs, and we were unluckily the butt of her jokes on that particular program.

I never saw Judy Garland in person following *Oz*. Our paths never crossed, but if they had, that might have been one of the things I would have brought up, because she left behind a legacy of untruths about us and we've had to fight to correct it. *Under the Rainbow* was an extension of those stories, and even though we had one of the *Saturday Night Live* players starring in the film and everyone knew it was a wacky comedy, people continued to believe the rumors. Why did I do the part? Money, of course. Billy wanted me to do the movie. I also thought the movie was so outlandish, nobody could possibly take it seriously. Unfortunately, I was wrong, because the rumors about us original Munchkins persisted. It wasn't until 1989 when Stephen Cox's book, *The Munchkins Remember,* was published that many of those stories were finally put to rest, backed up by the memories of about thirty of us surviving Munchkins at the time.

In *Under the Rainbow* I played a guy named Smokey Jones, which meant they supplied me with free cigars for about three months. (I was taking the things home from the set, they had so many.) Billy Barty was the main little person, playing a Nazi dwarf who gets caught up in the filming of *Oz* in 1938. In one scene, we're playing ball inside the hotel. I had a few lines, but a lot of my role was cut out. One of the scenes had a line of little guys waiting outside the hotel room of a whore. I emerged out of the room after having sex. I forgot what my line was, but it was funny. The whole movie was forgettable, actually.

There were only two of us from the original cast of *The Wizard of Oz* who appeared in *Under the Rainbow*. That was Ruth (Robinson) Duccini and me. We were the only ones. Many people have assumed that Billy Barty was in *The Wizard of Oz*, but he was too young, and he has never claimed to have been part of the cast. I don't know why the producers didn't hunt down and ask some more of the originals from the film, because there were many more alive back then, but they didn't. Billy helped cast the film, and he preferred mostly achondroplastic dwarfs, whereas MGM had hired only midgets for the original film. There is a noticeable difference in physical appearance. I know that was prejudicial back then, but that's the way MGM wanted it in 1938.

▲ Elizabeth and I watch some of the footage on the set of *Under the Rainbow* with Chevy Chase.

▶ Elizabeth and me on the set of *Under the Rainbow*.

▼ I played a character called "Smokey Joe" (because I smoked cigars) in the movie. You could hardly call it a character after the editing, because so much of it was cut out. Here, a line of "Johns" is waiting to enter the room of a midget prostitute, and I'm exiting the room with a smile on my face.

▲ Joe Namath happened to be at the set and came over and watched some of the filming of *Under the Rainbow*.
▼ The giant crew and cast of little people from *Under the Rainbow*, a movie based on the ridiculous rumors that haunted us for years. This 1980s film poked fun at the real Munchkin cast from *The Wizard of Oz*.

It was a windy day on that Tournament of Roses Parade float.

Johnny Leal and I were good buddies. I met him on the set of *The Wizard of Oz* and we became friends. Here we are posing in the early 1940s and later, the last time I saw him, in 1990 when he was in his nineties. At the time, Johnny was the oldest living Munchkin.

A group of us Munchkins reunited for an *Oz* festival in Liberal, Kansas. *(left to right)* Margaret Pellegrini, Emil Kranzler, me, Meinhardt Raabe, Lewis Croft, Clarence Swensen, and Ruth Duccini.

Looking back, *Under the Rainbow* made all of us on *The Wizard of Oz* seem lousy, irresponsible, and raunchy—like we were tearing the place to pieces and destroying the hotel and studio amidst weeks of filming. That never happened, of course. But they did everything they could on *Under the Rainbow* to make us look goofy, like having us swing from the chandeliers and drop things down the elevator shafts, slide down the lengths of the bar all drunk and throw up on the floor. Stuff like that. It was all for laughs, of course. I certainly hope no one believes that movie. It was a flop.

Little Reminders

In the past twenty years or so, I've been making personal appearances—not only as a surviving Munchkin from *Oz,* but as an elf, a greeter, a Leprechaun. You name it. If the job is brief enough and there are no lines to memorize, I'm there. I've never really wanted to officially or fully retire, which is why I take the jobs. I don't need to do it, but it feeds my ego and it keeps me going. Sometimes I gamble, bet on the horses with that money, so I don't feel like I'm spending my savings. It's playing around money, and I enjoy that. I mean, I don't drink, I don't do drugs, I don't shop obsessively. A guy's got to have some sort of vice. I have cigars and a little wagering on the side. That's life.

Once in a while a strange job will come up that I can't pass by. A number of years ago, the actor Martin Mull was getting married, and he and his bride wanted a novelty kind of thing. They wanted little people in tuxes to greet people at the door. It was at his home in Malibu. It was fun. Strange thing, but at his ceremony, I greeted a judge, a priest, a rabbi, and minister. I thought, what the hell is going on? As it turned out, he had gotten married by all of them. Lot of unusual people at that party.

It's funny, I'm not bragging, but I've done so many things in my life, and yet what most people ask me about is *The Wizard of Oz*. That's okay. The film never vanished from my life, and I never expected to ever be so closely associated with one movie appearance, but this one stuck. From the 1940s through the 1960s, I didn't think much about *Oz*. Then it started to become a staple on television every year, sometimes around the holidays. Generations of kids have grown up with the movie, and so many of them tell me it's their favorite of all time. How can you not revel in that?

I'm reminded of *Oz* almost daily. If it's not by way of my fan mail, then it's some reference in the funny papers or on television. One day I was working as a stand-in on the

(Clockwise from top left) Billy Curtis and I reunite with the Tin Man himself, Jack Haley, at a *Wizard of Oz* screening held a the Variety Arts Center in Los Angeles, May 12, 1979. Fifty years later, doing the Lollipop Guild bit in a snapshot. The 1973 Tournament of Roses Parade featured a massive float sponsored by FTD FLorists that paid tribute to *The Wizard of Oz*. The parade that year was themed "Movie Memories," and the grand marshal was John Wayne. Fellow Munchkins Hazel Resmondo, Billy Curtis, and I were reunited to appear on the float New Year's Day. Playing Dorothy was a local young lady, nine-year-old Alissa Bennington. Some of the actual costume pieces we were wearing were original wardrobe accessories which came from the film itself, borrowed from a collector back East. Billy Curtis is wearing a soldier's jacket from film and I'm wearing the barrister's robe. At a rare *Wizard of Oz* reunion in 1979, Munchkins Hazel Resmondo *(left),* me *(center),* and Billy Curtis *(right)* reflect on the filming of Munchkinland with the Wicked Witch, Margaret Hamilton at a screening of the film in southern California.

This was one of our large reunions, in Chesterton, Indiana, around 1992. *(left to right)* Ruth Duccini, Marcella Kranzler (spouse of Munchkin), me and Elizabeth, Mary Ellen St. Aubin (spouse of Munchkin), Edna Wetter (spouse of Munchkin), Meinhardt Raabe, Betty Ann Bruno (one of the child Munchkins from the film), Margaret Pellegrini, Karl Slover, Clarence Swensen, and his wife Myrna.

Hollywood's Cinerama Dome launched a national theater rerelease of *The Wizard of Oz* and brought in me and fellow Munchkin Jeanette "Fern" Formica (on the right) for the opening. My wife Elizabeth is in the center and we're examining some *Oz* memorabilia at a press conference, in 1989.

Michael Landon series *Little House on the Prairie*. We were doing some scenes over at the old MGM lot, which is now owned by Sony. Some of the workers had told me that on another soundstage, they had recently pulled up some of the old floorboards and what did they discover? Some of the actual yellow brick road that had been painted on the floor for *The Wizard of Oz*. Sometimes at the studio, they just lay down more levels of wood floor and that's what had happened on this particular soundstage. I would have loved to have seen it years later. I did return to our Munchkin soundstage for an interview with the

One of my favorite things is seeing the amazement of little kids. I never had kids of my own, and truthfully that's okay, but I love other people's kids nonetheless. Children have always been my biggest fans.

BBC for a documentary they were producing on *Oz* in the late 1980s, and I've returned to Stage 27 with some of the Munchkins on a brief visit of the old studio too. The soundstages are ripe with history and curiously they still smell the same.

In the past few decades, *The Wizard of Oz* has taken me places I never thought I'd go. When Jack Haley, Margaret Hamilton, and Ray Bolger were still living, Billy Curtis and I took part in several film tributes with them here in Los Angeles. As the main cast members from *Oz* died, the Munchkins became the survivors. In 1989, the fiftieth anniversary of the film, MGM gathered quite a few of us for a reunion, as did several annual *Oz* Festivals around the country. Many of us hadn't seen each other since we made the film. I

◀ Billy Curtis and I were part of the new *All New Truth or Consequences* television game show with host Larry Anderson in 1987.

▼ Steve Guttenberg and I costarred briefly in a sitcom called *No Soap, Radio* in 1982. I played Morris the bellboy. That was one of my best TV gigs . . . my own parking spot, great pay, prime-time television. It only lasted a few episodes, I'm sorry to say.

remember when I first saw little Nita Krebs, a tiny frail thing. She had been one of Leo Singer's most prominent midgets in her heyday, and here she was now in her eighties and reuniting with us Munchkins. She was one of the Lullabye League toe dancers; fans flocked to her to meet this little lady. I think she was able to attend two festivals before she passed away quietly one day at her home in Florida.

Every major anniversary for *Oz* brings a new request from magazines and radio stations for an interview or a photo shoot. In New York, five of us Munchkins posed for a *Life* magazine photographer in New York City on the same weekend we were appearing on Maury Povich's daytime television show. I've appeared with Howie Mandel on his talk show, Tammy Faye Bakker, Geraldo Rivera, among others. I've seen the actual ruby slippers exhibited by the Smithsonian Institution, as well as a pair from the film that belonged to a private

(Clockwise from top left) Billy Curtis and I were honored to reunite with Ray Bolger and Margaret Hamilton at a Motion Picture Academy tribute to *The Wizard of Oz* in May 1983. Sadie Delfino and me with Cheech and Chong in a photo shoot for their comedy record album titled *The Wedding Album*, in 1974. Sixty years after *The Wizard of Oz*, my fellow Munchkins Margaret Pellegrini and Ruth Duccini and I took a rare opportunity to revisit the Munchkin soundstage on the old MGM lot where we filmed our scenes. Appearing at the stately old Alex Theatre in Glendale, California.

A group of surviving Munchkins and spouses, along with our *Oz* choreographer Dona Massin, attended an *Oz* festival in Chesterton, Indiana.

collector. I've held costumes from the film and some props that survived. I posed for photos with Bert Lahr's actual lion costume, a prized piece that went up for auction. And fifty years after the movie, I even held my own costume, which an *Oz* enthusiast bought at auction for more than $25,000. But still, I've never been able to figure out what happened to the oversized lollipop I

used in the scene. It was a prop wooden lollipop, not too heavy, painted, and it had a ribbon tied around it. Boy, would I like to have that thing today.

Elizabeth and I were privileged and honored to be asked to take part in an NBC television movie about the life of L. Frank Baum, the man who dreamed up *Oz* in 1900. The movie was called *Dreamer of Oz* and they cast John Ritter to play Baum. He was a perfect choice, not only because he resembled Baum, but also because he was a professed fan of the original books and the MGM film. Elizabeth and I were Munchkins in one scene; however, the makeup and wardrobe more closely resembled the Munchkin characters from his original book. Since I was in the MGM musical, I felt that it was important that I

187

Karl Slover and I gaze upon one of the actual pairs of ruby slippers worn by Judy Garland in the film. This is the pair in the collection of the Smithsonian Institution that toured the country in 1996.

Margaret Pellegrini and I put our hands in cement at the Disney/MGM Studios Tour in Florida.

Answering questions about *Oz* at a festival appearance in Chittenango, New York, in 1995, with Clarence Swensen (in his replica soldier costume), Margaret Pellegrini (wearing her replica Munchkin villager outfit), and Karl Slover.

My wife Elizabeth (whose stage name is Elizabeth Barrington), Joe Griffo, and I were Munchkins in the NBC-TV movie *The Dreamer of Oz*, which starred John Ritter as the creator of *Oz*, writer L. Frank Baum. I was honored to be chosen to appear in the movie, especially given my long history with *Oz*.

take this role. It brought *Oz* full circle for me. It was one of those moments that was "meant to be," you know? The movie was a heartwarming story. This film officially dubbed Elizabeth a "Munchkin." In fact, I sometimes say she's an M.B.M.—that's "Munchkin By Marriage."

Once, while Elizabeth and I were making a personal appearance at an autograph show in Los Angeles near Universal Studios, a man approached us and asked if we would be the guests of Michael Jackson at the nearby studio. We said, "Sure . . . we'd love to." Michael Jackson had requested our presence and that of Al Lewis, who was Grandpa on *The Munsters*. We all got in a limousine and it took us to a soundstage at Universal where Michael Jackson was filming a new music video, one with extremely shiny, highly polished, reflective floors. They gave us little white cloth booties to put over our shoes so as not to scuff the floor, and we walked over to Michael Jackson, who was standing there, eager to meet us. He was terrific. He asked me about *The Wizard of Oz*, and we did a little dance step together. He had his photographer take some pictures and they promised us some, but we never received any.

Jimmy Kimmel and Adam Corolla hired me for *The Man Show* on Comedy Central

▲ This was probably the largest Munchkin reunion ever, held in 1990 in Judy Garland's home town of Grand Rapids, Minnesota. I can't believe how many are now gone.

▶ Here I am looking at my original Lollipop Guild wardrobe, an expensive ensemble you might say. I grew more than a foot since my Munchkin experience, so it definitely wouldn't fit me now.

several times, doing the strangest stuff. I think Jimmy has a thing about midgets. He loves midgets, he has said it. Here I am eighty years old, and they have me dressed as a young boy, swinging on a swing, and some half-nude big-breasted girls are pushing me. One time they had me in a bathing suit, jumping on a trampo-line. The director was a little surprised I was in my eight-ies, and I think they were easy on me with that trampoline. I didn't want to jack up my leg if I came down wrong from a jump. Right after me, Jimmy Kimmel climbed on the trampoline in nothing but a speedo and a hairy back and jumped for the cameras. And they thought *I* was a sight?

> **Mother Nature is a maaaad scientist.**
>
> —KRAMER, *SEINFELD*

Elizabeth and I got a call to do an episode of *Seinfeld* in February 1997. It was great because it didn't involve any lines at all—my favorite thing. The episode was called "Yada, Yada, Yada," and we had no idea what that meant. We went over to CBS Studio Center and reported to Stage #9 for our scenes. Being fans of *Seinfeld,* and knowing his show was the top-rated comedy on the air, we knew this would be a treat. In the story, Kramer was dating a girl of average height whose parents happened to be little people. That was us. We were filming scenes outside of the usual show performance done live with an audi-ence, kind of quickie things that I don't recall even requiring much makeup. There were two scenes, one involving Kramer and his girlfriend and another was a wedding scene in a

Elizabeth and I appeared on an episode of *Seinfeld* as the parents of Kramer's girlfriend.

chapel. Robert Wagner and his wife Jill St. John were in the wedding scene as well as the entire cast of *Seinfeld.*

On the set, Michael Richards came up to me, sat right down, and offered me a cigar and asked if I wanted to smoke it in the scene. I know he likes cigars, too. I said, "Sure . . . that'll be fine." We both lit up. He was interested in my career and asked me about *The Wizard of Oz* and some other TV shows, and what kind of cigars I've smoked and which were my favorites. He was a really nice guy; much more serious than you'd expect from a guy playing Kramer. Jerry Seinfeld came over to meet us, and after our scene he had everyone clap for us, which was nice. They do that for the guest stars, mainly to thank them right there on the spot for their work. Afterward, I sat in the diner set in those red padded seats and filled out my union forms and signed the contracts and such before Elizabeth and I left for the day. We had no idea that we were going to be part of probably the most popular, or at least one of the most memorable, episodes of *Seinfeld.*

It seems that's how my life has gone: Never knowing it, I've jumped from one classic to another, not to be revealed for years. But I'm certainly proud of it.

As for the rest of my career? Well, yada, yada, yada . . . and there you are.

Jerry Maren

◄ If I had a dollar for every time I've signed my name in my lifetime. Oh wait . . . I do!

▼ Oz parades are always fun events, when the weather is clear.

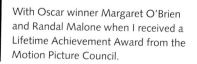

With Oscar winner Margaret O'Brien and Randal Malone when I received a Lifetime Achievement Award from the Motion Picture Council.

We received a Star on the famous Hollywood Walk of Fame on November 20, 2007, right next to Grauman's Chinese Theater where the film originally premiered in 1939. It was an astounding event, something I'll never forget. During the ceremony, I tried to remember all of my little pals who had passed on, and I wanted people to know that the award was for them, too. *(left to right)* Mickey Carroll, Clarence Swensen, me, Karl Slover, Ruth Duccini, Margaret Pellegrini, and Meinhardt Raabe. Three of the child Munchkins (non-midgets) who were in the film too joined us for a photo unveiling our Star. Behind us are Joan Kenmore (partially obscured by my lollipop—sorry!), Ardith Dondanville, and Priscilla Montgomery.

BROADCASTING SYSTEM, INC.

ONE CNN CENTER
BOX 105366
ATLANTA, GEORGIA 30348-5366

NORTH TOWER
(404) 827-1717

R. E. TURNER
CHAIRMAN OF THE BOARD

June 30, 1993

Dear Jerry:

It has come to my attention that you are celebrating 55 years in show business with your friends. I just wanted to extend my congratulations and thank you for your contribution to THE WIZARD OF OZ as one of the Lollipop Kids. This movie has brought many hours of enjoyment to young and old alike throughout the years.

May you continue to enjoy good health and success!

Sincerely,

R. E. Turner

INDEX

African Americans

IN

TELEVISION

D1262870

This book is part of the Peter Lang Media and Communication list.
Every volume is peer reviewed and meets
the highest quality standards for content and production.

PETER LANG
New York • Washington, D.C./Baltimore • Bern
Frankfurt • Berlin • Brussels • Vienna • Oxford

GREGORY ADAMO

African Americans
IN
TELEVISION

Behind the Scenes

PETER LANG
New York • Washington, D.C./Baltimore • Bern
Frankfurt • Berlin • Brussels • Vienna • Oxford

Library of Congress Cataloging-in-Publication Data

Adamo, Gregory.
African Americans in television: behind the scenes / Gregory Adamo.
p. cm.
Includes bibliographical references and index.
1. African Americans in television broadcasting.
2. African American television producers and directors—Interviews.
3. Television broadcasting—Social aspects—United States.
4. African Americans on television. I. Title.
PN1992.8.A34A32   791.45'08996073—dc22   2010021079
ISBN 978-1-4331-1040-5 (hardcover)
ISBN 978-1-4331-1039-9 (paperback)

Bibliographic information published by **Die Deutsche Nationalbibliothek**.
Die Deutsche Nationalbibliothek lists this publication in the "Deutsche
Nationalbibliografie"; detailed bibliographic data is available
on the Internet at http://dnb.d-nb.de/.

The paper in this book meets the guidelines for permanence and durability
of the Committee on Production Guidelines for Book Longevity
of the Council of Library Resources.

Printed in the United States of America

To the creators

CONTENTS

Acknowledgments

This research began with conversations I had with my good friend James Gordon when he worked in Hollywood in the early and mid-1990s. Jim, who is African American, has been a public relations specialist for over thirty years. Our discussions, mostly about television, often veered into areas of race. For example, when he was working for Steven Bochco of *Hill Street Blues, Doogie Howser, M.D.,* and *NYPD Blue* fame, James spoke about a television show Bochco was developing. Called *Capitol Critters,* the animated program portrayed mice, rats, and roaches residing in the White House. James was taken aback by the fact that the roaches had the dialect and stereotypical mannerisms of inner-city African Americans. He discussed his dilemma of whether to speak up about his concerns, warning the producer and writers that these portrayals could be perceived as racist. As a public relations executive he was, "glad the press called me about it which gave me a reason to confront him about." James said Bochco "softened" some of the images. The show was a ratings failure and ABC cancelled it after seven episodes. James' story made me aware of an issue that other African Americans, working in Hollywood in greater numbers than ever before, might be facing. Some might involve the shows they were working on but others could include issues faced by African Americans in any kind of workplace. For example, James said that that if he did not wear a jacket and tie on the studio lot he would be mistaken for a deliveryman, an issue that I, as a White man, had never run into in any work situation. Jim kept telling me that the story of African Americans working in Hollywood needed to be told. These discussions intertwined with my doctoral work at Rutgers University and thus this research was born.

My interests were encouraged by two wonderful mentors. Linda Steiner of University of Maryland, College Park, is a great educator and good friend. Allan DiBiase, philosopher/hiker/professor of Franklin Pierce College, is a model of intellectual inquiry and teaching.

I want to thank all the writers, directors, producers, and actors who gave their time and shared their experiences and stories. Without them this work would have been impossible. The encouragement and connections of Michael Ajakwe, Felicia D. Henderson, and Sharon Johnson were particularly important in keeping this project going. Shirley Salomon, a former student, was the first person I interviewed for this project when she was at MTV and an executive at BET when I interviewed her again in 2005. Seeing nice people do well in the media business is a real joy.

Special thanks go to those whose comments on my manuscript inspired me to see this project to completion: Elaine Inguilli of Richard Stockton College, Todd Steven Burroughs of Morgan State University, whose knowledge of African American television shows is amazing, and my son Colin of Yale University. The pride and joy of getting feedback from my son is indescribable. My editor, Marsha Houston, was extremely helpful with all her comments, questions, and suggestions. And thanks go to my graduate assistants over the years, particularly Joy Thompson at Morgan. One of the great things about teaching is having students become lifetime friends.

And I want to acknowledge those whose advice, counsel, and friendship over the years have been so important. Tara Crowell, Donnetrice Allison, Mary Ann Trail, Arnaldo Cordero Roman, and Paul Lyons of Richard Stockton College, Baruti Kopano and Laura Dorsey-Elson of Morgan State, Marcy De Veaux of Cal State — Northridge, Radha Hegde of New York University, and Robert Kubey of Rutgers University. Thanks to John Devecka of Loyola University and Deran Browne of Morgan for some last-minute formatting help. And to Jessica Schiffman of the University of Delaware, our friendship and talks helped show me that it is possible to balance scholarship, work, and most important, family.

Finally, I thank the most important people in my life: my mother and father for always stressing the importance of education; Jeanette, a woman I can call my friend; and my children Kerian and Colin for always showing me bright moments.

We want television to show us to be all the things we truly are: pimps on one side, preachers on the other; doctors as well as prostitutes; nurses; professors; people who attend conferences as well as those who go to the red light district. We want the power to show that we are as good or as bad as anybody else, in all departments. And until we have the authority and the power to control our own images, we will be disadvantaged and dissatisfied. It is not enough that good White people, out of best intentions, should themselves continue to make the images by which Blacks will be seen, even if those images present Black people as angels. Better we should have some less-perfect images presented by ourselves, than to have images that are handed down, even if they are handed down from heaven. I end as I began, talking about the only thing that matters in all this: power.

Ossie Davis (1917–2005), actor, writer, and producer, 1982

Prologue

The Beginning of the New Normal: Black Television in the Nineties

Watching *Grey's Anatomy* on ABC in 2009, and knowing it's a popular drama created and run by Shonda Rhimes, an African American female, it sometimes is hard to remember that it wasn't always this way.

Ten years is a long time in television. In 1999, I was watching the series finale of *Sister, Sister,* a sitcom that started on ABC before moving to the WB Network. (The merging of the WB and UPN into the CW in 2006 led, unfortunately, to the eventual cancellation of Black sitcoms *Everybody Hates Chris, The Game,* and *Girlfriends.* It was the end of an era.) The fact that *Sister, Sister* could be on the air at the same time as UPN's *Moesha* in 1999—both programs produced and written by African Americans, both programs from the worldview of young African American teenage women, within their own Black middle-class cultural aesthetic—was an amazing way to end the decade that, from my view, changed everything in television.

A decade can also considerably change a society that television attempts to reflect. As the 1980s became the 1990s, a new generation of Black young people, under thirty and with disposable incomes, now established itself as a new, urban demographic, ready to be marketed to. Born in the late 1960s and early 1970s, they wanted to see television that was more relevant than *Diff'rent Strokes* and *Webster* of the previous decade. Turning twenty throughout the late 1980s and early 1990s, it needed no more White shadows to guide them into televised adulthood, thanks to the efforts of Oprah Winfrey, *The Cosby Show,* his fictional Hillman College, immortalized in the *The Cosby Show* spin-off *A Different World* (complemented by and contrasted with Spike Lee's bizzaro version, Mission College, in his 1988 film *School Daze*), August Wilson plays on Broadway, the two presidential campaigns of Jesse Jackson, the struggle against South African apartheid and the campaign to free Nelson Mandela, politically charged hip-hop (Public Enemy, Boogie Down Productions, Poor Righteous Teachers and X-Clan immediately come to mind), Spike's film version of the life of Malcolm X, and, last but not least, the continued grass-roots popularity of the always controversial Minister Louis Farrakhan of the Nation of Islam.

This book tells the largely victorious story of a transforming time in American television history. The 1990s started with network broadcast advances—"the Huxtable effect" of *The Cosby Show* stretching into NBC's *The Fresh Prince of Bel-Air* and Fox's *Living Single* — and ended with cable triumphs, such as HBO establishing itself as a premium space for Black television movies (*The Josephine Baker Story, The Tuskegee Airmen, Miss Evers' Boys*) and anticipation for the family drama *Soul Food*'s 2000 series premiere on Showtime.

Five factors allowed television to move forward significantly for a changing Black America between 1990 and 2000. First, Fox's late 1980s programming strategy of using "urban" (read: Black) sitcoms to gain a toehold in America's major television markets succeeded. (Fox, which had research showing that African Americans watched television for greater lengths of time, abandoned this strategy by the mid-1990s, when it purchased the rights to broadcast NFL games and began to schedule more White-oriented dramas. But it had proven that Black programming could produce revenue.) Second, Black creators in Hollywood, long at the margins of Televised America, knew they had a responsibility—and opportunity—to reflect their new, multi-generational cultural reality, and so they used their hard-won reputations in the industry to do just that. Third, the expansion of four networks to six—UPN and the WB were both created in 1995—helped, because both used Fox's "Black-first, White later" strategy. The fourth factor was the explosion of channels when cable went satellite and digital, allowing more original programming to be created. Fifth is the triumph of hip-hop culture in American life, becoming not only America's unofficial youth culture, but the core of its popular culture as well.

As a result of result of those five factors, African Americans in the 1990s slowly (or quickly, depending on one's perception) became showrunners of network programs—sitcoms and "dramedys" that began to reflect a larger spectrum of (African) American life. They created programs that emphasized Black popular culture. It's not that racial stereotypes didn't continue to abound in the new era—just one look at UPN disasters such as *Homeboys in Outer Space, The Secret Diary of Desmond Pfeiffer,* and *Malcolm and Eddie,* along with Fox's *Martin,* showed that. But more often than not, this dues-paying generation of Black Hollywood writers, producers and directors used the chance given them to put on commercial television a variety of Black images and realities, using Black America's increasingly intra-racial class, generation and gender differences to comedic and dramatic advantage. The days of the blatant one-note "Big Three" stereotypes of Beulah, Eddie "Rochester" Anderson, J. J. "Dy-n-omite!" Evans and Huggy Bear were now gone, dismissed to video libraries or DVDs or "Nick at Nite" and TV Land; those stereotypes would emerge in the new generation of Black shows only as historical parodies or tongue-in-cheek Blaxploitation homages. In the same vein, the middle-aged racial tokenism of the 1965-era *I Spy* or the 1970-era *Julia* or the 1981-era *Benson* was also thrown in the dustbin of television history. The 1990s was a new, young time, with new, young programming for new, young, urban audiences. And this programming would make visible major parts of the African American community, on (admittedly somewhat mediated) African American terms.

Especially important is that either these Black showrunners, and/or the shows' stars, had formed their own production companies to produce these Black-oriented shows and other programs for the networks. Entertainment history will record that the 1990s was the first decade in which Blacks produced their own television shows en masse, and the diversity and depth of the content shows in their respective products. This power did not cede without a demand, so this book documents the struggles Black showrunners like Tim Reid, Mara Brock Akil, and Felicia D. Henderson had to wage to (a) get and keep power over their cultural product and (b) keep the integrity of their concepts. The road was not always rosy for these new showrunners. They still had to deal with getting their ideas green lighted and understood by White network executives and even White writers and crew members. They had to serve as cultural ambassadors for the Black reality they would attempt to reflect in a White, corporate environment.

This book takes on these topics one at a time. Chapter one explains the importance of listening to the stories of African American television workers in order to understand both the obstacles and opportunities they face. Chapter two details how writers, directors, and other creators enter the television business and move ahead in the system. Chapter three outlines the culture of production and how television shows are created, while Chapter four explores the workplace, issues of difference and African American workers often "otherized" by the majority-dominated industry. Chapter five discusses the role of African American writers, how they are sometimes limited in the kinds of work they are allowed to do and their desires to create images that reflecte their lived experiences. Chapter six tells the story of three African American showrunners, women who have created and produced successful television programs centered on Black characters. These women recognized that their place in the system would not have been possible if not for the groundbreaking work of African Americans who came before them. The final chapter, seven concludes with an exploration of the rapidly changing television workplace and industry. While there is greater diversity than ever before, television is facing stiff competition from new technology that is drawing the audience away to the point that broadcast network television is on the verge of disappearing. Yet our increasingly multicultural society prevents the industry from ever going back to old habits of playing to the White mainstream as the audience for all media is too diverse for that.

The generation of Black showrunners examined here had to educate those in power about what they were doing, explain (or downplay) the political and social significance of their ideas and, most importantly, show how it would make money. So they did. And a decade of television, the last of the twentieth century, was forever defined.

CHAPTER ONE

Introduction

"I give to you responsibility."[1] Imagine Sidney Poitier saying that to you. In his 2005 Oscar acceptance speech actor Jamie Foxx recounted his first meeting with Poitier. That there was little comment in the media on that part of Foxx's address is not surprising. At the turn of the twenty-first century discussion concerning responsibility in the mainstream media is rare. Few, if any, majority group members talk about a responsibility related to their race. So why would someone receiving one of the entertainment community's highest honors talk about responsibility? Indeed, with regard to the media, what does responsibility mean?

Foxx's account is tied directly to his cultural identity, prefacing his remarks as living, "this African American dream." Blacks must deal with a long history of media misrepresentation and non-representation, stereotypes, both negative and positive. The 1915 film *The Birth of a Nation, Amos 'n' Andy* on both radio and television, *The Cosby Show* in the 1980s, and *The Chappelle Show* in the 2000s are all examples of how some of our most important and popular media productions have helped to depict and define how U.S. society sees African Americans.[2] There has been one constant in the responses to the question of representation. Beginning with the African American newspaper editors who encouraged investment in an independent Black film industry to counter the images in *The Birth of a Nation* straight through to the civil rights groups' condemnation of the television industry at the end of the twentieth century, critics of the mass media's portrayal of minorities have stressed that one way to rectify the situation is to have more minority producers.[3] Finally responding to that criticism, in 1999 the major television networks signed their first agreements with the National Association for the Advancement of Colored People and a coalition of Latino, Native American, and Asian American groups to, among other things, increase minority employment.

But what does it mean to be a minority producer? Do African American workers see themselves as "minority producers"? Do they believe they have the power to create images depicting the variety and complexity of African American life? Do they hope to create images that can change the way other people view African Americans? Now that they have a presence in the production system do they feel free to openly acknowledge such goals? What responsibility do they feel to create a certain type of image? These are some of the questions that this book addresses. My goal is to find out how members of a minority group long denied access to positions of power in television respond to the opportunity to create television programs.

Entertainment Media Production: Early Studies and Current Reality

Focusing on media production, the business and the people who work within that system, can reveal the complex personal and organizational structures within which the content is created and how those relationships affect what ends up on television. In his influential study of entertainment television in the early 1980s, Todd Gitlin claimed that understanding television's relationship to social reality depended in part on understanding "who put the images on the small screen and for what reasons."[4] One problem is that many of the important studies that looked at the people who produced entertainment television were done in the 1970s and 1980s, when there were almost no women or minority producers.[5] Most of these researchers admit that few minorities were working in the television industry when they conducted their research. For example, in the introduction to their 1983 book *The Producer's Medium*, Horace Newcomb and Robert Alley point out the problems inherent in television content created in a system that lacks input from minority groups:

> The limited numbers of women and minority members in the production community indicate to us that dialogue is flawed, narrowed, in ways that must be corrected if social equity is to be rectified not only in the television industry, but in American society at large.[6]

What has changed since these studies were conducted is the entrance of African Americans, women, Latinos, and openly gay people into the production of television programming.[7] Members of minority groups that had been denied access to one of the most important forms of communication in modern society now have some place, some voice in the production process. Twenty years after Gitlin's call to look at the people who put the images on the screen the same question needs to be asked in today's more diverse (at least in the sense that there are more African Americans and women) workplace.

The involvement of greater numbers of minorities in the production of mainstream television and film has the potential to empower them to create work that portrays the variety of their experiences. Some critics of media images have argued that media creation is the true expression of independence for a minority audience working to free itself from influence of the dominant culture.[8] Stuart Hall stresses the importance of the relationship between minority identity, representation, *and* production in seeing mass media,

> not as a second-order mirror held up to reflect what already exists, but as that form of representation which is able to constitute us as new kinds of subjects, and thereby enable us to discover places from which to speak.[9]

Yet the importance of economic and organizational structures in the production system mean that increased minority participation will not automatically translate into more authentic representations. As Krystal Brent Zook shows in her study of the Fox network of the early and mid-1990s, opportunities for African American authorship were due mainly to that network's short-term need to attract an underserved audience.[10] Once Fox established itself as a player in network television with the acquisition of NFL football, it began to respond to advertising pressure for a younger and Whiter audience. In addition, the complexity of cultural identity and its relationship to production prevents making any automatic link between the presence of minority producers and the production of more diverse and complex images. What must be acknowledged are the *possibilities* associated with the increased involvement of minority producers. Possibilities for media representations that begin to reflect variety and complexity of minority life.

Hall's Circuit of Culture Model

In thinking about my own research I have found useful Stuart Hall's "circuit of culture model" as shown in Figure 1.[11]

Circuit of Culture
- Production & Identity

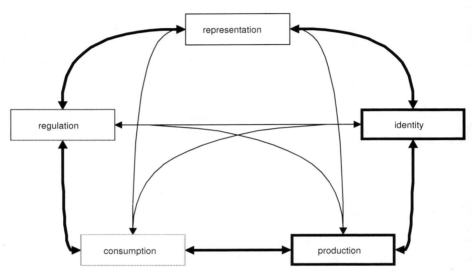

Figure 1.1 Circuit of culture model.

Hall's model illustrates the interrelationship and importance of all five elements in the communication of culture. One can see how all parts are interrelated, with, for example, identity influencing the audience and the producer. I have modified the model to highlight the areas of interest in this book, identity and production, without denying the role of the audience, image, and regulatory factors. Even though the identity of the people producing television content is the strongest relationship here, the fact that these creators are also consumers cannot be denied. In fact, many of the people I interviewed referenced shows they watched as children, shows they loved even though they included few if any African Americans. In many cases their current work was shaped by the desire to create minority characters to fill the void they saw as consumers of television.

Although the entertainment television industry has changed in the past 20 years with the growth in cable and satellite services and the competition for viewer's time from the Internet, the American public maintains a strong attachment to television, with the average number of hours of home television use remaining fairly stable.[12] Television remains "the central cultural experience for a majority of working- and middle-class Americans"[13] as it affects all aspects of contemporary social life, including the shaping of identity. Television is one place where the construction of reality, the interpretation of events, the representation of shared beliefs, and social change are struggled over and played out.[14] Questions concerning race and television center on television's construction of ideas about race and ethnicity and the role racial identity plays in the construction of these images.

Hall contends that the media "construct for us a definition of what race is, what meaning the imagery of race carries, and what the "problem of race" is understood to be."[15] Television is the most dominant form of media in contemporary America and as such it helps define what we know and think about people different from ourselves. While film, radio, and music all have problematic histories concerning racial representation, Herman Gray regards entertainment television as the medium that is "most completely saturated by representations of Blackness."[16] He adds that situation comedies, music television, and other forms of entertainment television are programs "that African Americans, in particular, watch with the expectation of finding Black images."[17]

Historically, television has failed to portray a full spectrum of African American images. In the early 1950s, television's formative years, White ideas concerning race were communicated through the adoption of the radio and film caricatures of *Amos 'n' Andy* and *Our Gang*. Except in a few isolated cases, television shows in the 1950s and 1960s either had no Black characters or relied on stereotypes. Even as television programming progressed after the civil rights movement of the 1960s, programs rarely illustrated the diversity and complexity of African American life. A successful African American-centered series like *The Cosby Show* was criticized for both its unrealistic images and its failure to comment on the economic and social disparities faced by many Blacks.[18] When a program that began to portray the richness of Black life, *Frank's Place*, got on the air, network executives did not know what kind of audience it would attract and where to place it on its schedule.[19] Though the 1990s saw a great increase in African American–centered programming, most creative programs, such as

Roc and *South Central,* faced greater scrutiny by the network and were eventually cancelled.[20]

Focus: African Americans in the Television Industry

I am particularly interested in how African American workers see themselves in the production process. While many minority groups have been long denied access to creating media images, Blacks present the central example in American society of a group that has been impacted by media representations and the lack of power to create self-representations. No other minority has endured, to the same extent, the combination of demeaning portrayals or the absence of images while at the same time being denied access to the mainstream production process. Cornel West ties the problem of Black invisibility and misrepresentation directly to the "lack of Black power to represent themselves to themselves and others as complex human beings."[21]

The legacy of invisibility and representation not only presents a problem, but an extra responsibility for Black producers as these "media producers shoulder the burden of satisfying the need for alternative representations in a racist society while being true to their art."[22] Studies of entertainment television have asked television producers about the social impact of their programs and if and how their social consciousness was reflected in their work. But they were not seen to have the special responsibility placed on Black actors to create work that responds to the legacy of misrepresentation.[23] In his book *Blacks and White TV* J. Fred MacDonald has one answer to why African American actors have historically been held to standards far different than Whites:

> There is an aspect to most Black performance in popular culture that is unique. Because there is comparatively little minority representation in radio, film, and television, and because each performance by an African American is regarded as a chance to make a statement about Black realities, each appearance takes on added weight. Since few African Americans have as yet enjoyed the recurring exposure granted to the stars of hit TV series, when the Black actor does achieve such success he or she is vulnerable to special criticism. If a role seems too accepting of White social dominance, the star as well as the character he or she is portraying may be attacked as too acquiescent. If the role is one of a middle-class suburban Black, it may be assailed as too bourgeois and unsympathetic to inner-city "brothers" and "sisters." If the role involves no racial politics, it may be censured as not

"Black" enough. And if it is critical of social injustice, it may be assailed as hostile, radical, or heavy-handed.[24]

The criticism Bill Cosby faced with *The Cosby Show* illustrates the dilemma faced by African Americans television producers whose work is closely scrutinized mostly due to the scarcity of Black producers. While Gray credits Cosby for producing images that corrected some distortions of prior images of Black life, he also criticizes Cosby for failing to comment on the economic inequities facing millions of African Americans.[25] Sut Jhally and Justin Lewis' study of audience interpretations of *The Cosby Show* found that the show fostered or reinforced White attitudes that fault Blacks for not overcoming the inequality in society.[26] Popular culture is always ripe for criticisms. But White male producers rarely are asked whether their work represents anything more than their personal background and interests.

This book began with two questions: Is there a minority voice in television production? If so, where is it? The answer is found in the voices of almost twenty African American media workers. In interviews conducted over the past ten years, I hoped to find how minority producers survive and succeed in the production of culture. The interviews focused on how individuals think and talk about workplace values, the production of racial representations, and the responsibilities of minority workers. I have followed the call to listen to African Americans talk about their everyday experiences, an endeavor particularly important for those interested in understanding the contemporary experiences of Black Americans.[27]

Listening to Stories

Nichelle Nichols tells the story of her frustrations during her first season as Lieutenant Uhura on the original *Star Trek*.[28] Unhappy with the limited way her character was used — primarily as a twenty-third century telephone operator — Nichols considered quitting the show. Upon meeting Martin Luther King, Jr. she mentioned her plans. "Don't you know you have the first non-stereotypical role in television?" she recalls King saying. "For the first time the world will see us as we should be seen — people of quality in the future. You created a role with dignity and beauty and grace and intelligence. You're not just a role model for our children, but for people who *don't* look like us to see us for the first time as *equals*."[30] King's response helped convince Nichols to stay on the show. Nichols' story illustrates how audience, producer, and identity are entwined in relationships that impact each other in innumerable ways, just as Stuart Hall's model would lead us to expect.

This book is about stories, not as fiction, but as personal accounts of professional lives. The stories told by Nichols and others give a unique perspective on the entertainment industry. They are both the background and foreground of the people who in turn create the television stories that entertain us. Stories enable the listener or reader to explore the importance, impact, and responsibility of minority workers. At its essence, television is about stories. Individual programs tell stories within their twenty-two or forty-four minute allotment of time. Good programs stretch their stories, with the blessing of their network, over a full season and sometimes many seasons. Television itself also tells us stories about ourselves. The mythical innocent 1950s told us the norm was a nuclear family with a father as breadwinner and a stay-at-home mom. The story of the turbulent 1960s was told on the evening news or in the interruption of an entertainment show to report another assassination of one of our leaders. In the 1970s societal changes erupted into comedy programs, either directly on programs such as *All in the Family* or more indirectly on a show like *MASH.* In the 1980s a former movie and television star became president and told us war stories from movies as though they were from his own lived experience. Yet for much of its first thirty years of existence television failed to tell any of the stories of African Americans. As histories such as J. Fred MacDonald's *Blacks and White TV* and Donald Bogle's *Primetime Blues* recount, for more than half of its history American television relegated African Americans to minor roles, stereotypes, or invisibility on the screen. These historical studies also remind us that even with limited opportunities, African American–centered television programs can entertain, succeed, and even open up new ways of understanding cultural identity. The lack of advertising support did not prevent Nat King Cole from creating his 1950s music and variety show, although it cut short its run.[31] Though *Roots* may have been framed around the traditional television story of a family triumphing over adversities, it also exposed America to a history that had largely been ignored in the media and schools.

In his 1991 documentary *Color Adjustment* Marlon Riggs explores and questions television's history of negative stereotypes and Black invisibility through the stories of people such as Diahann Carroll,

Esther Rolle, and Tim Reid. The film gives voice to television stars whose role as minority workers is rarely told. Rolles' tale of refusing the starring role on *Good Times* unless her character on the program was given a husband gives a personal insight into a minority worker taking a stand. Not a major star at that time, Rolle risked losing a lucrative position because the images she was helping to create mattered so much to her. Eventually *Good Times* did devolve into caricature and stereotypes as the producers played on the popularity of the buffoonish character J.J., and Rolle's television husband was written out of the show. The power of an African American actress was limited in comparison to market forces and racism that prompted producers to overemphasize popular if buffoonish characters and writers and producers intent on perpetuating the stereotypical one-parent household so often depicted on television.

"The biggest fights with the networks were not about money and ratings. They were about different ways of seeing the world."[32] That is how writer-producer Ralph Farquhar explained his work to Krystal Brent Zook. Her thesis in *Color by Fox* is that the wave of African American programs of the early and mid-1990s presented brief but important instances of African American authorship. One example was Fraquhar's *South Central*, a Fox network show about a working class mother of three children. The show premiered in April 1994, and was cancelled after ten episodes. While the focus of Zook's chapter on Fraquhar's work is a strong textual analysis of *South Central* the quotes from Fraquhar are evidence of the dilemma faced by African American creators.

The Numbers Story

I am not out to discount the impact of quantitative work concerning the numbers of minority television workers. In fact, statistics on the lack of minorities behind the camera helped inspire the most recent cycle of change in the industry. The Writers Guild of America (WGA) reports tracking minority employment, begun in 1988, have brought attention to the issue of ethnic, gender, and age inequities.[33] Throughout much of the 1990s the industry claimed that progress was being made pointing to the increase in African American–centered shows. But in May 1999, when the *Los Angeles Times* began a series of articles on the lack of diversity on television with the finding that almost thirty network shows had no minorities in leading roles, the industry was forced to act. They began to add minority characters to their shows, but these were Band-Aids on a long festering problem. When a group of minority writers took a two-page ads in *Daily Variety* and *The Hollywood Reporter* in the fall of 1999 they hoped that their statistics showing the almost total absence of African Americans writing on White-themed shows would intensify the pressure on the networks.[34] The strategy worked. Within months, the networks signed diversity initiative agreements with the advocacy groups.

By the turn of the century, minority influence in the industry had become more complicated. The "progress" seen in Darnell Hunt's statistics showing that African American characters were over-represented on the television screen during the 2001 and 2002 seasons is outweighed by the data showing television's segregation.[35] Hunt finds that the most prominent Black characters were "ghettoized" on the least-watched network (UPN), in situation comedies, and on Monday nights."[36] Hunt, who supervises the Bunche Center/UCLA's longitudinal study on race and television, also sees continued White control of the industry as minorities are "underrepresented in key behind-the-scenes creative and decision-making positions."[37] This is a crucial point. Critics, scholars, and many of the people I spoke to in the industry point out that no African American has ever had the authority to "green light" a program for airing on network television. Until that happens real change will not occur.

No statistical analysis can explore the responsibilities that a minority may face. Numbers do not explain different ways of seeing the world. Understanding the human dimension comes from talking to the people involved in creating television, and hearing not one definitive story, but many different stories with common threads. It is these stories and these threads that help paint a more complete picture of the creation of entertainment television in America.

Background on the Interview Process

In order to get at issues of power and control, to make comparisons to prior research findings, and to better understand the workplace environment, I set out to interview producers and writers. Research has shown the key role that producers play in television production.[38] Investigation of the role a writer plays in contemporary television can also be helpful in understanding how the system of production works. The producer often writes and many producers start out as writers. In fact, in television production, except for staff writers, almost every writer is also listed as some type of producer with titles often reflecting increased responsibility in the production of a television program. Take a close look at the opening credits on a television show, and you will see titles such as supervising producer, coordinating producer, and executive producer, people who have a direct impact on what ends up on the screen.

Since I did not want to cut myself off from some potentially significant perspectives, I also interviewed other workers involved in television production, including directors and network executives. Three of the interviewees also had experience as actors. Talking with a variety of workers allowed me to make comparisons between people at different levels of the industry. For example, are there similarities among respondents even though some are able to exercise more power? Do those at higher levels feel a greater responsibility to use their power to make a difference? Do those at lower levels in the system feel they have to "pay their dues" before they can make a difference? How do explanations of career goals change? What are the differences in conflicts with the system? Talking to professionals at different levels within the system also allows investigation into whether and how various people think about issues of power relating to race.

The majority of the interviews were conducted in the summer and fall of 1998. I did follow-up and additional interviews in 2004 and 2005. Most of the interviews were in Los Angeles with a few taking place on the East Coast.[39]

I did not go into these interviews expecting to hear a single story explaining how individuals view their work. On the contrary, I anticipated finding as great a variety of views among Black producers as prior researchers found among White ones. What I did expect was that my respondents might have had similar experiences, including a struggle to get to their current position, interactions with White supervisors and coworkers, and incidents of discrimination. My focus was on how each reacted to these situations. Did they feel a sense of responsibility to make certain representations? Did they feel a need to speak out? What prompted it?

While I hoped to uncover some of the experiences of discrimination of African American media workers, I tried to begin with an open mind. I did not know whether all the people I spoke with would tell me they had faced overt acts of racism or how many of them would believe institutionalized racism was a part of the production of entertainment television. I was not interested in determining whether my interviewees could pass some litmus test regarding attitudes toward race and television. Neither was I interested in condemning media producers for racism. I wanted to find out how cultural identity, informed by experience, relates to the creation of media images.

In addition, I looked at how the respondents interpreted and evaluated their own experiences.[40] For example, did they talk about their experience as having any relationship to the situation of fellow African Americans or other minorities? How much emphasis did each place on being a racial minority? Did an interviewee talk only about their professional roles and play down issues of race? In this way I could find out how individuals saw themselves in the system of production. I was also able to find similarities and differences among the various workers. Interview material can be viewed as another text, an interpretation of experience rather than a recounting of fact.[41]

The Challenge

Early on in formulating this project I attended a lecture by Cornel West.[42] The focus of his talk was the powerful quote that W. E. B. Du Bois uses to open his book *The Souls of Black Folk*: "for the problem of the Twentieth Century is the problem of the color-line."[43] Du Bois' prescient statement is often quoted in the literature on race and culture. West cut to the core of the issue by asking the audience, "What does it mean to be a problem?" He gave the examples of African Americans going to school, moving into a neighborhood, in the workplace, and for males even walking down the street—all of which are seen as being "a problem." West asked Whites in the audience to really think about the significance of that concept. He challenged us to ask African Americans what it means to be seen as a problem. For me it hit home. In an uncomfortable way, this is what the project I was planning was about. For the history of African Americans and television is centered on the problem of representation, or more commonly, the lack of representation. But it is also the problem of lack of opportunity. And more recently the problem for the television industry is the pressure from critics and advocacy groups seeking more employment and power for African Americans and other minorities. But had anyone asked the people working in the industry what it was like to be seen as a problem? No one that I could find had done so. It is an awkward question to ask. But, few have even tried to really find out what it is like to be a minority in such a high-profile industry. West said that Whites would be surprised at how many African Americans are willing to talk about race, that the problem of discussing these issues is really one that Whites have.

So the chapters that follow are a way to help answer that question. More important, they are a way to give a more complete picture of the roles that African Americans play in the production of entertainment television. This is far from a complete picture, but it is what Edward R. Murrow would term "the little picture," a story that gives insight into larger issues. In this case it is little pictures of some of the people who help to create television.

My interviews reinforce Gitlin's finding that television is a "talker's business."[44] Once granted an interview, I had little problem getting the respondent to talk about his or her experiences in the business. While all seemed to freely express their opinions and experiences, some were more candid than others. I attribute the variable openness to personality: some people are just more talkative than others. I found no correlation between an interviewee's degree of openness and their positions in the system. Some, like producer Tim Reid, were very willing to discuss the industry, how they were treated, and how race played a factor in their careers. Others, like Vida Spears, another successful producer, were hesitant to go much beyond the surface level of their experience in the industry. It should be noted that since Hollywood is a business dependent on personal relationships, I expected most people not to be overly negative. If they were, they might not get calls returned and offers of future work.

Being a White researcher is not inherently a disadvantage in studying issues of race. Just as minorities can occupy different subject positions, it is possible for Whites to shift locations, be sensitive to issues of race and domination, and have some understanding of how people can see the world differently.[45] I brought some of this understanding to the interview situation in the hope that these workers will want majority group members to comprehend the situation of minority workers in today's media industries. In fact, that is just what I found. Some of the interviewees were eager to tell of their experiences and apparently had no difficulty doing so with a White researcher.

While there may be problems with differences between interviewer and interviewee, this is true of much social science research. It is part of the "process by which each of us confronts our respective inability to comprehend the experience of others even as we recognize the absolute necessity of continuing the effort to do so."[46] Chapter two is the first step in understanding the people who create television as I explore the stories of how people enter the business, move up within the system, and sometimes move out of the system.

CHAPTER TWO

Getting In – Staying In

Understanding how workers enter the television production system, learn policies and procedures, and move into positions of power helps reveal what kind of people may ultimately create the programs that we watch. There are no clearly delineated steps for entrance and advancement in the television business. Education, personal contacts, internship and professional development, and mentoring opportunities all play a part in who gets access to the power to create media images. Historically, African Americans have been denied this access. Hiring patterns in the media, as in many other large institutions, tended to reflect the dominant racial, class, and gender patterns in the United States.[1] Even minority workers who were in the television industry in the 1970s and early 1980s had little chance for advancement, because moving up in the Hollywood system was dependent on social connections.[2]

African Americans can now move into positions of power in television production. Some of the workers interviewed here have been able to create images and produce programs that express their cultural identity. A few were even able to move fairly high up in the network hierarchy. Yet many of the respondents described hurdles they encountered simply because they were African American. Their stories included tales of opportunities and obstacles as African American professionals in Hollywood.

Socialization can be seen as one of "the most basic activities of humans in communities of other humans: learning to fit in."[3] Failure, whether to learn how to act, to comprehend the unwritten rules to move up in the business, or to develop contacts, usually means a short-lived career in television. The stories included here reinforce the idea that there is no "one way" to enter and succeed in the television business. But they also show that a person who goes to an elite college, attends industry-related workshops, and develops relationships can "fit in."

This chapter explores the ways these African American workers worked to fit into the world of television production. Included here are descriptions of the respondents' educational experience, involvement in internship and professional development programs, contacts in the industry, mentoring opportunities, and the extent to which they learned through observation of other professionals. Listening to their stories gives an idea of the multitude of ways people respond to a system that often views them as "other." The goal is to begin to get a picture of the variety of ways that these African American workers are socialized into the profession.

Education

Almost all of the people I spoke with attended competitive colleges; four graduated from Ivy League schools. In some cases college contacts proved to be a key element in entering the entertainment field. For example, an executive with a cable network entered the industry though a networking opportunity provided by her Harvard education. Late in her senior year she met an African American television producer at an event that brought Harvard alumni back to campus. She gave the producer her resume, which led to being hired as a researcher/production coordinator for a documentary he was then working on.

A similar experience proved pivotal in Martin Jones' decision to move to Hollywood. Jones was attending Denison University, a fairly elite midwestern liberal arts school. When Disney Chief Michael Eisner, a Denison alumnus, came to give a speech on campus, Jones was able to get a few minutes alone with Eisner, and he asked for some career advice. Eisner told him that the most important thing Jones could do to get in the business was move to Los Angeles. Once he moved to the West Coast his Denison connection proved helpful. For example, one job came from the fact that film producer David Irving was also a Denison graduate. According to Jones, when Irving saw Denison listed on Jones' resume he said, "Oh, you're in."

Former CBS and Universal executive Frank Dawson told me how his educational experience affected him socially and politically. Even though he grew up in a New York housing project, he said, "I integrated an all-White boarding school in the mid-1960s, which changed my entire life and my perspective. Going to school with all these rich

White boys changed my whole view of the world." Dawson went on to get his bachelor's degree at Cornell and master's at Syracuse. Attending Cornell in the late 1960s had a profound impact. During his freshman year he was involved in a building takeover, a result of a protest over racial issues on campus, an event that ended up being depicted on the cover of many of the national newsmagazines.[4] Dawson says

> That was my coming of age, and it had a profound effect on me in terms of how I dealt with this business. It put some severe limitations in terms of how far I could go as an executive because of a certain sense of consciousness that I have.

As part of the first class of African Americans recruited to Cornell from the inner city Dawson said it was this background that played a part in these students "challenging what we were being taught from a Euro-centric standpoint." Dawson explained:

> The few Black students that they had [previously] at Cornell [were] basically middle class kinds of kids. They started a special program in 1965 and in 1968 they felt they were ready to recruit in the inner cities and here we came. Because of that time we tended to be more politically aware and really hell bent on making some changes.

He concluded, "That spirit has kind of stayed with me."

Dawson saw that his education gave him credibility when dealing with the Hollywood business world. He said he would not have been able to take advantage of many career opportunities had he not had "a sound academic background." Dawson explained that his Ivy League education was important when he challenged the television industry's status quo:

> At the times that I have stepped out on a limb to do things, I think because people knew my education [and that] I could represent myself articulately. I think it made a difference in them having to take a second look. It was "I don't agree with what he has to say but he says it well. And he has the background to know something about what he is talking about."

Conversely, Shirley Salomon, a Production Manager at MTV,[5] described the effect of not attending a well-known college. Salomon has a degree in communication from the College of Staten Island/CUNY. She was very aware that most of her co-workers, people who attended more prestigious schools, have better connections, and more mentoring and job opportunities available to them. Salomon, who, like Dawson, comes from a less privileged background, told me:

> You look for people like yourself, and you're like "where are they?" You just don't see them. You see one or two. But you don't get the sense that all those kids you went to school with, or who told you that's what they want to do, are doing it.

The only time MTV co-workers showed any interest in Salomon's education was when she mentioned that she took some film classes at NYU. Reaction to her educational background prompted Salomon to favorably compare her work ethic to that of some of the people who attended more prestigious schools:

> They don't have the want and drive that I did. They want to work for MTV because they want to go out and party and go to premieres, and that's not really what it's about. They think it's the party network. But people are working hard 23 days in a row and doing all these hours. And I think maybe, they don't fight for it as much. When they come up against an obstacle they say, "OK I've had enough, I'm turning back."

Sharon Johnson, who attended an Ivy League school majoring in the arts with a concentration in writing, claimed that she did not get much practical experience in college. She said the pedagogic philosophy at Columbia University was "you can't really study anything well at the undergraduate level." Consequently, her education lacked the hands-on experience she thought she needed for a career in media until she entered the masters program in media studies at the New School for Social Research in New York City. There she was finally able to tie her writing to her interest in media production.

One sitcom writer, on the other hand, explicitly linked her undergraduate course work to her career in television. This writer explained that while majoring in television production at a large state university she wrote a script for one of her classes. The script sparked her professor's interest enough to ask her if she ever thought about pursuing a career as a writer. Up to that point the answer was no. It took this event for her to make the connection between her interest in writing and her desire to work in television. He encouraged her to go on to a master's program in drama at the university. She had little interest in writing for the stage. Her heart was in television. But she made a compromise with this same professor who allowed her to write sitcom scripts for some of her assignments. "I wrote a couple of plays but generally I wrote sitcoms, and he had to rush home and watch the sitcom in order to know if it was good. I taught him, too."

Similarly, *Eve* writer Michael Ajakwe Jr. had a professor he believes "changed [his] life" by encouraging him to hone his writing and to read plays and screenplays. It was writing professor Bruce McAllister of the University of Redlands who challenged him like no other. [6] "No one before or since made me realize that having talent in an area is not enough—you have to refine your talent by constantly working on your craft." Ajakwe said that after expressing interest in a career in the entertainment field, "McAllister helped get him an internship at Paramount Studios with the show *Cheers* whose creators, Glen Charles and Les Charles, also attended Redlands." Paramount Vice President Rose Catherine Pinkney, a graduate of Princeton, cited the importance of a course on African American images that "really opened" her eyes to America's history of Black misrepresentation.

Though education may form a foundation for professional life, college course work only seemed to play a strong influence on an interviewee's career when it involved a professor taking personal interest in his or her studies. In many cases it required the connections or reputation of an elite college to develop their careers. Going to a prestigious school sometimes meant access to contacts in the industry. For some a college's reputation occasionally conferred needed status for a minority employee. Frank Dawson, for example, saw that his Cornell education made a real difference, especially when he spoke up about a perceived injustice. Those in power paid more attention to what he had to say because of his elite educational background. In contrast, for Shirley Salomon attending a less prestigious school seemed to make advancement harder. As she saw it, class sometimes played a more significant role than race. A White male alum from the same school as Salomon working in television production described facing similar snobbish attitudes from graduates of colleges such as NYU.

Dawson's achievement of an executive level position at CBS and Universal, shows that someone who "grew up in a housing project in New York" can do well in the business, supporting the argument that class background is less important in non-news areas of the media.[7] The difference for Dawson may be his Ivy League education. He credited his Cornell degree for opening doors into the executive side of the business. The fact that some of the people I interviewed used their education at elite institutions to enter and advance in the industry refutes Schiller's claim for a strong relationship between class origins, an individual's schooling, and their employment opportunities.[8] Over the past thirty years, some African Americans from lower-class backgrounds have gained access to these elite educational institutions, allowing them some advantages that otherwise only come with upper-class roots.

Affirmative Action

"The issue is not just letting people in. It's having them stay in and move up in the hierarchy." That is how Rose Catherine Pinkney saw the challenge of affirmative action. She said some people are shocked to discover that she is a product of affirmative action. Pinkney is proud of the fact:

> I always want to stamp it on my forehead and say, "Yes, I did get my start through affirmative action." And it can work, given companies who support people who come through such programs. Companies that don't think of these programs as a short-term chance for minorities to get a look inside, but think of these programs as a chance to mold people to be the kind of executives that the company need them to be—executives who just happen to be people of color.

For director Leonard R. Garner, the false impression that he was an affirmative action hire meant that he was perceived as unqualified for his position by his White co-workers. He said that early in his career he had to endure comments and jokes from Whites that the bar was lowered in order for him to enter the system. This reveals one of the drawbacks to affirmative action: it can be used by Whites to disparage the qualifications of African Americans. It is a somewhat new weapon in the arsenal of racist comments and denigrating attitudes that not only marks Blacks as "other" but also as not being truly qualified for their job.

Conversely, Shirley Salomon accepted that at one job she had been hired mainly because she is African American. Salomon said that she was deeply offended when she found out she was hired as a director's assistant on the daytime soap opera *One Life to Live* principally because of her minority status. She realized that she was never going to be anything more than a token: "They groom you for that position and they keep you there just to fill their quota." She said that discovering she had been an affirmative action hire was the reason she left the show to work at *Cosby*.

Director Oz Scott saw affirmative action as a small and necessary policy for gaining access to the system. He said affirmative action was a way for minorities to get their "foot in the door." Scott compared this to White people getting jobs because of nepotism. He cautioned, "Your father being the head of the network or my being Black only lasts so long, at which point you [have to produce]." Scott recounted a discussion with a White colleague:

> After being asked, "Do you feel badly about getting a job because you're Black?" I turned to him and said, "Do you feel badly that your uncle got you your job?" That's for me the same thing. I said, "Because the one thing that is different between your uncle and my affirmative action is your uncle will keep getting you a job. Affirmative action only works once. And if I don't do the job, nobody's there to look out for me."

The variety of opinions and experiences concerning affirmative action is a reminder of why African Americans cannot and should not be viewed as being united on any issue, even an issue that can bring employment to group members. The dilemma is that while affirmative action can open doors, it can also mark workers as unqualified, or consign them to jobs with no room for advancement. The strongest message is given by Rose Catherine Pinkney; when used to effectively socialize a person into the profession, affirmative action can be a valuable program for the television industry.

Internships/Professional Development

Many of the people I interviewed cited their involvement in internship and professional development programs as key to their entrance and advancement in the business. Nonetheless, their responses show no uniform definition of an internship program. Some described traditional college programs where students received credit for working in the industry while others mentioned their involvement with in-house internships similar to management trainee programs in other industries.

Many of these workers mentioned internships when describing how they got their first break in the business. Shirley Salomon credited her work on *Saturday Night Live* and network soap operas with getting her first position as a production assistant on *All My Children*. Public relations executive James Anderson cited the internship program at Denison University for bringing him to New York to work for

Saturday Night Live creator Lorne Michaels' production company, Broadway Video. The internship gave him the background and the connections to start as a production assistant on *The Cosby Show,* another program based in New York.

Producer and writer Felicia D. Henderson entered the industry through a more structured internship/training program receiving a fellowship from NBC that paid for her second year of graduate school at the University of Georgia.[9] After that Henderson was accepted into NBC's management trainee program designed for minorities, adding: "It was White blonde women as minorities, if you know what I mean." From what she observed, any affirmative action benefits of the program went to White females. The training program involved rotating through different departments in the network. Henderson's true interests lay in comedy writing. She submitted some of her scripts and was accepted into the Warner Brothers Writers Workshop, a prestigious program that helped open doors for her, such as a job as an apprentice writer on the mid-1990s success *Family Matters.* Within five years, Henderson had risen to her position at the time of our initial interview: supervising producer on *Sister, Sister.* She contrasted her rapid success to that of other people she knew who took more than a dozen years to get to a position like hers, stating: "Times have changed." Henderson acknowledged African Americans who entered the business before her, including some of her own contacts and mentors, for helping to make her relatively rapid rise possible. Henderson was aware that these minority workers had to face a struggle that in the end helped to facilitate her own success.

Frank Dawson's story of gaining entrance to an in-house management internship program at CBS in the late 1970s shows the kind of persistence that was necessary for African Americans to open doors in the television industry. Although Dawson had worked his way up to a writer/producer position in network promotions, he still yearned to advance to the executive level. He knew CBS ran a management training program that could help him reach his goal. Dawson explained:

> CBS had an internship at that time to move into the programming department. It had been created for the sons and daughters, nieces and nephews of the executives working in the business. They would hire these kids straight out of UCLA and USC, and they always turned out to be related to someone in the business.

According to Dawson, at his insistence, the CBS Employees Association questioned the network management as to why employees were excluded from participation. CBS's response was to open one slot for employees. The selection process involved a series of interviews, which Dawson navigated successfully, gaining him the single internship position. He cited his profile at CBS with helping him land the position. Some of the CBS executives knew him from his work as a writer/producer. Others were familiar with him from his efforts in helping to establish a Los Angeles chapter of the CBS Black Employees Association.[10] Dawson said people at the network were impressed with the way he and the other African Americans promoted the issue of minority advancement. According to Dawson, he and his colleagues relied on research and negotiation, not confrontation to make their case that the network needed to make a greater effort to increase minority employment.

Dawson's yearlong internship involved working in different CBS departments, including promotion, late night as well as daytime programming and research. The experience allowed him to see the inner workings of the network:

> Every department that I went into, people were open with information. I sat in offices while they were on the phone negotiating big deals and business affairs. They kind of knew you were not going to be around for long, so you were not a threat. They also knew that you could possibly become an executive, be their boss, so they wanted to be nice to you.

After completion of the program Dawson became an executive in dramatic programming at CBS.

For many workers, internships profoundly affected the direction of their careers. For example, one network executive said that while she was working on her first job after Harvard, as an assistant on a television documentary, she was considering other career paths such as law school. But then she heard about and was accepted into a six-month internship at major television production studio. The program led to a job as a junior executive at the company and her career in television. Kim Sizemore, stage manager on *The Parent'Hood*, first became involved in television in the 1970s through a government funded CETA[11] program in New York that led to a production job at CBS news. After moving to Hollywood, Sizemore applied to the American Film Institute and was accepted into its Center for Film and Television Studies. According to Sizemore, she was the AFI's first Black female cinematographer.

These internship programs benefited both the minority talent and the industry. For these new workers the internship experiences allowed them to find out how the industry functioned, how people did their jobs. For industry executives these programs were a way to evaluate and then hire new talent. For example, television director Leonard R. Garner explained how he moved from being a struggling actor to becoming involved in the Directors Guild of America's training program in the 1970s where they assigned him to different jobs:

> My first couple of jobs were at Universal as a trainee. You show up at a place and an A.D. [Assistant Director] tells you "this is what you are doing today." And you follow orders and you learn, you start learning like that.... There were a lot of things I liked. You're working on big shows with big stars. I'm not just being a production assistant on a low budget movie.... I got on *The Rockford Files*, which was great. On a big show, big star. Universal had all the shows at that time, *Beretta*, *Kojack*. They were a machine.

Garner did mention race in describing the program:

> Obviously there were not that many Black people who had done that before.... There was one guy who would always keep referring that I had gotten in through some sort of an equal opportunity thing, which the trainee program really isn't. The training is based on testing and scores.... Yes, they do try to have an ethnic mix but they don't lower the curve at all.

Garner did not dwell on the false perception among some in Hollywood that recruiting African Americans into the system required some lowering of standards. He said that he accepted this attitude as a fact of life in a work environment, which at that time, the 1970s and 1980s, had few minorities. He was resigned to the notion that some Whites were going to think that way and he just had to "deal with it." For Garner, being the lone Black was a routine experience. He related it to growing up in Scranton, Pennsylvania: "I was used to being the only Black man in certain situations."

Garner, Dawson, and Sizemore were the only people I interviewed to specifically raise the issue of race when describing their involvement in training programs. All three entered the industry in the 1970s, which suggests that Blacks faced more obstacles compared to people such as Felicia Henderson and Meg DeLoatch who entered in the 1980s and 1990s. And except for Dawson, who explicitly noted the difficulty of gaining access to CBS's program, they did not complain about their internship experience. It seems that the current groups of minority workers face a more open atmosphere in the industry.

Felicia D. Henderson credited those African Americans who came be-fore her for making that possible:

> Four years ago I was a staff writer. Today I am the co-executive producer of this show [*Sister, Sister.*] Other people and [my] mentors have taken thirteen, fourteen years to do that. But times have changed as well. Some of the reasons I was able to do it was because it took them ten, twelve years to do it.[12]

Meg DeLoatch, creator and showrunner of *Eve*, used her time in the "Cosby Workshop" to create the original pilot script of the show. Officially titled *The Guy Hanks and Marvin Miller Writing Program*, it was established by Drs. Bill Cosby and Camille Cosby in 1993, at the USC School of Cinema-Television. The program was named in honor of Camille Cosby's father, Guy Alexander Hanks and Bill Cosby's producer, Marvin Miller. According to the program's Web site, "The 15-week intensive workshop was designed with a twofold purpose: To assist writers in the completion of a film or television script. To deepen the participants' appreciation for and comprehension of Afri-can American history and culture."[13] Although not an affirmative ac-tion program, it certainly reflects the Cosbys' commitment to promotion of the understanding of African American culture. DeLoatch, a graduate of American University, said it was a wonderful experience for a number of reasons, including developing friendships with people in the industry. She said the workshop's emphasis on Af-rican American history had a huge impact on her:

> For someone who had been to college, and had taken some courses in Black history. I grew up in the suburbs. But I thought I was pretty aware. And I learned so much. I just sort of had my conscious awakening of, "Holy cow, it's amazing, this history of people that I come from."

Writer Michael Ajakwe Jr. seconded DeLoatch's sentiments about the impact of the workshop: "The most insightful part of it, for me, was the African American history portion. I learned more African Ameri-can history in those fifteen weeks than my entire life before or since." Ajakwe like DeLoatch, a part of the first class of the Hanks & Miller Screenwriting Program back in 1994, cited the value of the experience for providing him "lifelong professional and personal relationships."

Contacts and Networking

One advantage of involvement in an internship is the opportunity for networking. Internship programs can lead to contacts, jobs, and support systems. Most of the people I interviewed had few, if any connections, relatives, or friends within the industry at the beginning of their careers. Few mentioned race as an issue here, but instead explained how networking could substitute for the connections that come with having family or powerful friends in the business. For example, Carsey-Werner's Senior Vice President James L. Anderson said that he always mentions his internship when he talks about his background because it "set up the path for me. It connected me, certainly opened the door." This initial experience helped not only lead to his first job as a production assistant on *The Cosby Show*, but after driving producers around for that series in New York, Anderson was offered a position on their next show, *A Different World*, which was being developed in Los Angeles.

When production director Kim Sizemore, arrived in California in the late 1970s, Oz Scott, a previous co-worker from the New York theater scene, helped get her a job on a film he was working on. Scott had recently come out to direct Richard Pryor's film *Bustin' Loose.* Subsequently Scott helped Sizemore get television work at Universal, where he had also worked. Sizemore said that even though she had other good references, Scott's recommendation made them "more predisposed to hire me." Her job on *Bustin' Loose* led to five years of work as a production assistant on Richard Pryor films. Sizemore said she was able to use this association to become, at one point, one of the highest paid production assistants in Hollywood. She explained that when Pryor signed on for a film he let it be known that he preferred to have crew people he had worked with before. Often the production company would initially offer Sizemore less money than she had earned on her previous Pryor film. Sizemore said if negotiations "got sticky" she would say:

> "I'm not sure I can take this job. I will have to call Mr. Pryor and have him get involved." And the next day they would call and say "We think we can pay you the money that you asked." No one wanted to ruffle his feathers.

Though Sizemore did not mention race when talking about the help that Scott and Pryor provided, what she was describing is networking among African Americans in the business, how Blacks help other Blacks.

In Hollywood, where the payoff is high and often comes quickly, people regularly hire people they know. Many of the people I interviewed were insulted by the industry practice of hiring relatives and friends, which they found detrimental to minorities looking to get their feet in the door. Director Oz Scott said people often hire those they are most comfortable with, people they don't mind "spreading the wealth to." One writer was especially critical of this practice. He thought the primary consideration should be a person's talent and stressed the importance of working with people who may question a producer's approach. The writer gave the example of his show's White executive producer:

> He took a chance. I don't know many White showrunners who would say "I am going to admit I am not aware of teen sensibilities, especially teen Black sensibilities and I am going to bring in some quality Black people who are going to enhance the project I am trying to do."

This writer added that his producer was the only White writer/producer on an otherwise Black staff, which he asserted as, "unheard of."

A couple of the interviewees described networking opportunities that developed through long-term relationships. For example, Vida Spears met Sara Finney while working as a receptionist at Norman Lear's production company. Finney was an assistant to a producer there, and the two shared the same aspirations of becoming writers. They even worked together writing sketches for the company Christmas shows. Spears went on to work as a secretary for a producer on *Silver Spoons*. Finney approached her about becoming her writing partner, as she wanted to work as a team. They then pitched scripts for *Silver Spoons*. Spears explained: "Usually you need an agent to get in and pitch, but [people on these shows] all knew each other. And the producers from different shows let us come in and pitch. So we sold our first story together on the first pitch." Spears and Finney went on to write for *The Jeffersons, 227, The Facts of Life,* and *Family Matters,* where they eventually became producers. They then teamed up with Ralph Farquhar to co-create and executive produce *Moesha*. Spears explained that neither she nor Finney had experience as executive producers, something she knew studios would be looking for. She liked Farquhar's sensibilities and the fact that he

was co-creator of the Fox series *South Central.* In describing her relationship with Finney, Spears never mentioned the fact that Finney is
also African American.

Although many of the people I spoke with described their success
with the industry's networking system a few expressed frustration.
For example, Shirley Salomon said:

> Nepotism runs very deep in this industry and I have no one. Every job I get
> on my own. And I work hard at it. There is no one saying: "Shirley, hey, I
> know about a job.... My friend works here. Just tell him that I sent you."
> Now in the last seven or eight months, people are starting to know my
> name, they call me for movies, for certain things. But all of that I got on my
> own.

Her experience observing how other people, both Black and White,
obtained jobs though relatives and friends in the business has inspired Salomon to go out of her way to assist those without connections. She told of a young person who called MTV about an
internship, sending resumes but getting no response. When he called
her, she told him, "Send it to me and I will personally walk it over
and give it to them."

Director Leonard R. Garner criticized Hollywood for being such a
"people business." He wished the industry was different: "I really
want my relationship with the network to be based solely on work....
I don't go to a lot of the parties. I don't do the scene, I'm about the
work." He said the fact that he does not get a lot of "quality" pilots to
direct or that he does not do much work at networks other than NBC
results from his lack of interest in networking. Garner asserted that
the quality of his work and the fact that he directs a hit series should
speak for itself. Yet, he maintained that his disinterest in socializing
would continue to affect his ability to get additional opportunities.

In contrast, Martin Jones, General Manager of New Millennium
Studios at the time of our interview, enjoyed the networking aspects
of the industry. When breaking down how the industry works, Jones
claimed: "The ironic thing is, in my twelve years in Hollywood, and
thirteen or fourteen jobs, I never got a job from an application or from
a want ad. It was always because of knowing somebody." In his case,
he said, "Personality has played a very large part.... Hollywood is a
very people business and I guess I 'do' good people." Jones said success requires staying in contact with former co-workers and supervisors. He mentioned that he recently formed production and foreign

distribution deals with people he knew from one of his first jobs in the business, working in a production company mailroom.

While Jones tied his success to his ability to be a "people person," he also mentioned that, for people of color, Hollywood is not an easy place to make connections. He described Los Angeles as a racist and segregated city where people can be "pretty closed minded." Jones has observed that people in the industry rarely have contact with those unlike themselves. He tried to describe working in this environment:

> Movies are shot on location.... And even when [workers] get into areas, they are very isolated, they are in this pack, this club. Even though they are in someone else's neighborhood there are people there whose job is to insulate them, to keep the outside world out. Even, to some extent, the people who get down there and see things still are holding on to stereotypes because they haven't really been there.

Former network executive Frank Dawson connected the cultural isolation of some White creators to the current state of television programming. In his view, the segregation went beyond any particular work environment. Dawson said many White network executives have limited parameters of contact; they often base their programming decisions on the people they know, people like themselves:

> If you go through any network suite, the people who are calling the shots and taking the meetings, they are the people from *Friends*. You look at the characters on *Friends*, the people who populate those offices look just like that. They are twenty-eight year old White guys and their girlfriends. They make all the creative decisions now. And that's why all the stuff they are buying for network television looks just like that.

Joseph Turow's study of Hollywood in the early 1980s found that, "Inexperienced Black writers find it harder to develop the trusting, helpful contacts they need in the overwhelmingly White TV community."[14] Some of the people I spoke with described their success as due in part to the preceding generation of African American television workers. They could go to these more experienced creators for advice and assistance and some African Americans feel a responsibility to help other Blacks. Thus, the importance of networking and the fact that there are now more Black creators enhances the possibility that diversity in the industry will increase; more African Americans in the business should mean increased opportunities for new entrants into the system.

Mentoring and Observation

If, as mentioned earlier, socialization is about learning how to fit in, then receiving guidance from people with experience in the business can be a priceless resource to a person's career. New workers can find out how an organization works, how they can move ahead, and how to avoid problems along the way. For most of us career advancement usually requires caring, effective mentors.[15] Felicia Henderson described the tutelage she received on her first writing job, *Family Matters*. Sara Finney and Vida Spears were co-producers on the show when Henderson arrived. "From the moment I walked in the door [they] just embraced me and schooled me," she recalled. Henderson said that Finney and Spears were discreet in the way they offered help: "With my first script (they whispered), 'this is between us, let us read this first.' And they gave me notes... before I ever turned it in, without the showrunner ever knowing." Such feedback on a writer's early work can increase the chances of the script being accepted for production. Notes can give a writer an idea of what the network is looking for in a script; whether their characters follow a series' premises; whether their work is moving the series in the directions the producers expect. This type of assistance is one of the reasons Henderson credited African Americans who came before her for her success, although she did not express any specific racial angle to Finney and Spears' mentoring. Instead, she cited them as two of the most positive, "non-negatively competitive" women she has ever known.

Henderson's positive experience at *Family Matters* is somewhat ironic in light of her apprehension before joining the show. She said that when she first arrived she anticipated some resentment because of her impression that one African American writer already worked on the show. Henderson described what she expected: "A sort of in-tra-racism that is the most hurtful. You sometimes find that when there is a Black person there, so much of their power comes from their being the only one. That they don't want other Blacks around." In fact it was the opposite that occurred. The other African American workers on the show, such as Finney and Spears, helped to create what Henderson described as a very welcoming atmosphere.

Finney and Spears continued to advise Henderson even after she left to write for *Fresh Prince*. When Finney and Spears created *Moesha* they asked Henderson to join them on the show. Henderson recalled that she was excited about "writing this Black girl's show from a Black perspective, working under Sara and Vida." Henderson said that the relationship with Finney and Spears continues and the advice they give strengthened her work at *Sister, Sister*. The foundation laid by people like Finney and Spears translates into a more hospitable and creative environment for African Americans entering the business in the past fifteen years. The fact that Henderson went on to help create *Soul Food*, the longest running African American television drama, is a testament to her television "ancestors."

Passing this legacy on Henderson works with young writers and writer trainees, people who can observe and learn from the way she does her work. She stressed the importance of being proactive, asking for a trainee, not waiting to get one assigned. Henderson specifically referred to race and its relationship to production in describing why she mentors others:

> You are always feeding the machine of the next generation of people who look like you in hopes of even next time, by the next series of shows, there won't even be this battle.... You have to make time. That is the future of the images that I see on television.

Though not the same as professional mentoring, Henderson described the responsibility she feels to guide young people, including a group of girls who live in a group home. When she was working on *Sister, Sister* Henderson brought these girls to the show "every so often to sit down and have pizza and talk about their future... and show them the career opportunities behind the camera."

Early in his career Tim Reid looked to experienced writers and producers for advice. But, he contrasted his attitude to that of the new generation of creators. While praising Hugh Wilson and other television writer/producers whom he considered mentors, he expressed frustration with today's younger workers. He told the story of a young Black director who, after he got in "over his head" on a production, had someone call Reid to request that he come over and talk to him. Reid was insulted, feeling that, with his successful record, the director should have come over to Reid's office. "That arrogance of his kept him from having someone help. I have never been afraid to go to Black, White, I don't care who they are, to learn something."

According to Reid, the case of the young director was not atypical. He contrasted his experience breaking into the business to those of the latest group of writers:

Younger people don't want to hear it. I wanted to hear it. I chased them [successful writers and producers] down. Young people don't have it in them, the humility that you need to go and learn from people who have information by living experience.

Yet, some younger workers are interested in getting advice from experienced creators. MTV Production Manager Shirley Salomon said that before she left her job at *Cosby*,[16] she approached Bill Cosby for career advice. Salomon said he was happy to give her a little time to discuss her career goals. She recounted what Cosby told her:

You know it's not always about helping other people, sometimes it's first about helping yourself and not really worrying what other people think and what they need you to do. You just keep focusing on your goals and keep focusing on what you want to do and eventually you'll get it.

Some people mentioned race in discussing mentors and mentoring, while others played down the issue. For producer and former network executive Frank Dawson, being able to go to other African Americans for advice was important. While acknowledging the small numbers involved, Dawson said he was part of a second wave of Black executives in television. He said he would contact Stan Robinson, who was part of the first generation of Black executives, for advice. At one particularly trying time, when Dawson was transferred to a less influential department at CBS, he went to talk to Robinson:

Stan really got me focused. He got me calmed down. He got me to understand that it wasn't anything personal against me. And he really got me to sit down and look at the situation and determine what I really wanted to do and how I could use it to my advantage.

Robinson eventually told him to contact Universal about a job because he knew Dawson was respected there which led to Dawson leaving CBS and taking the position at Universal.

Most said race was not a factor in mentoring and that both Blacks and Whites opened doors to up and coming workers. For example, director Leonard R. Garner said that he considered actor and producer James Garner (no relation), with whom he worked on *The Rockford Files*, a mentor "because of the way he treated me and the way I saw him treat people around him." James Garner showed him that he didn't have to "buy into the bs" of Hollywood. Leonard R. Garner mentioned that he looked to Ivan Dixon as a mentor because he was the first Black director that he had an opportunity to observe. Dixon, a fairly successful film and television actor, was one of the first African

American television directors. His work, starting with *The Bill Cosby Show* in 1970, included multiple episodes of *The Waltons, The Rockford Files,* and *Magnum P. I.* Leonard R. Garner added that James Garner opened doors for minority workers, pointing out that he was instrumental in having Dixon direct episodes of *The Rockford Files* and other programs he produced.

Sitting in her office at New Millennium Studios in Virginia in 2005, actress and media executive Daphne Maxwell Reid recalled that when she started out there were few role models in television for African American women, "except Diahann Carroll." Maxwell Reid told me that her first mentor was actor Robert Conrad, citing his kindness, advice and opportunity for work. "The confidence that I got from working with him gave me the confidence to go on and seek some more [work]." For Maxwell Reid opportunities to mentor young people is one of the rewards of running New Millennium Studios. The studio has employed ninety interns over the past eight years with a number "going on professionally in the business." Maxwell Reid said she tries to give these people a clear picture of the television industry:

> The mentoring that I do is more about reality and taking the stars out of your eyes about this business. It is not a glamorous life. The rewards can lead to personal glamorousness but the work is hard, it is long, it's politically charged. It is difficult. They are not prepared when they come out of school to do this work. They need to be prepared starting in grade school in tenacity, in gumption as we used to say.

Leonard R. Garner echoed the sentiments of many of the people I interviewed in describing mentoring not in terms of receiving advice, as an opportunity to watch how people work and live their professional, and sometimes personal, lives. For one network executive it was observing one of her bosses, a White man who she described as "an extremely flamboyantly gay guy":

> [He was an] incredibly creative, sort of very big personality and I learned from him that you don't have to feel constrained about who you are. That you can really sort of take the best of who you are and let that shine. He did that every day.

His example was important because the network "was a pretty conservative place." Her boss was able to survive a number of regime changes at the network, something not every executive in Hollywood is able to do. "People thought he would get fired and he just said, 'I've got to be who I am, I'll be responsible and get the shows made.'"

Carsey-Werner's James Anderson told me that people he considered mentors might be amazed to hear that because these are people he works side by side with. Anderson described how he observed their work habits and patterned his work on some of their positive actions. He also mentioned how surprised he is when people tell him that they consider him a mentor. Two people, one Black and one White, have told Anderson that his advice, his professional actions, and the way he listened have helped them with their careers.

Shirley Salomon tied her ability to learn through observation to some of her success in the business—moving from production assistant on a couple of soap operas, to *Cosby,* to Production Manager for the *MTV Summer Beach House* series to production executive at BET. "I'm a very observant person. I look at everyone's job description, see what it is they do, and see if I can help out with that." She said that most of the time little direction is given to production assistants. In order to understand her job it was essential to be attentive. Salomon watched how others performed their duties then tried to help them. She also saw that people who advanced in the system were problem solvers and people who could think fast.

In the high-pressure world of production there is often little time for specific instructions, so listening and observing is sometimes the only way to survive. Production Director Kim Sizemore recalled that early in her career working with movie producers Cliff Coleman and Hope Goodman gave her the opportunity to see the importance of pre-production: how a script gets broken down piece by piece; the scheduling involved; and the questions that people ask themselves concerning how each scene is to be produced. She said she continues to use these skills in what she referred to as the more "regimented" world of television production.

For most of these workers mentoring and modeling behavior were rarely cast in terms of race, possibly because there were few experienced African Americans to observe. In fact, Vida Spears speculated that one of the reasons she lacked a mentor was that so few African American women were producers. Spears added: "That's why I try to do that as much as I can for people, because I know how difficult it is. Hollywood is a hard business for everyone, but it is especially hard for minorities and especially, especially hard for minority women."

Unlike sociologists Joe Feagin and Melvin Sikes, who find "few (or no) White managers willing to be effective mentors for Black employees,"[17] most of the people I interviewed said they could look to Whites for help. But in such instances the issue of mentoring was often framed in terms of minority status. For example, there was the network executive who cited the importance of working with a gay White male supervisor. He did not hide his "otherness." Her supervisor's behavior sent the message that it was possible to do one's job well and succeed in the business without compromising one's individuality.

Conclusion

Getting in and staying in the television business remains dependent on social connections.[18] When discussing almost any aspect related to socialization, these workers described how contacts with experienced creators helped their careers. Even interactions that were fairly mundane could be instrumental to a worker's advancement in the business. For example, Jim Anderson's driving duties when he was a production assistant on *The Cosby Show* helped lead to his career in Hollywood. The producers he drove around New York assisted him in getting work on one of their company's new projects, *A Different World*. Sometimes the connections were more direct. *WKRP* creator and producer Hugh Wilson not only allowed Tim Reid the creative leeway to create the iconic character Venus Flytrap, he gave the actor the opportunity to write for the show. Their relationship also led to Reid's first work as a producer, when he and Wilson created *Frank's Place*.

Television production, for the most part, has an absence of direct training programs. Having a mentor, someone to go to for advice on negotiating with authority figures and handling constructive criticism can be key for inexperienced workers. For many of the people I interviewed a support system that gives feedback on scripts, contacts for jobs, and counsel, important in a business dependent on personal relationships, is the difference between survival and failure in the business.

A responsibility to help those who came after them was a common sentiment among these workers. This was true for people who have reached a level of success, such as Vida Spears or Felicia Henderson. It also applied to Shirley Salomon, who, as a Production Manager at MTV at the time, may not have mustered a lot of power, but saw the importance of going out of her way to help people without connections. Many respondents mentioned examples of living up to this responsibility because they felt an obligation to assist and sometimes mentor less experienced workers. They all seemed to take great joy in these efforts, some seeing it as one of the tangible benefits of moving up in the television industry.

The industry has changed positively for African Americans over the last thirty years. People who entered the business in the 1970s and early 1980s had few role models or mentors of color. Some were fortunate enough to have White executives, producers, or actors who helped guide them. Those African Americans who persevered and succeeded have created a community that makes it slightly easier to get one's foot in the door, learn the ropes, and maintain a position in a very competitive field. Part of that legacy is structural and institutional, such as the writers' program created by Bill Cosby and Camille Cosby. But the growing numbers of African American television workers have created what is for the most part an informal network that mentors new workers, filling a role that slowly builds the numbers who can get and stay in the system.

The following chapter explores the routines of entertainment television production through the experiences of African American writers, directors, and producers.

CHAPTER THREE

The Production System

A writer has an idea, be it an adult drama concerning family relationships, the joys and sadness shared by a group of friends, or the challenges faced by the new owner of a restaurant in New Orleans. Getting that idea from initial spark to the fully realized television show for twenty-two weeks is a daunting process. Approvals, producers, casting, network green lighting and then feedback, audience considerations — all must be addressed. The fact that some spark of that initial idea ever makes it to the viewers' home could be considered a miracle. This chapter will explore the production system and how those involved describe navigating from concept to seeing their program on the television screen.

The Television Production Cycle

The television production cycle often begins with an individual idea for a show, be it from a writer, producer, or television executive. From thereon production people, studios, and networks are involved as idea moves from concept to reality. This is a fluid process that follows a fairly regular schedule. Figure 3.1 illustrates the sequence of events necessary for bringing a show from concept to the television screen. The schematic should be helpful to understanding the interviewees' description of the organizational aspects of television creation. One can see that writers, writer/producers, and producers often have to convince production "gate-keepers" such as a network development executive (Step 1), and then that executive has to shepherd the show from concept to script through pilot production (Steps 3–7). This is one example of how much control of the success of the production is out of reach of the producer. It should be noted that the increasing competition between and among the broadcast and cable networks has destabilized this process. For example, it is becoming more common for networks to rearrange their prime-time schedule in response to their competitor's announcements.

Figure 3.1. Television production cycle.

Television Production Cycle

Step 1. Show idea/Concept

The basic idea and outline for a show

Step 2. The Pitch

Face to Face to:

- Network Development Executives

- Production Studio Representatives

- Personal Contacts at the Networks (friends/nepotism)

- Diversity Executives

The Selling season, when ideas are pitched, runs July through October.

Note: Most, but not all, show ideas are pitched with writers attached.

Note: This can be a two-way street. The networks can come looking for a writer/producer to develop an idea into a fuller concept.

Note: Development of Drama shows move faster than Comedy shows.

Step 3. Script Is Written

When a network likes an idea they order a script to be written.

This occurs during the selling season once a pitch is accepted.

Note: Networks develop 50–80 projects accepted a year to end up with 10 projects to schedule.

Step 4. Early Judgments

Immediate principles in Network Drama and Comedy Development Departments have discussions early. — October–November

Examples: "Script was not good enough and needs more work" or Idea just does not work and should be dropped."

↓

Step 5. Winnowing Down the Scripts

Network President asks Head of Drama and Head of Comedy — November

"Which looks real?" "Do we really like them?"

Scripts are winnowed down to 30–40

↓

Step 6. Ordering Pilot

Drama pilots ordered — 10–15 depending on network — January

Comedy pilots ordered — 10–15 depending on network — February–March

This includes costing out production of pilot.

Step 7. Early Screening

Pilots are screened by network.

Note: For some this is the end of the process. Networks don't bother to test screen
because the pilot is just not good enough.

Step 8. Testing

Audience screen testing — Concurrent with screening by network executives

Test

- Favorable responses to individual characters

- Line scores — with audience dial ratings

- Focus/discussion groups

–   Mailing to test in homes and response questionnaire — DVDs

Step 9. Series Pick-Up

Series approved for production and scheduling.

Step 10. Scheduling

Network schedule is set in mid-May.

Step 11. Upfronts

Selling the show to advertisers.

Within a few days of series pick-up sales to advertisers.

May and June

Step 12. Production

Writing and producing are concurrent

From July on

Start all over again with pitch

The Pitch

Much of a network's power derives from its ability to approve a show
for scheduling. Producers must pitch their ideas to network
executives in order to receive financing from studios or the network
itself. But it all begins with an idea, most often from people already
working on a show. For example, Vida Spears and Sara Finney came

up with the idea for *Moesha* while they were both writing for *Family Matters*. Spears said their pitch to CBS was based around the characters—an African American teenager and her family. "CBS bought it within the first ten minutes of the pitch. They really liked it."

Unfortunately, Spears said, although CBS agreed to produce the pilot, the network decided not to put *Moesha* on its schedule.

> It was sort of a bumpy process because it was "OK we like this because it's different" and then they kind of get nervous because it's different. My agent said one reason CBS gave for not picking it up was they didn't have anything similar to pair *Moesha* with. So they passed on us for the fall season.

Spears explained what she thought made the show challenging for CBS: "Well, I've never seen anything like *Moesha* on CBS. I mean that's just, real." She added that there UPN was a good opportunity and the show, "had a nice run there."

A network executive gave some indication what contributed to that decision. She compared CBS's audience at the time, which was older, more rural, White, and female, to *Moesha's* target audience: younger, Black, female, teenagers. She predicted the show would be a hit for one of the new networks or for cable but that it would never have worked on CBS. In fact, six months after CBS rejected *Moesha,* UPN decided to pick it up for broadcast. There it ran for five years and had a successful run in syndication.

These same considerations seemed to persist almost ten years after *Moesha's* 1996 premiere. CBS was given an opportunity to schedule one of the most highly touted new shows for the 2005 season, *Everybody Hates Chris*. By then, CBS and UPN were both part of the entertainment giant Viacom.[1] CBS Chairman Les Moonves scheduled both networks. For the 2005 season he choose not to put *Everybody Hates Chris* on CBS, a network with a much larger viewership than UPN. Its audience is also much Whiter than that of UPN. Network scheduling is not a science. It involves risks, and when race is a factor, schedulers are less willing to take more risks. Not scheduling the show on CBS drew attention. Moonves told a *New York Times* reporter, "Everyone in the press wants to know why that show is not on CBS." He explained why he did not take advantage of its larger audience: "But if we put it on, that would destroy the credibility of UPN as a network. *Everybody Hates Chris* may put them on the map."[2] Moonve's explanation may be a dodge to fend off criticism for a poor decision. Less than a year latter UPN was no more as it combined with WB to form CW. Moonves's judgment regarding *Everybody Hates Chris* did little for UPN and prevented a critically acclaimed sitcom from reaching a wider audience.

"They said this wasn't realistic" was how Felicia D. Henderson described a network's response to a proposal she pitched in the late 1990s. She explained that the plot line revolved around a mother who encouraged her daughter to become a doctor. The mother objected when the daughter wanted to join a singing group. Henderson said the network executives could "not conceive that a Black mother would think that it's beneath her daughter to sing and dance." Henderson responded by telling the network people they should talk to her friends who live in middle-class neighborhoods and send their children to private schools. "They are not sending those kids to school so that they can sing and dance. And they don't feel any less Black for that."

Henderson was also told by White network executives that one of the African American characters in her pilot was "just not real." She said network programmers don't want to deal with multifaceted minority characters — and they want to avoid conflict that might come from cultural differences. She offered her theory as to why executives seldom understand complex minority characters: "If you think about it, for the most part the people making these decisions, what they know of Black people is what they have seen on television." Henderson's observation is as good as any I've heard to explain why certain decisions are made in Hollywood. It is also a real life illustration of Stuart Hall's circuit of culture (see chapter one) wherein a media-created world becomes reality. White people whose primary knowledge of minorities comes via one-dimensional media depictions may not be able to conceive of a multifaceted African American character. At the same time, Whites can be reluctant to deal with the issues and the conflict that can arise in dealing with race. Yet Henderson, in her 1998 interview, said she was interested in producing television in which people work out these conflicts.

Television critic Fredrick McKissack speculates about the pitch meeting for *Homeboys From Outer Space,* a primarily Black show that UPN aired during the 1996 season: "Let's send two funny Black guys into outer space. It'll be like *Star Trek* meets *Sanford and Son.*"[3] A former executive at CBS I spoke with, was at one pitch meeting for *Homeboys In Outer Space.* While she acknowledged the criticism of the show's stereotypical characters, she said its two Black writers were very sincere about their work. She said they thought their idea was really funny: "They were in their mid-twenties, and they just thought this was hysterical." CBS was not interested.

The executive attributed some of the criticism of shows like *Home Boys* to a "certain generational, even a class bias." She said, "A broad working-class audience of African Americans isn't necessarily as interested in watching the things that Ivy League-educated Black professional writers are interested in watching or writing." She said the same thing is often true of shows that White writers pitch and sell. But she added White writers "are just allowed to write, maybe, a broader selection of shows."

Tim Reid saw network relations, including pitching shows, in terms of power differences. He said network decision-makers are well aware of their ability to make writers and producers wealthy. When creators pitch show ideas they accept this relationship. This means that a pitch meeting can be intimidating. Reid said that for African Americans an added layer of tension may arise from racial differences. He explained the attitude he projects at these meetings:

> We will deal with each other on a level of power, your power vs. the lack of mine. But we will deal with it in a realm of honesty and I will force you to deal with me on a level of respect, just human respect.

Reid said that demanding respect and refusing to accept any form of racial intimidation is one reason he is "constantly" in adversarial and even confrontational situations. While his attitude may cause him problems in certain circumstances, Reid credited his assertiveness for his overall success in getting what he wants, in making the kind of shows he believes in.

In listening to a pitch studio executive Rose Catherine Pinkney looks for show concepts that can be sustained over many episodes. Pinkney often hears writers pitch an idea that could work for a film but not something that people would come back to week after week, which is a requirement in television. She also wants to know, "Can we get a mass audience to watch?" Not that Pinkney ignores a minority audience. She simply knows that a concept must attract a fairly large group of people to stay on the air. Pinkney is encouraged to see "talented writers of color... being trained, rising up through the ranks, learning to run shows and how to develop shows." Pinkney takes great pride in her involvement in shows created by minority writers and producers. When a producer of color does not make a successful pitch, she admits, "I feel twice as bad when I call them and tell them we have to pass. But it's my job to develop the ideas with the most potential."

Priorities and Power

"On a daily basis I look for ideas that we can sell to networks" is how Paramount's Vice President for Comedy Development Rose Catherine Pinkney described her job. One step in getting a show on the air involves selling an idea to a production studio. A development executive is one of the people who listens to pitches for new shows and develops the ideas to sell to a network. Once a network decides it wants to air the show, a development executive may shepherd the show through the initial production. Pinkney explained that, "As a development executive, once you get a show on the air you stay with it for the first 13 episodes, and then it is time for you to move on and start developing other shows." Current executives, who manage the shows that are in production, take over from that point on. When I mentioned to Pinkney that I had interviewed Frank Dawson she smiled and said that he was around when "there were no development executives of color." In what one contact in the industry calls "the small Black world in Hollywood" many people know him as a trailblazer for people of color. Dawson said that as a network and studio executive in the 1980s, he was "really committed to getting more African American-themed programs and images on the air." He admitted he was frustrated that he had never managed to achieve a position with "green light" power, the authority to approve a program idea for production. Dawson explained that at CBS he helped supervise the development of scripts and coordinated production of successful shows such as *Magnum, P.I.*, *Cagney and Lacey*, and *Falcon Crest*. Toward the end of his tenure at the network in the early 1980s he moved from drama to comedy development, despite the fact that his interests did not lie in comedy. The change was the only way for him to reach one of his primary goals: supervising his own shows. In drama Dawson was partnered with a senior executive, complaining that he was, "stuck as an associate program executive." He also saw other White colleagues at CBS get promoted while he was left in a position with limited authority.

Frustrated in his efforts to move up in the network hierarchy, and thinking he would have a greater chance to supervise shows and more opportunities for advancement elsewhere, Dawson finally left CBS to become Director of Comedy Development at Universal.

At Universal Dawson moved up from Director of Comedy Development to Director of Programming. During this time he was the studio's executive for programs such as *Charles in Charge* and *Miami Vice*. He also developed *He's the Mayor*, an ABC sitcom about a young African American who becomes mayor of his hometown. Dawson believed that his next step should have been to a vice presidency at Universal, a job that presumably would have given him the authority to hire any writers, directors, and producers he wanted. Instead, Universal brought in someone from cable television for the position. Dawson thought he was more qualified and openly said so. He was told to be "patient," that he might get the next opening for a vice presidency. Unsure that this would ever happen, he left his inside executive position when Universal "offered" him an outside production deal with the company.

Dawson's experiences led him to view the business as restrictive for those who are not already part of the power structure:

> There are these small circles of people who do business with the studios and the networks. They tend to be the friends of the people in power and they pay one another. One guy loses a job [and] the guy who he gave work to hires him. It's this real tight little circle. And what I was doing was kind of expanding that circle. They are not interested in expanding that circle. Some of it has to do with racism. Most of it has to do with pure greed. They knew that me going into that position was going to expand that circle ....

The issue may be less about expanding the circle than taking a seat at a limited table. The real tension of affirmative action is that there are not enough seats at the table and a Black seat equals a White loss.

While Leonard R. Garner agreed that power dynamics played an important part in his work environment, his view differed from Dawson's. A television director of shows such as *Wings* and *Eve,* Garner works in a system based on a division between creative and craft relationships. He explained:

> Below the line — above the line is the power line: who has any creative input, who has any residual control, a piece of the residual action on a project. That's the line and whether you are considered creative or not. And the line falls at actors and directors, producers, writers .... An Art Director, he is on

the line, in certain situations he might be right there. In general DPs [Director of Photography], Art Directors, anything else on down you are in the crafts.

Garner saw the fact that he was "above the line" as a sign of real success, one with money and power. There was no bragging or talk about these relationships in an egotistical way. Rather, Garner was proud of how he had worked his way up in the system to the point that he can now have a creative impact on a show, such as by offering casting and script suggestions.

Garner described the pressures he faced to become a director, using the example of his job as an assistant director (A.D.) on *Miami Vice*:

> The first assistant director ... in certain situations is the fall guy .... You tell the producer you've got more work than you can do in the time allowed to do the work. And they say "just do it" and you find yourself in a situation, when you are running over, you are a half day behind. Then they fire you. You are set up for failure.

Garner lasted two months at *Miami Vice*, one of approximately ten A.D.s the studio hired and fired that season. After *Miami Vice*, Garner worked in cable television, as a stage manager on a Showtime sitcom called *Brothers*. There he received his first opportunity to direct. But his big break came with the NBC sitcom *Wings*. Garner added that people used to refer to *Wings* as "one of the Whitest shows on television" since none of the main characters were Black and there were rarely any minority actors on the program. This was not a problem for Garner. What was important was that he had worked his way up through the system to a regular directing job on a successful network show.

The discrepancies in how Dawson, Pinckney, and Garner talked about power may be due to two factors: their jobs and the era during which they worked. Dawson and Garner started in the business around the same time, the late 1970s. But, Garner, as a director, was able—indeed forced—to focus on the day-to-day work of getting a show completed. Dawson, who never had that opportunity, became more focused on power relationships. Unlike either Garner or Dawson, Rose Catherine Pinkney became a television executive in the 1990s, a time when there were programs and even networks tailored to African Americans. She is not the first or the only African American at her level of power. The production culture in which she works is dramatically different than the one faced by Dawson and Garner in the 1980s.

Network Notes

An important part of the network–creator relationship involves "notes," the guidance that network executives give to writers and producers. Network notes are usually given verbally, in a fairly casual manner. They may cover specific script suggestions, character development, or story lines. For a program already on the air, notes are the principal means of communication for the network. Depending on how strongly network executives feel, they may be sent as suggestions or as orders. But former network executive Frank Dawson stressed that the way notes are communicated is as important as what is said, since "producers usually don't want to hear any criticism."

When describing how she saw notes, one network executive said she is "always thinking" about the needs of the network as well as what would work best for the particular show. With *Under One Roof*, for example, a drama centered on an African American family aired by CBS in 1994, the executive said network notes were intended to remind the producers and writers to avoid themes and characters that would make the show "feel earnest and soft and kind of feel good/do good." She explained that the network's perspective was that such understated, earnest shows inspire viewers to say, "This should be on the air," but unfortunately they don't watch them week after week.

For producer Vida Spears, notes are a fact of life in a collaborative business such as television: since the studio and network pay the bills, it is vital that writers and producers listen. Spears explained her view of network notes:

> Even if you don't agree with them, try to make them work when you can. And I think if you try to work with them, when you disagree they will be more apt to work with you, when you feel really strongly that something is not right.

Without going into specifics, she remembered that early in the production of *Moesha*'s third season the network had some "first episode jitters" when they saw some of the scripts. Spears explained that she and the other producers worked to calm network concerns to eliminate problems and make things run smoothly. She attributed studio and network nervousness to increased competition from the new broadcast and cable networks as the late 1990s was an unpredictable era for the television industry. The producers wanted to introduce a bit more edgy material, subjects such as the temptations of drugs and teen sex, work that might be tame for cable but was new to a family show on broadcast television. Two years later Spear left the show. According to *Mediaweek*, UPN fired Spears after she objected to a gang-related story line pushed by the network. *Mediaweek* quoted a "source close to Spears":

> For four and a half years, Vida has protected, championed and treated the images on *Moesha* with great respect. This story line is not only an affront to what Vida has done, it's an affront to all of Black middle-class America. It's as if these programming executives believe that all Black males own guns and belong to gangs.[4]

Director Oz Scott said he paid attention to what the networks and studios have to say in their notes and used his expertise as a director to carry out their advice. He added that he has been in the business long enough to notice changes in the interaction between networks and producers over notes. For instance, he recalled that in the late 1980s one CBS executive told him he intended his notes to be used as a guide to where the network wanted the show to go, not precise directions for the writers and producer. Ten years later Scott saw the networks using notes to micromanage a production. Scott sees such micromanagement as stifling creativity and being at least partially responsible for the uniformity of the current crop of television shows.

One sitcom writer/producer said that staffers received notes from just about everybody: the network, the production studio, the cast, and even the mother of one of the characters on the show. She explained that the network is one that often pushes "family values" topics. It wanted the sitcom to be a family show and sometimes the writers and producers deal with issues, such as Black history, that the network doesn't "understand." But satisfying the writing staff wasn't sufficient. The writer/producer said that she's been surprised when the network approves a script only to have the production studio raise objections. It was her prior experience that once a network approved a script the writers could "call it a day." But, she said, "With this show the studio seems more concerned with the image of the show than the network." The implication was that a sitcom centered on an African American teenager can run into conflict concerning the image it projects, particularly when dealing with issues outside the conventions of the typical sitcom.

Another writer's philosophy on network notes was that writers and networks have always clashed because the producers' vision of a show evolves while the network is not always willing to accept changes. She speculated, "There are shows that battle frequently and there are shows that are left alone. Probably the networks don't say much to the *Frasier*s." This opinion was based on guesswork, since she had never worked on an Emmy-winning show like *Frasier*. The implication was that both the success of *Frasier* and the fact that it was a White show meant it might not get questioned the way that, at least in her experience, a typical African American–centered show does.

Studio executive Rose Catherine Pinkney said that when it comes to giving notes, the role of an executive is to "make any material that we are working on better than it is." She remembered that there were often notes on *In Living Color*, a show that aired on Fox while she worked at the studio. Her recollection was more of "explaining to White folks why some jokes and sketches were OK and why some stuff wasn't OK." "It's a cultural thing," she would have to explain. Pinkney accepted that role as a fact of life. "That seems to be part of what all of us do. At least as African Americans in the mainstream media world."

When she was a production assistant on Cosby in the mid-1990s Shirley Salomon had the opportunity to observe how network people dealt with at least one African American with a tremendous amount of power. As the individual responsible for the most popular program of the 1980s, Bill Cosby is one of the most marketable and powerful television personalities in the industry. Salomon said she could tell that the network executives who came to the set were well aware of Cosby's power as she saw them change their attitudes when they had to deal directly with Bill Cosby:

> They will say [among themselves] "this is how it's supposed to go, we've got to get him to do this, we've got to get him to do that." But when it gets to telling him, it's an entirely different story. It's like "Oh well, would you be able to?" It's the communication. When they're away from him they speak like executives. When they are next to him they speak like friends or people with good intentions.

Salomon may well have been observing what Frank Dawson described regarding notes: the way network executives communicate their ideas plays a part in whether their notes are followed. When it comes to a person with the clout of Bill Cosby the notes are expressed in deferential manner.

Audiences

Who is the audience? This is a question of essential importance for network executives who "green light" a project or set the broadcast schedule. Those involved in producing entertainment television usually have some conception of their likely audience. Responses to the question of how these creators conceived of the television audience varied according to their job. For example, network executives described target audiences and scheduling considerations. Producers focus on the quality of their shows, believing that if they do their best work the show will attract an audience. On the crafts side of the production process, stage manager Kim Sizemore mentioned the importance of the studio audience, whose laughter and reactions help motivate the cast: "It brings everybody's level up. The actors are 'on.' And they are delivering everything, getting all the laughs that they haven't been getting during the week [in rehearsals]." While observing the production and taping of an episode of *Eve* in 2004 I got to see what Sizemore meant. The studio audience, through laughter and applause, gives feedback that contributes to the creative environment.

Yet the studio audience is a minor consideration to producers and executives. A network executive said that in buying and selling program ideas mass audience considerations are paramount:

> I was at CBS for a long time. Their audience was older, more rural, and more female .... [We] had to keep that audience happy and yet [the network] wanted it to be younger, hipper, all of those things. So you are constantly trying to keep that one audience and build it. You look for great writing, smart, inventive ideas that are not on the air and feel compatible with what it is that you are going after, who your audience is.

When these concerns are combined with network politics it can be almost impossible for an established network to try something outside the box. In explaining why in the mid-1990s CBS was not interested in scheduling *Moesha*, one executive used the example of what happened to a high-level network programmer who tried to skew CBS toward a younger audience with a young adult-oriented show, *Central Park West*. Even though the program enjoyed a tremendous amount of promotion it received dismal ratings. The show was quickly cancelled and the executive behind the idea was fired. She said that if *Central Park West* couldn't succeed, then *Moesha*, which was aimed at an even younger audience, would not work on CBS's schedule.

Network scheduling can be an important factor in a program's ability to attract an audience. When Frank Dawson was at Universal Television he became frustrated with the way ABC scheduled, *He's the Mayor*, one of the programs he developed. The show centered on the youngest and the first Black mayor of a city in Pennsylvania. Before the season started ABC scheduled the program for Tuesdays at 8:30 p.m., following *Who's the Boss*, a hit show staring Tony Danza. Dawson saw great potential for promotional ties between the two shows. He said the audience demographics and flow from one show to the other were also a good match. Nevertheless, the show's final placement on the schedule made Dawson believe that "all the network could see was that it was a Black show." He explained that the summer before the show's fall debut, NBC canceled *Diff'rent Strokes* staring Gary Coleman. Though *Diff'rent Strokes* had a long and successful run, its ratings were down. Yet ABC decided to pick it up and use it as the lead in for *He's the Mayor*. Dawson offered his take on the network's scheduling change:

> Well gee, they've got these two Black shows, they have to put a Black show with another Black show …. [They] yanked us out of our hammock position behind Tony Danza, which they give to *Growing Pains*, which goes on for eight years of success, given that hammock launch as a lead in.

Dawson said *Diff'rent*, a show that at that time harbored few viewers for itself, brought *He's the Mayor* no audience and the show was canceled after 13 episodes. He believed race was the main factor in the network's decision:

> Audience flow, all that stuff that is their Bible, goes out the window when race is introduced. All they could see was that it was a Black show so they had to put it with anotherBlack show. So they "Black blocked" it on Friday and that's what happened to it …. Tremendously frustrating.

Eve producer Meg DeLoatch said it is important that there is now more industry interest in minority audiences. "UPN, thank God, is committed to the urban audience so there's somewhere for people to go. A lot of my friends watched *Sex and the City*, *Friends*, and I did too.

But it's nice to know there is something you can turn on and go, they look like me too."

Producers Vida Spears and Tim Reid downplayed the idea of creating work targeted to a specific audience. Spears said she concentrates on what she would like to see in her characters while also asking "do I have characters that are going to appeal to everybody?" Tim Reid maintained that a well-written, well-structured story with rich characters will find an audience. "I think *Seinfeld* proved that. I think *Touched by an Angel* proved that. *Cheers* proved that." Neither Spears nor Reid mentioned race when discussing the audience. Yet, by creating characters and writing scripts that interest them, they in fact create programs that reflect their identity. No wonder Spears' *Moesha* and Reid's *Linc's* did not shy away from issues of African American life. *Moesha*, centered on a Black teenager, at times explored topics such as African American history while *Linc's* was an adult sitcom about a D.C. bar where discussions of race were commonplace.

On the other hand, when Reid described the writing process, he said he had to consider how network management represents a type of audience, one that can alter his scripts. He made the point that a producer may succeed in pitching an idea to a network, but by the time the program airs it "is going to be a skeleton of the original concept." Reid explained his strategy for getting a "quality" show on the air:

> I think in terms of layers and layers and layers of story and character within one premise. So as they strip these layers [away], by the time they get the thing down to the naked truth I still have hidden enough substance in it so that I feel the integrity of what I really want to do will be involved there, at least some. And you have to fight to do that and you have to be clever.

When writing for *Sister, Sister* in 1998 Felicia Henderson said she was "always thinking of Black kids first and then kids in general." She said that if she were writing for a show with an adult audience she would not feel the same level of responsibility to her race that she does while working on *Sister, Sister*.

Conclusion

In 1997 Barry Levinson the executive producer of crime drama *Homicide: Life on the Street*, then in its sixth season, gave filmmaker Theodore Bogosian full access to the production of one episode of the show. The resulting documentary, *Anatomy of a Homicide*, is one of the few inside views of the creation and production of a television episode from discussion of the initial idea to writers' room, on the set production, to editing, and final audio mix. Save for an interview with President of NBC Entertainment Warren Littlefield, any view of the networks role in this process is unseen but heavily felt. So network notes are only heard about on the writer/producer's side of a phone conversation with the network and the resultant rewrites to meet NBC's demand regarding the script's near-profane language. Obtaining a full inside view is one of the real challenges of any study of contemporary television, particularly when it comes to the issue of television and race. While I did get insightful opinions from writers, former executives, producers and directors, how network executives fully see the cultural identity as a consideration in the cycle of production is filtered through network diversity offices or off-the-record stories. But the stories I did hear are evidence that by the 1990s the television business allowed and sometimes encouraged a greater diversity of images and stories. That reality was made possible by creators who at times demanded that space and by advocacy groups that shined a spotlight on the system's failures in diversity in hiring and in the images the network produced. This progress was made through the lived experience of getting work, of being the only African American or female in the writers' room, of, at times, being marginalized as a minority, and yet still maintaining and using one's own creative energy to produce work that reflects one's life experiences. This is part of the story that is told in the following chapter where I explore the work and how race intersects with the workplace.

CHAPTER FOUR

Workplace Culture

"The truth is, as in a lot of areas, White men are presumed to sort of be the neutral element that can do everything." That's how one network executive described television work at the end of the 1990s. What does that reality mean for African Americans working in entertainment television? How does that translate into the day-to-day interactions in the workplace? What is the reality of the writers' room, the soundstage, and the business office? To get a more complete picture of the production of entertainment television we need to understand the political climate in which television programs are produced.[1] The increase in African American workers and African American–centered programs means a more racially diverse climate than documented by Cantor and Cantor and Gitlin a quarter-century ago.[2]

This chapter explores the way African Americans talk about the political elements in the workplace of entertainment television. In so doing, it shows how these workers are, at least at times, treated as "other." How they responded to this system varied by their job, seniority, and sensitivity. Some of these workers explicitly protested discrimination. Others tried to educate their White co-workers about how to avoid stereotypes. Conversely, some respondents often felt it was not their place to take a stand. A workplace culture that is in most respects predominantly White can also heighten awareness of the double consciousness that Du Bois describes for African Americans, the sense of always looking at one's self through the eyes of others.[3]

Even as he documents an increase in minority television workers, Darnell Hunt describes network television as a "highly insular industry in which White decision makers typically reproduce themselves by hiring other Whites who share similar experiences and tastes."[4] I have spoken with some of the African Americans who are breaking what Hunt calls the "vicious employment cycle"[5] of television, not only by entering the system but by rising to levels of creative power where they can hire other African Americans who share their cultural experiences. What follows are stories that focus on the elements of the organizational culture in which they work.

The Creative Process

"We sit in a room and laugh" is how one respondent described the process of writing a situation comedy. "Basically it's a bunch of grown folks sitting in a room laughing, and joking, and telling stories. Every now and again we get something on paper." The system starts with one of the writers bringing a script to the rest of the writers for feedback. The goal of the writing team is to create "the funniest and the best product." The group process can sometimes make for a long day as the writers all weigh in with their opinions. When the writers of the script are not open to changes the executive producer has the final say.

James Anderson described the production process for *A Different World*, something he witnessed early in his career. He said these sessions often included intense debates about how to address issues such as race and class:

> Every episode of that show, sometimes it was painfully worked out, not to the point where the creativity was beaten out of it, but to where it finally felt authentic. If you noticed the subjects were never banged over your head, felt preachy, or took one particular side.

Anderson's description of the creative process on the show gives some idea of how thoughtful, diverse images are created. He said that everyone was allowed to voice his or her opinion on such issues as how the college students portrayed in the show dealt with being "Black in America." Anderson said that the production's free and open discussions, where a diversity of opinions were openly challenged and defended, were one of the reasons *A Different World* was able to portray African Americans from "different backgrounds within the same culture." The show, and Bill Cosby's commitment to it, including using his *Cosby Show* success as a time slot lead-in, and the ideas it explored are evidence of what can result when an African American has the power and will to bring a more complete picture of Black life to the television screen.

When I first interviewed Felicia D. Henderson in 1998 she was a writer/producer on *Sister, Sister*, a successful sitcom staring Tim Reid, Jackee, and the twin sisters Tara Mowry and Tamera Mowry. The show began on ABC in 1994 but moved to WB in 1995 where it lasted for four years. One of the more successful African American-centered shows of the time, it had a fairly diverse staff of writers and producers with a White showrunner, Rick Hawkins. While crediting Hawkins for being open and cooperative, Henderson said Hawkins brought with him some misconceptions regarding the uniformity of Black opinion. She explained that Hawkins previously worked on *The Wayans Bros.* show, another Black program. Henderson described a script where one of the sisters says "Oh yeah and now I'm free." According to Henderson:

> Hawkins said "Oh no, you never say that. Black people don't like it when you say they are free ... we have always been free." It was this political thing that he got from the Wayans. I [said] "No, what are you talking about?"

The White producer had gotten the impression that African Americans would be offended by a Black character saying they were now, "free." This is a small point but an illustration of how some Whites become sensitive to issues of race from working with minorities but then take the opinion that all minorities will see things the same way. The writers on *Sister, Sister* influenced Hawkins' thinking, explaining that they were not offended, illustrating that there is a variety of opinions among African Americans. Henderson said he had a better understanding of "what our [the Black writers on *Sister, Sister*] experiences represent."

A diverse workplace can sometimes open space for confronting offensive racial characterizations and stereotypes. Henderson recalled that a *Sister, Sister* script apparently called for one of the female leads, played by African American Jackee[6], to use the phrase "you are going to get the back of my hand." At a script meeting Henderson took exception, saying they had done a similar joking threat on a previous episode. Hawkins wondered why she objected. According to Henderson, Hawkins said he was trying to do the "strongest thing" for the character. Henderson replied, "This is not a joke ... that I would ever do on a White show. This is a distinctly Black show joke and I don't want to do any more of them." While crediting Hawkins for his openness to these discussions, Henderson said he didn't realize the level of racism involved in using the kind of jokes that say "I'll hit you—you better get out." She thought Hawkins would never pitch those kind of jokes if he was working on *Seinfeld*, and was frustrated that someone could think these jokes are acceptable on a Black show. She said they reminded her of the old *Sanford and Son* show, where Aunt Esther was always saying, "You fish eye fool, you better get ...." The stereotype of the tough and sometimes violent Black woman can be found in American popular culture from *Amos 'n' Andy*, where, if they depicted women at all they were, "loud, abrasive, violent, and emasculating,"[7] to the blaxploitation films of the 1970s with what Freydberg refers to as the "superbitch."[8]

Henderson's experience is not unusual. Another writer told me that explaining Black life to Whites is common in the writers' rooms. On an African American–centered show there are often discussions of jokes that are "really funny to some percentage of the people and really, most importantly, the main viewership of the show but that has to be explained to people that don't know it." Studio executive Rose Catherine Pinkney said, "you live and die on how you, as a minority executive producer, react to consistently having to explain things that to you are a given." Henderson's objections to the "back of my hand" line in the script may have been due to the fact that *Sister, Sister* had a White showrunner. On *The Cosby Show*, one of Bill Cosby's most famous lines was, "I am your father—I brought you into this world, and I can take you out!"

Staff Diversity

Many respondents discussed how diversity of the working environment, or lack thereof, affects the production process. For example, Sharon Johnson said her most "pleasant" writing experience was the short-lived situation comedy *Buddies*, a show "specifically about Black/White friendship:"

> It was a really integrated environment, truly integrated, not just, "OK, there is a token here." You saw people at all levels doing different jobs. So I really felt good and that was, I guess because of the tone of the show. It lent itself to discussion.

Writer/producer Felicia Henderson appreciated the advantages of working on a show with a primarily African American staff. While Henderson said that she had always worked at Black-oriented shows,

Moesha represented her first experience working under a Black executive producer:

> I found that it really allowed you to relax. There was a whole level of battle that you were never going to have. And then it frees you creatively. You are never going to have to say "gosh that is racist." You don't have to work, that was just freedom.

Another writer I interviewed echoed Henderson's sentiments recalling the open and collaborative work environment of a mostly African American writers' room. Conversely, when she was the only Black writer on a show with an interracial cast the only contributions she was expected to make involved explaining African American life to the White writers.

Director Leonard R. Garner had the unusual opportunity to direct two almost totally White shows: *Wings* and *Just Shoot Me*. He said that race is rarely an issue at his workplace, although the uniqueness of his situation is sometimes the subject of questions from less experienced workers. African American stage managers and assistant directors who want to move up to directing often ask what it is like to work on a White show, curious about how he handles an all-White cast. Garner has even been asked whether he acts "in a different way?" He said that he understands these questions—they reflect how little these minorities know about what goes on at White programs. He maintained that these questions also show the lack of opportunity some Black workers have to work on White shows. Garner outlined his work philosophy:

> Discover who you are and be yourself and just do that. I can't change that from show to show. And artists are going to respond to me across the board for a certain level, but I can't pander to anybody on one side of the board or the other.

During an interview in 1998, Shirley Salomon struggled to communicate what it means to be the only Black on a production team. She said: "If you're comfortable with yourself it's not a problem." Yet there were situations, such as when a security guard on a set treated her with a lack of respect, when she's asked herself whether she was dealt with differently because of her race. Salomon said she was "just tired of going to places and being the only African American girl there." Solomon moved up to an executive position in program development first at MTV and then in 2005 at BET. She told me that at MTV she got along great with the people she managed. However,

Figure 4.1 Leonard R. Garner, Jr., director of numerous shows including *Just Shoot Me*, *Girlfriends*, *According to Jim*, and *Eve*. (Courtesy of Leonard R. Garner, Jr.)

when first taking on a production job, such as developing a new show, she often finds a certain attitude, one questioning whether she is up to the job, among the male staff. Solomon said she has learned to project a "take charge" demeanor from day one, an attitude that sets the right tone on the rest of the project.

Frank Dawson recalled what it was like to be the only Black executive at Universal Television and his responsibilities as the only one who took an interest in the work of other African Americans:

I am providing access. I know a lot of good writers, producers and directors who are people of color. I am having them come in to pitch to me. I am seeing White people too. I know my job is Director of Comedy Development, my job is to find the best people possible for the studio to work with. And that's what I am figuring I'm doing. No one else at the studio is seeing anybody Black. I am the access way.

Dawson said that the fact that he was the only executive meeting with any Black creators was so obvious that when an African American came for a meeting the security guard's automatic response was "Oh, you're going to see Mr. Dawson?"

Dawson's interest in the work of African Americans also drew disapproving attention from his superiors. He remembers people at Universal telling him that he was talented and had good instincts but that he tended to lose his objectivity when it came to Black people and Black projects. They thought he was more interested in promoting something because it was Black than because it was good. He said he was taken aback by this response to his efforts to open up opportunities for Black creators. He also wanted to produce programming to reach African Americans, an audience that, at the time, in the mid-1980s, was underserved. He said, "All the statistics are telling me that minority audiences are watching more television than anybody else." According to Dawson, Universal could not understand what he was trying to do. He recalled, "I don't care what kind of arguments I could make, [they] didn't mean anything, because I was a Black person." The prejudices that Dawson faced as the only African American in the workplace fueled his frustrations.

Rose Catherine Pinkney, Senior Vice President for Comedy Development at Paramount told me in a 2004 interview that she sometimes discusses with other African American executives the fact that they have to be "bilingual." She saw this as a strong case for having more minority executives:

> When you hire an executive of color you are really getting a two for one bargain because you're getting somebody who has to be able to function incredibly well in the mainstream world. Plus you get the benefit of somebody (if you choose correctly) somebody who knows other cultural worlds as well.

Diversity in the workplace often enriches what ends up on the screen. In discussing television's portrayal of minorities, one network executive said, "It is much more important to have a variety of people behind the scenes with a whole variety of voices and attitudes and opinions so that they can be out there with a wide range of characters." She asserted that the greater the ethnic and racial variety of people in the decision-making process, from production to program acquisition, the less individual minority group members will feel they need to represent all parts of their culture.

A diverse work environment, a place where depictions of African American life would be explored, was a priority when Felicia D. Henderson had the opportunity to help create a show. She made it a priority to hire African American writers and directors for *Soul Food*, the longest running African American drama in television history. "I just knew I couldn't be in that position and not hire people who looked like me."[9]

Producer and director Tim Reid reported that people had asked him why he demanded a multiracial cast on his programs. He was advised to "just get in the door" first and then worry about other issues. Reid stressed that a creative environment means being able to look around the set and see a "familiar world." He described the set on *Linc's*, a series he had recently produced for the Showtime cable network:

> If I am creating a show about Black people, about culture, about a bar, whatever it is that I'm creating, I should, out of my own belief in the system, surround myself with as many people who represent as much about what the story is, or about the place, or the issues as I possibly can. So that when I turn away from the camera I am still immersed in that world. So here I am doing a show [set] in Washington, and I said "Let's submerge ourselves. Washington is a multiracial city, it's very different." The cast and the crew reflects that. *Frank's Place* was the same thing. *Snoops* was the same thing. You've got to demand that.

Reid accused many Black television producers of forgetting the importance of a diverse creative team and workforce and that the most that some do is promise to include one Black on the crew. He claimed that, "the average person in the dominant culture doesn't forget" to have other Whites on their crew and cast. Reid maintained that diversity helps him creatively:

> I like to look around and see people of color .... It's a good feeling, creatively. It's very interesting, women, Black women, White women, Asian. Multiracial crews work better and there is an element, I don't know what you call it, essence of the production. It's much better when the crews are more diverse. I worked on enough [shows] in the three decades I have been in this business to know that's a fact. Most people don't understand it, though.

A June 2000 *New York Times* profile of the HBO production of the mini-series *The Corner* discussed at length another African American television professional, who, like Reid, requires a multiracial crew.[10] The director of the series, Charles Dutton, not only demanded a diverse workplace; he also wanted the series to reflect the experience of African Americans. In a follow-up to the *New York Times* article on its Web site, Dutton explained the benefits of a diverse work environment:

> The few diverse crews I've worked on, I've had the most fun. There's more to talk about. The creative energy rises. And everyone has the chance to learn about each other, to rediscover their humanity with one another and think "I've not only made a few friends, but I've changed my mind about a couple of things—I've had more than a 'film experience.'" I don't know if you can get that in a factory, but what we do is create—it's called art. To me, there's something sacred about that. It shouldn't be about racism, prejudice or inequality. It should be as close to a utopia as possible.[11]

Both Dutton and Reid attest to the enormous difficulty of creating an integrated workplace. "They weren't all White. But almost," is how the *New York Times* described the crew that Dutton saw on his first day of production on *The Corner*.[12] Dutton demanded that the producers hire more African Americans. His insistence offended some of the Whites on the production, with a few of them agreeing that "Whiteness was a liability on the set."[13] Dutton's tenacity and the reaction it produced among Whites recall Tim Reid's description of the reactions to his business style. Reid said his position on hiring an integrated crew and his refusal to be intimidated contributed to his reputation for being "confrontational":

Dutton was also very explicit in describing racism in the industry:

> There isn't a Black actor in Hollywood, on the star level or the lowest level, who doesn't in private vehemently rail against the industry .... Because somewhere along the line they are still reminded, "You know something? You're a big star but you're just another nigger."[14]

While most of the people I interviewed did not directly condemn the industry, Dutton's statement is simply on the far end of a continuum that depicts how African Americans see themselves treated as "other." Tim Reid, one of the few people I interviewed with even more experience and power than Dutton, was just as outspoken. He clearly linked television's business practices to racism. For example, Reid compared his efforts to create a production studio in Virginia to that of a runaway slave:

> When the slave ran away, they caught him. They could care less about the fact that they got him but they had to set an example. Because they did not want the word to spread to too many other slaves. And what this [studio]

represents is, if I am able to pull this off and be self reliant, and operate outside of the system, we may send a signal [that there is] someone who could do them damage, who can affect their power base.

The content and the tone of Dutton's and Reid's comments are identical. By invoking slavery Dutton and Reid are not simply condemning the business, they are declaring that the problems African Americans face in the television workplace are strikingly different from any obstacles White workers encounter. Their responses reveal that, for African American creators, economic, creative, and racial issues are tightly connected. In starting his own production studio Reid is not only establishing some economic independence, he is forging a racially integrated work environment and a place to produce images that reflect the ethnic diversity of American life.

Both Dutton and Reid have created a body of work that comments on the condition of Blacks in America. Yet they know that their success comes by taking a hard line. Making demands of the White power structure has enabled them to produce the type of programming they want. Reid and Dutton combine their reputation for quality work with an unwavering stand for diversity on the set with the goal of producing television that begins to portray the complexity of African American culture. Though bitterness threads through their comments, it has not seemed to affect their resolve to continue the struggle. These responses are evidence that Blacks who reach even relatively high levels of power must continue to fight for what they want: a work environment that allows them to make television that begins to show what Michael Eric Dyson calls the "vibrant diversity" of African American culture.[15]

Being "Otherized"

Being perceived as "other" was a question intertwined throughout discussions of work. Sometimes it was small incidents, such as when a White security guard at the *MTV Beach House* addressed Production Manager Shirley Salomon with "Hey, girl." Salomon said she responded by asking the guard, "Did I give you any indication that's how I like to be spoken to or that's my personality?" James Anderson said he would sometimes run into people with whom he had been dealing solely on the phone. They are surprised that he is African American, because to them and in their words he doesn't "sound

Black." Most of the people I spoke with said that they are used to these types of interactions, one stating that he treats them as a moment of ignorance and he moves on.

Asked about incidents of discrimination, Tim Reid replied that nothing in the entertainment business could compare to what he lived though growing up in the segregated South. "If anything, I think that I have used the ignorance of race that has been tried to be put upon me as a weapon, a sword to get through it all. I think it's been a motivator." He tied this to his success in the industry:

> Doing all the things they say you can't do. You can't build a studio in the middle of Virginia. You can't go from [producing] a half-hour [television program] to an hour [program], go from hour [program] to half-hour [program]. You can't, so don't even do it.

Reid said his persistence has helped him deal with racism in the business. He recalled how, early in his career, when auditioning for television roles, he often faced Whites' misconceptions of how Blacks should act. For example, in the early 1970s, one of the White casting directors for whom Reid was auditioning decided to show the actor what he was doing wrong:

> And this guy decided to stand up and teach me how to be Black. To watch this nice young Jewish boy from New York shuck and jive was fascinating. I sat down, he auditioned for me. And when it was over, I said, "You should play the part of the Black guy. You are Blacker than I am.'

Norman Steinberg, one of the other writers he auditioned for that day, offered Reid some guidance: "You know who you remind me of? A young David Niven. The tragedy of it is that they are not writing any parts for Black David Nivens, but if they ever do, you are the man." This was pertinent advice for Reid. Niven had been one of his heroes, but he realized that he needed to develop David Niven-style parts for himself. Steinberg's suggestion helped motivate Reid to begin writing his own scripts.

The most blatant racism director and producer Martin Jones experienced was when he worked in music videos. Jones saw that the music video companies that were run by White people, that featured White artists, or that had White directors received more money for their productions than Black productions. "To me that's the worst kind of racism, it's economic, it's blatant—'You're a Black company you get this much.'" Jones found the business starting to change in the late 1990s: the budgets rose on video projects for Black artists; Black musicians started to demand specific directors who were Black.

On the other hand, Jones cautioned against being too quick to accuse people of discrimination: "I think it's easy for people to let the specter of racism get in the way of the reality of maybe you didn't really make a good movie." Leonard R. Garner likewise admitted difficulty in determining whether racism has anything to do with the way he's treated.

> I get confused as to how much is racial and how much is not. I mean there is definitely a racial thing …. I feel that I am battling the next step in getting to the level of directing the pilots I want [to direct]. Then on the other hand, so much of it is a game.

People who have entered the business in the last ten years were less likely to raise the issue of discrimination or being made to feel different. Not that these things did not happen. If I asked about it, most would laugh and say, "of course." The difference is that they are in a workplace and society that has changed in the past twenty-five years. The times of being "the only" or token Black person are ending. Workers now have a support system of other African Americans in the business to go to for guidance and networking.

Star Treatment in Black and White

"It is like the White guy has always got to be the star," was how Frank Dawson saw the television industry managing African American stars in the 1980s and 1990s. In recalling his work on *Miami Vice*, Dawson found stark differences in the press attention bestowed on the White and Black leads, Don Johnson and Phillip Michael Thomas. According to Dawson, when the show started, the two were co-stars. But as *Miami Vice* evolved, most of the promotional efforts and character development focused on Johnson. Dawson accused Universal Television and NBC of not knowing how to develop and promote an African American star. He recalled attending a major event with Thomas and the top executives of Universal where women, Black and White, all fawned over Thomas. Dawson said these executives did not know, or even want to know, how to use this Black television actor's star power to his full potential, thus missing out on potentially lucrative programming possibilities. He called the treatment typical "of the worst things that happen as far as images, particularly of minority people in network television."

Tim Reid said that television still had a problem promoting African American stars in the late 1990s. He was amazed at the lack of attention the stars of *Sister, Sister*, Tia Lowry and Tamera Lowry, received, considering their success:

> This show is probably ranked number one among crossover shows in America, on all of television. It is a big hit in Spain, in England .... The Spice Girls wanted to meet them. And these girls don't get any respect .... They get no respect from the Black creative community and they get no respect across the line. And I think these girls are major stars. Again, I think it's a look at the so-called incorrectness of race in America. We all deny it and say opportunities for all.

In 1999, a year after Reid made these comments the two stars received one of the prizes bestowed on media stars—commercial endorsements. Tia Lowry and Tamera Lowry were featured in a series of television ads for Old Navy. It was not a major development, but compared to the way Frank Dawson described the opportunities lost on Phillip Michael Thomas, it represented a step in the right direction. It took Disney in the early 2000s to fully develop the star potential of a young African American. Raven-Symoné, who got her start at age four on *The Cosby Show* before moving on to four years on *Hangin' with Mr. Cooper*, got her own show in 2003, *That's So Raven*. It was Disney Channel's highest-rated and longest-running series, the first on that network to air more than one-hundred episodes. *That's So Raven* spawned a Disney franchise, including soundtracks, dolls, episode DVDs, and video games. Raven-Symoné is one of the most successful "tween" stars of all time; evidence of how this generation is comfortable with multicultural icons and corporations like Disney now fully exploit that fact.

Recently television has seen more shows centered around African American stars. The success of *The Cosby Show* did lead to sitcoms centered on minority comics, from Steve Harvey to Wanda Sykes. Many were Black family sitcoms such as *Family Matters*, *My Wife and Kids*, and *Bernie Mac*. Some of these shows had fairly long-term success, mostly on UPN and the WB, networks that focus to some degree on African American audiences. The success that rap singers have had as film actors along with the fact that rap and hip hop drive much of today's youth culture has also meant that African American stars can carry much more clout in Hollywood. By the early 1990s Hip-

Hop/R&B was Pop. And artists from that genre had proven their success on the small screen: Will Smith on *Fresh Prince*, Queen Latifah on *Living Single*, and Brandy on *Moesha*. They had shown they can attract the all-important eighteen to thirty-four years demographic. It may have been one of the things that helped Meg DeLoatch's project *Together* get on the air. It was not pitched to the studio, Greenblatt-Janollari Studio, or the network, UPN, with any single person in mind. But it was Eve, a rap star from Philadelphia, who was given the script and, according to DeLoatch, "loved it." The show was renamed *Eve* setting the tone that this was her star vehicle and hopefully bringing her audience to the small screen. The fact that a network can use the star power of an African American pop star to launch a show is evidence of how the industry has evolved over the last twenty years. Frank Dawson described how pitching an idea works in 2004:

> The script I am working on right now is going around packaging agents knowing that if we're going straight with the script the chances of getting it sold are slim and none. So you go to an agent saying who can we get involved, a star acting talent, start director, or star producer. Star shows run, [they] eliminate that fear factor of the executive saying, "if I go out there with this and this doesn't work my job is on the line."

Television has always been star driven with people like Jack Benny, Bob Hope, and Ozzie Nelson setting the tone for the medium in the 1950s. The first African American with real success in the medium, Bill Cosby, had already established himself as a successful comedian before starring on *I Spy* in the 1960s. The fact that African American comedians and pop stars are not only as mainstream as ever before in American history but are also central in attracting the youth demographic, translates into more opportunities for minorities.

It's About the Work

One constant among all the people I interviewed was the pride they take in their work. For Meg DeLoatch it was the joy of running a show. She talked passionately about *Eve*, a situation comedy about three twenty-something friends running a fashion boutique. The program is diverse both on the screen and on the creative side. DeLoatch explained her goals in staffing the program:

> First of all, you want people who can do a good job. We are really into having just good positive people around. I wanted to make sure that I had a

really diverse writing staff but I wanted it to be we're fairly representative of people of color. This is the most diverse writing staff that I've ever been on. The way it's fallen it's great that I've got to help pick it .... I think it's important to have various people represented because everybody brings their experience, and to bring that to the show what's in front the camera.

The balance of having fun and getting the work done was evident as I watched a taping of an episode of *Eve*. DeLoatch and some of the writers of that episode including Michael Ajakwe offered small suggestions to polish up a joke or two. The atmosphere for the most part was both relaxed and on task. This was due in no small part to the fact that Leonard R. Garner was directing that episode. When I first interviewed Garner six years earlier he described his directing style as one that encourages actors to be "creative." One of his tactics is to get them to be comfortable and open:

> I am just trying to have fun. That is my approach to it. It is fun to be on the sets. I like to be around them. Even as a director now, keep it alive, this is why we are doing it, I like to do comedy. I don't want to have to get people to work. I don't want to have to motivate you to come out and work, I don't want you to have to motivate me to come out and work. I want to meet and have some fun.

One African American writer who had worked on a program that Garner directed years earlier told me that Garner's style of work seemed to cause a problem for some of the show's White writers. "They talked about the Black director. They would say that he was taking too many calls on his cell phone, he was smoking, he wasn't doing his job." [16] The respondent was curious enough about the situation to ask one of the African American actors on the set if he thought this was true. The Black guy said:

> No. As a matter of fact, he is the best director we've had so far, as far as actors are concerned, because he really talks to us and gets feedback from us, where some of the other directors don't care.

This information reinforced this writer's perceptions of her White co-workers' "racism." It should be noted that this took place on a show with a primarily White staff—a bit of evidence in favor of using more diverse crews. But what do we mean when we say diverse? No one I spoke with ever mentioned a certain number of African Americans, women, or other minorities in defining diversity. Instead these workers were looking for a commitment, or at least awareness, by the people who hired the crew that there is a need for diversity and the will to carry through on the commitment.

Kim Sizemore, stage manager on *The Parent'Hood* at the time of our interview in 1998, emphasized the necessity of teamwork for a successful work environment. Her philosophy was that each worker has an important role in the production and no one on the stage crew should be considered a star. For Sizemore, collaboration "fosters a good-natured attitude," making it easier to produce a show on a tight schedule. She did, however, express frustrations with some of the younger employees she worked with on a few music videos she managed, finding among them some with lackadaisical attitudes. Sizemore described the difficulty some of them had waking up at 5:30 a.m. for an 18-hour day, noting: "Everybody wants to be in the business but nobody wants to get up on time." I should underscore that Sizemore's criticism of her co-workers did not seem to imply that one race was more blame worthy than another. In fact, Leonard R. Garner and Michael Ajakwe, who entered the business many years apart, both question the work ethic of many of the people now entering the television industry. Ajakwe said that people think television is a glamorous business. While not denying that there are many perks that go along with the work, he stressed that it can be incredibly difficult. Ajakwe added that those who don't realize that don't succeed, making his job more difficult because he has to work harder to pick up the slack. Garner said it was harder and harder to find people, no matter what their race, who wanted to do the tough work sometimes required in television production. He's found many people in the business simply for the ego gratification.

Gendered Racism

Intertwined throughout some of the responses from the female creators is the issue of gender. At times gender seemed to be even more of an issue than race when it came to workplace interactions. This can be no clearer than in the writers' room, a place long dominated by White men, and an environment where the banter can get rough. One sitcom writer complained of having to deal with male writers who would go off on "tangents about women's breasts, and penises" with hours often "wasted" on this type of talk. Felicia Henderson found a similar sexist environment earlier in her career when she was a staff writer for *Fresh Prince*. But instead of making overtly sexist comments, Henderson said, the four White male writers on *Fresh Prince* would usually censor themselves. Apparently the sole female writer on the program, Henderson said the experience was unpleasant at times: "They try to make you feel uncomfortable because they don't really want you there, because you make them uncomfortable. They can't tell all the 'dick' jokes they would have told if you weren't there."

Television writer Sharon Johnson faced one work environment fraught with the stress of racism and sexism. As staff writer on *Goode Behavior,*[17] a situation comedy with a primarily Black cast, Johnson was one of only two African American women on a writing team with eleven White men. Johnson had heard this type of racist and sexist talk on other shows and had become somewhat inured to it. But workplace interactions became particularly strained when one of the White writers, in a tangential conversation, commented: "I don't like it that Black people can say whatever they want and get away with it." He gave two examples: Jesse Jackson's Hymietown comment and basketball player Charles Barkley saying, "I hate white people." Johnson responded by raising Daniel Patrick Moynihan's old comment about benign neglect for the poor. According to Johnson, the White writers didn't know what she was referring to. One of the executive producers then asked Johnson if she thought O. J. Simpson was guilty. When Johnson replied that she did not, the producer apparently replied, "If that's the way you feel, I can't even talk to you." Johnson said that things cooled down a bit the next day when the writer who made the comment that Black people can say whatever they want, apologized to Johnson, telling her that when he later told his wife about the interaction, she pointed out that he was wrong.

Many of these interviews took place in the summer of 1998, little more than two years after Simpson's trial for the murder of his ex-wife.[18] Yet, Johnson wasn't the only respondent to raise the issue of O. J. Simpson. Former network executive Frank Dawson said that the Simpson trial illustrated how differently Blacks and Whites reacted to issues of race and class. He noted that while Whites were outraged by the verdict, he and other African Americans viewed the trial as demonstrating what many Blacks have long understood about America: "We have a judicial system that favors those that have substance," referring to the idea that people with money get favorable treatment in the courts. Producer and studio manager Martin Jones described how tense Los Angeles was during the riots and the Simpson trial. He found more women clutching their purses when he walked by or getting out of elevators when he got on. Jones said that in order to work in the city he tried to "block out most of those things."

Tim Reid used the Simpson situation to illustrate how Blacks are often judged by the actions of other African Americans. He went on to explain that he often takes a firm stand in business negotiations. Apparently, he is so adamant that other Blacks tell him, "Stop being so confrontational, because you are making it bad for us." Reid believes that African Americans are somewhat afraid to be associated with him "because we so rarely get to the table .... Darn if you've got someone in there creating a lot of turmoil." He made an analogy to Simpson and how some Whites bring their frustrations with the Simpson verdict to their interactions with Blacks:

> Believe me, if I could get in the room with O. J. for ten minutes I'd kick his butt. Certainly, the tragedy ... of it is one reason. But, the reason would be for the repercussions that [I] and other Blacks have suffered because of some person not being able to get off that anger towards him. I come in the room and I catch some extra flack just because of the O. J. trial.

White reaction to the Simpson trial made visible a common problem: minorities are often held responsible for, or are associated with the activities of other minorities. The fact that these attitudes can affect and even poison workplace interactions needs to be acknowledged by Whites as evidence of White privilege. Being immune to the responsibility of the actions of others from their ethnic group allows Whites to operate at a much higher comfort level in social interactions. Whites, even those who don't themselves hold minorities responsible for other members of their race, become complicit unless they recognize that minorities do not share that privilege.

Black women found themselves victimized by stereotypes. Johnson, for example, found herself marked as an assertive Black woman. She said a friend, who was working on the primarily Black show *Living Single*, mentioned to her that someone added a notation on Johnson's resume that "Sharon is sassy." Johnson explained:

> I told this to a woman that also went to Barnard, an intern .... [The intern's response was] "You know sassy is code word for Black woman." You know the snappy thing, the neck rolling, whatever .... It may not be overt. In these little ways, this is how you let people know, Black.

Another writer decried the way African American women are often categorized: "When they are sending Black women with strong opinions, what's the word? Difficult. Then I guess I know a lot of difficult women." While many people in Hollywood have been known to be demanding and troublesome, African American women who are assertive seem to be readily labeled as difficult and aggressive, and thus viewed as a problem that agents and producers might want to avoid hiring or promoting.

A strong African American woman can act as a role model for those around her. For example, in commenting on the absence of a mentor when she first entered the business, Vida Spears could only find a few African American producers, none of them women, whom she could look up to. Later in her career, however, she was able to fulfill that mentor role for Felicia Henderson. For Meg DeLoatch, seeing Yvette Lee Bowser run a show inspired her. DeLoatch recounted Bowser telling her, "'You can do this.' That was really important for me early on." DeLoatch, Rose Catherine Pinkney, and Feleica D. Henderson are proof that strong and competent African American women can succeed in the business, in part because they had people like them break down some barriers and they themselves have helped to create an environment more welcoming to minorities.

You Are a Black Guy, So You Must Be Funny

"You are a black guy, so you must be funny. Because all the Black people that we knew do funny stuff," Oz Scott said in mocking the attitude of many Whites in the film and television industry. Whites in Hollywood often assume that Blacks should work in comedy as opposed to drama. One writer described a drama script involving differences in light and dark skin color. The pitch meeting went well but the response was to purchase the script and have another writer develop it. The studio assumed this African American was "more suited" to writing comedy, although the writer's background centered on writing dramas. "We didn't do anything in the pitch that was funny. It was a serious story; there was no laughing."

In the early 1980s Frank Dawson, then a CBS executive who wanted to supervise his own shows, struggled with his desire to stay in dramatic programming. Dawson said he approached Harvey Shepard, then President of the network, to discuss his career goals.

According to Dawson, Shepard attributed the problem to Dawson's conservative boss. He told Dawson he would have to move into the comedy division if he wanted his own shows. Dawson's response: "I don't want to be in comedy. You guys always want to put Black people into comedy. You want laughs, to be funny. I want to do serious stuff." In recounting the story, Dawson said he would never forget Shephard's reply: "You know Frank, it's your choice. You do what you want to do. You came to me and said you wanted to move ahead. I'm telling you how you can move ahead." Realizing this was good career advice, Dawson moved into comedy, eventually supervising the sitcoms *The Jeffersons, Alice,* and *Private Benjamin.* But Dawson did regret never having the opportunity to succeed in drama.

One person I spoke to described how Whites' assumptions about Blacks and comedy are communicated. This writer explained that the network official gave no specifics regarding the network's vision of the direction of the show, but instead requested that the producers add a White writer, in order to add "some smarts to the show":

> We are sitting on a staff with people who went to Ivy League schools, Northwestern, all these great schools, and you are saying we need it to be smarter? So the assumption is still: if we want it smart we better hire White writers. If we want it jokey, and for the most part, on Black shows they want it jokey [then we keep Black writers]. They want the modern day *Jeffersons.*

Director Oz Scott emphasized that his success across a variety of genres, including those outside comedy, only came through a determined effort on his part. He explained that when he was directing the sitcom, *The Jeffersons,* the producers offered him twenty-four episodes for the season. He agreed to direct twenty shows so that he would have time for other shows such as the dramatic series, *The Mississippi.*

Scott cautioned that he saw little middle ground for many Blacks, little opportunity for work that mixed serious and somewhat lighter subjects. He has been able to do both comedy and drama, directing shows like *Hill Street Blues, Archie Bunker's Place,* and *The Practice.* Nonetheless he suggested that some of the limitations that African American writers faced stemmed from their own lack of interest in writing things that mixed comedic and dramatic elements. Scott said he found this attitude when he was working on a project a few years ago:

> I was developing a script and I went to a few Black writers to try and get a writer to go in with me on a film. And I found that, other than sitcoms, most

Black writers only had heavy dramatic writing samples. You were either writing sitcoms or you were trying to write heavy stuff. Where is the middle ground?

While most of the interviewees saw their work limited by expectations that they work in comedy, some also mentioned that they enjoyed the challenge of doing significant comedic work. Oz Scott used examples such as the scene in *Bustin' Loose* (where Richard Pryor's character mistakenly encounters a Ku Klux Klan rally) to illustrate how he liked to use comedy to define the pathos of a situation.

Similarly, in 1998 writer/producer Felicia D. Henderson discussed what she called her "passion project." The show would involve a basketball player-turned-executive whose alter-ego follows him around, questioning if Black people think he might be "kissing up" to Whites or if he should sit with the Black people in the commissary because Whites wonder why Blacks always congregate together. She said:

> I want to talk about those issues, but they scare people. And I want to do it with humor because if it is going to be done at all that's the only way you're going to get it done. I want to talk about what it's like to have that double consciousness, to have to live in both worlds, in a humorous way.

Speaking Up

Many of the workers I interviewed mentioned that they spoke out about issues of discrimination, mistreatment, or stereotypes. The degree to which each would speak up varied by their position and their degree of sensitivity. For example, Shirley Salomon said when she was a production assistant their were times she was tempted to object to what she regarded as a stereotype. But, she said, complaining to a producer or a writer was something a production assistant would never do. Salomon did describe how on *Cosby* she occasionally noticed some kind of stereotype in a script and would say to herself "are they kidding?" but didn't dare to speak up. She observed that the show's star/producer Bill Cosby would say something about the same stereotype and a change would be made.

Likewise, Kim Sizemore, stage manager on *The Parent'Hood* when I interviewed her in 1998, said her reluctance to speak out stemmed from the fact that she worked in "nuts and bolts production." When asked her views, she would give only a guarded opinion. "You have to be careful who you talk to," she asserted. She implied that "someone" might go back to the writer, something that could affect Sizemore's future job prospects.

One writer said that being one of only two minority writers on a show made speaking out difficult, "especially when you are low on the totem pole and everyone else was higher than you." This writer found her current situation, on a show with nearly all Black writers, a much more open environment for voicing her opinion. Felicia Henderson said that on *Fresh Prince*, where she was the only Black and only female writer, she was conflicted about speaking up. She thought if she did, it would merely solidify the view of her as "the Black expert" who interpreted African American life. She was afraid the White writers and producers might end up not caring about her other skills. As an example of her dilemma, Henderson recalled one script in which the White writers had a character going to a barbershop instead of a beauty parlor to get her hair braided.

> You are torn, because if you say one thing then everything [becomes] "Now, Felicia, would they dance this way?" And they turn to their resident Black expert, [and ask] "don't you know what all Black people in American do?" And my experience is so different from anybody else's experience that I know. But at the same time, if you don't speak up she will be going to the barbershop to get her hair braided.

Director Oz Scott said that most of the time he has been fortunate to work with producers who listen and react positively when he takes a stand on an issue of race. Yet he finds it frightening when people "don't get it … don't understand." For example, when he worked on a program that portrayed an interracial relationship, Scott told the producers the show was a good opportunity to make some funny comments about how some Black women view White women who date or marry Black men. He said the White executive producer did not understand his point, so Scott turned to the two Black writers and even the Black secretary for support. None of them wanted to address the issue. Scott said, "It's amazing in this town how quickly you get deserted."

Scott said he is especially troubled when people "worry about what's in front of the camera and fail to see what's behind the camera." He cited his experience working on a dramatic television series in the late 1980s. The program was set in the South and shot on location. Scott said that the producers attempted to illustrate the fictional town as primarily Black by hiring a large number of African Americans as extras. Scott's complaint, however, came with the lack of diversity on the crew:

> I looked around the room at this production meeting. We had about thirty-five people, heads of departments, head of make-up, head of wardrobe, head of construction .... At the end I raised my hand. I am sitting at the head of the table and I'm saying to the producers, can I ask you one question. If the majority of people in this town are Black and if you want the majority of the people on this show, the extras, to appear Black, how come I am the only Black person sitting around this table? And the answer was, "Well, we have a lot of Mexicans in the grip department."

Scott claimed the producers were "very conscientious but missed the big picture." He had not confronted the issue to criticize or impose his will on the production. Rather, his goal was to make people whom he liked and respected, people whom he thought had written a great show, aware that creating more realistic images involves something more than using African Americans as extras.

Vida Spears acknowledged that speaking out can always make someone unpopular, but, "there are times when you just can't sit there and say 'I am going to let this pass.'" She explained that often people don't mean to be offensive and that stereotypes are sometimes created because of White ignorance of African American life. Even when she thinks that people don't know any better, Spears still feels an obligation to object to an offensive joke or image. Spears said that one person with whom she had worked felt that "when I'd speak up I was saying that he was racist." She tried to make it clear to him that she wasn't accusing him of racism. Spears would explain: "I know that people will find this offensive if you do it. You might just be going for a joke but you don't understand what that joke means to certain people."

"We don't understand why that would offend anybody." How does an African American respond when a White person makes that statement? One interviewee recalled trying to clarify the complexity of the situation:

> I said being offended is an emotion. Most of the time when I am offended I'd prefer not to be. It's not a good feeling .... For the most part when someone is offended it is a true and honest and pure reaction to something they are seeing of their kind of experience. So the fact that I can't explain to you why it's offensive is a nature of being offended. But if I say to you, I've had ten calls from [viewers] who were offended, you might want to hear that.

Raising the specter of audience reactions may be the most effective tactic. The potential of bad publicity and the financial implications of airing a show that viewers can find racially offensive is something White executives should understand. But what cannot be lost is that in Hollywood it is African Americans who, being the first, and sometimes only workers to recognize the offending image, are left with the responsibility to speak up. They face the additional dilemma of dealing with White co-workers that may be uncomfortable with talking about race and afraid of being accused of being racist.

Frank Dawson said when he was at CBS in the 1980s he and other African Americans objected to the way they were being treated. They "were grumbling that they had better educations, better backgrounds, were more qualified than people they were working for, yet there was no movement within the company." Dawson's own action was to help establish a Los Angeles chapter of the CBS Black Employees Association, at a time when New York already had a chapter but not the West Coast. He said CBS's reaction to his effort was essentially "Who was this guy? What is he doing? Why do you guys want to separate yourselves?" CBS sent management from New York to meet with the Association. Dawson thought they were impressed with the way the Black Employees Association approached these conversations:

> We didn't go out and get [protest] signs and placards. We did research. We had access to statistics from personnel. We were able to sit down and document all the departments that had Black employees at all, what level they were at, what level of education they had, what their salaries were. And [we] looked at other people in their departments, including people whom they worked for and saw that they were not moving ahead in their careers and other people were. And so once the company sat down and looked at that in Black and White, they were, "I guess we need to do something about this."

In this case, "speaking out" proved helpful for Dawson and the other Black employees. CBS also realized that the Association could be a positive asset for the corporation. Dawson explained that the following year, "the CBS Black Employees Association was listed in CBS's personnel brochure as one of the resources they had in the company."

Dawson claimed that he never hesitated to speak up about employment discrimination or media stereotypes. He admitted he was often naive in certain situations, such as when he raised issues he expected that people should know and agree on but they "didn't at all." Dawson said he always tried to be as diplomatic as possible but people were often taken aback when he spoke up. As a result he was sometimes viewed as "this radical militant guy." Dawson speculated that this reputation might have hurt him in his efforts to reach higher and more powerful positions in the industry.

Advocacy Groups

The television workplace can often be affected by organizational pressure from advocacy groups.[19] The NAACP and members of the Congressional Black Caucus have each questioned network production and employment practices.[20] African American workers can be the main beneficiaries of the work of these outside groups. One network executive noted that the reports published by some of these groups can be helpful. She cited studies conducted for the Writers Guild of American (WGA) that track minority employment in networks and studios as a beneficial device for keeping these important issues in people's minds. According to WGA President Daniel Petrie, Jr. when the first report was issued in 1987, "the Guild leadership believed the announcement of the employment realities for women, minority, or over forty would create a catalyst for change."[21] The 1998 report showed minority membership in the Guild doubling during those years to six percent of membership. Petrie said that figure "must double and double again before our industry can applaud itself."[22] The 2005 WGA report shows that there have been increases, although small, with the number of minority writers in 2004 at slightly less than ten percent.[23]

Hollywood's practice of fast turnover in executive suites makes it difficult to get the networks and studios to transform. Members of advocacy groups told me that it can take time to establish a relationship with the president of a network or studio only to see the person gets fired or otherwise leave before significant change has been institutionalized. One person complained, "So it was sort of start all over."

A constant refrain from advocates, workers, and industry observers is that only when civil rights and other groups are active do studios and networks tend to be more concerned about minority employment. "But when the pressure is put off people go away quietly," one advocate said. Frank Dawson found protest activity cyclical, occurring every seven to ten years. When he read one recent newspaper article criticizing industry practices concerning minority hiring, he thought it was a re-write of something he had read years before. Only the names had changed. Dawson said the article included the usual lame industry responses: "Audiences just aren't interested. The [minority] talent just isn't out there."

When the networks revealed their fall 1999 lineups there were close to thirty comedies and dramas on the four major networks. Yet not one of the new shows featured any minorities in any leading or even secondary roles. A series of articles in the *Los Angeles Times* drew attention to this lack of diversity on network television. Civil rights groups challenged the industry's excuses. In a speech to his organization's national convention, Kweisi Mfume, President and CEO of the NAACP, condemned the television industry, calling the fall 1999 network schedule "a virtual whitewash in programming."[24] Mfume outlined his organization's "Television and Film Diversity Campaign" in a guest commentary for the *Los Angeles Times*.[25] He proposed litigation and civil action, including boycotts of the networks. Latino, Native American, and Asian American organizations joined the NAACP to form a multiethnic coalition to press for diversity. In the fall of 1999 the Coalition of African American Writers placed a two-page ads in *Daily Variety* and *The Hollywood Reporter* highlighting the absence of African American writers working in prime time television. (See Figure 4.2.)[26] The ads listed the total numbers of writers on each show, noting, "only eighteen of the ninety-five network sitcoms and dramas on the fall line-up employ African American writers." The ad also pointed out how few Latino, Asian Americans, and Native Americans work as writers—less than two percent of the total.

Meg DeLoatch was involved in the Coalition of African American Writers research on television employment and placement of the ads in *The Hollywood Reporter* and *Daily Variety*. "When we called, often posing as college students doing a survey, we often spoke to assistants who willingly gave up the information .... Those of us involved did it under the cloak of secrecy to avoid reprisals, but it felt good to take a stand."

DeLoatch said industry reaction to the ad was for a brief time "very intense." "The networks were embarrassed to see those numbers out there and it did help spur some much needed conversations." Her efforts may have had an impact on her career. The following season DeLoatch was staffed on the CBS show *Bette*. She explained:

To this day, that is the only White show on my resume. I don't know that it was a direct result of the ad, because I wasn't hired because of a mandate. The showrunner, Jeffery Lane, simply liked me and my writing and thought it would be nice to have a diverse staff. If there were more people like Jeffery in the business, that ad wouldn't have been needed.

DeLoatch looked back on her experience working with the Coalition. "As for regrets, I have none and I doubt any of the others who participated do either. We had a choice: to allow the inequality to continue or to speak out. Instead of choking on our frustration, we spoke out."

Sharon Johnson, chair of the Guild's Committee of Black Writers from 1999 to 2001, said she believes the ad "publicly embarrassed" the industry. She predicted that the ad, as well as pressure from the minority coalition, would have a positive impact for minority workers. In fact, in January 2000, the NAACP announced an agreement with NBC that "established goals and timetables to increase opportunities for people of color at the network."[27] The pact included promises for minority training programs, diversity workshops, and network funding of an additional writing position for a minority on every second-year show. Johnson said the significance of this last item is that it would place minority workers on the staffs of already successful White shows. NBC West Coast President Scott Sassa said, "Working on a successful show is the best way for a writer to become a showrunner."[28] Soon after the NBC announcement, ABC signed an agreement with NAACP that tied bonuses for management with the goal "to increase opportunities for qualified people of color in the network television industry."[29]

Frank Dawson said that this latest effort to change the industry might succeed. He explained, "This time it's different. The talent pool is there, up and down the line—writers, directors. This is really an opportunity for people to get their feet in the door." Dawson said some of the people he's taught at the University of Southern California screen writing program were now staff writers and that this might allow them to move on to "show running" positions. He pointed out that currently almost all show running executive producers were White.

Sharon Johnson stated that in the past the television business "considered [itself] different because we are creative." She said that

1964: RCA Introduces Color TV. 1999:

In recent weeks, the media has focused its attention on the lack of racial diversity in the casting of network television primetime shows. The major networks have responded by belatedly adding 17 minority characters to a few of their new and returning series. This same lack of diversity also exists behind the scenes; however, there has been no mention of diversifying the writing staffs of any of these series.

The lack of diversity in writers' rooms throughout television is even more startling than the lack of diversity on the air. **Out of the 759 writing positions on white-themed shows, 9 (or 1.1%) are held by African Americans. In contrast, 40 (or 50%) of the 80 writing positions on black-themed shows are held by white writers. It seems acceptable for white writers to work on black-themed shows, but unacceptable for African American writers to write on white-themed shows.** In fact, only 18 of the 95 network sitcoms and dramas on the fall line-up employ African American writers. Of the 839 total writers employed on primetime shows, only 55 are African American. And an overwhelming 83 percent of these 55 writers are segregated on black-themed shows.

When a pattern such as this is so blatantly pervasive, is it a matter of happenstance? Oversight? Or is it racial discrimination? We'll let the numbers speak for themselves.

The Facts

Fall 1999 Primetime Schedule
There are 95 sitcoms and dramas on the six networks' fall schedules.

On ABC, only 9 of the 171 writing positions are held by African Americans. (5.3 %)
On CBS, only 2 of the 144 writing positions are held by African Americans. (1.4%)
On NBC, only 1 of the 189 writing positions is held by an African American. (0.5%)
On FOX, only 3 of the 160 writing positions are held by African Americans. (1.9%)

Of the 839 writers employed on the 95 shows, only 55 are African Americans. (6.6%)
Only 1 white-themed show currently employs more than 1 African American writer.
45 of the 55 African American writers work on black-themed shows. (83%)

Only 9 of the 759 writers employed on white-themed shows are African American. (1.1%)
40 of the 80 writers employed on black-themed shows are white. (50%)

Only 5 of the 9 black-themed shows have African American show runners. (56%)
Zero white-themed shows have African American show runners. (0%)
Only 8 of the 55 African American writers are employed on the 39 dramas. (14.5%)
Only 8 African American writers out of 839 total writers are employed on dramas. (0.95%)

33% of all African American writing positions are on Moesha and The Parkers on UPN.
77% of all African American writing positions are on black-themed shows on UPN and The WB.

Only 11 Latino writers are employed on series on the fall schedule. (1.3%)
Only 3 Asian American writers are employed on series on the fall schedule. (0.3%)
Zero Native Americans writers are employed on series on the fall schedule. (0.0%)

African Americans, Latinos, Asian Americans, Native Americans and other minorities make up over 30 percent of the U.S. population. Yet, together, these groups account for only 7 percent of primetime network writing positions.

Most Writers' Rooms Still Cast in White.

	Total Writers	African American Writers		Total Writers	African American Writers
ABC			**Stark Raving Mad**/20th TV	9	0
Boy Meets World/Disney	11	1	Suddenly Susan/Warner Bros.	15	0
Dharma & Greg/20th TV	13	0	3rd Rock/Carsey-Werner	9	0
The Drew Carey Show/Warner Bros.	17	0	Veronica's Closet/Warner Bros.	11	0
The Hughleys/Greenblatt-Janollari	11	5	Third Watch/Warner Bros.	5	1
It's Like You Know/Dreamworks	10	0	Will & Grace/NBCS	10	0
The Norm Show/Warner Bros.	10	0	The West Wing/Warner Bros.	10	0
NYPD Blue/20th TV	8	0			
Odd Man Out/Warner Bros.	9	0	**Fox**		
Oh, Grow Up/Greenblatt-Janollari	10	0	Action/Columbia-Tristar	8	0
Once & Again/Disney	8	0	Ally/20th TV	1	0
The Practice/20th TV	6	2	Ally McBeal/20th TV	1	0
Sabrina the Teenage Witch/Viacom	9	0	The Badlands/Regency	8	1
Snoops/20th TV	8	0	Beverly Hills 90210/ Spelling	9	0
Spin City/Dreamworks	14	0	Family Guy/20th TV	18	0
Sports Night/Imagine	8	0	Futurama/20th TV	12	0
Two Guys and a Girl/20th TV	13	0	Get Real/20th TV	11	1
Wasteland/Miramax	6	1	Harsh Realm/20th TV	8	0
			King of the Hill/20th TV	19	0
CBS			Malcolm in the Middle/Regency	10	0
Becker/Paramount	7	0	Manchester Prep/Columbia-Tristar	4	0
Chicago Hope/20th TV	8	0	Party of Five/Columbia-Tristar	8	0
Cosby/Carsey-Werner	9	2	The Simpsons/20th TV	20	0
Diagnosis Murder/Viacom	5	0	That 70's Show/Carsey-Werner	9	0
Early Edition/Columbia-Tristar	10	0	Time of Your Life/Columbia-Tristar	8	1
Everybody Loves Raymond/HBO-IP	10	0	The X-Files/20th TV	6	0
Family Law/Columbia-Tristar	4	0			
Jag/Paramount	5	0	**The WB**		
Judging Amy/CBSP	5	0	Angel/20th TV	5	0
King of Queens/Columbia-Tristar	12	0	Buffy the Vampire Slayer/20th TV	6	0
The Ladies Man/Columbia-Tristar	10	0	Charmed/Spelling	14	0
Love or Money/Paramount	10	0	Dawson's Creek/Columbia-Tristar	8	0
Martial Law/CBSP	13	0	The Downtowners/Castle Rock	6	0
Nash Bridges/Rysher	6	0	Felicity/Imagine	6	0
Now & Again/Paramount	6	0	For Your Love/Warner Bros.	13	5
Touched by an Angel/CBSP	10	0	Jack & Jill/Warner Bros.	8	0
Walker Texas Ranger/CBSP	4	0	The Jamie Foxx Show/Warner Bros.	7	7
Work With Me/CBSP	11	0	Popular/Disney	7	0
			Roswell/20th TV	8	0
NBC			Safe Harbor/Spelling	4	0
Cold Feet/Warner Bros.	6	0	7th Heaven/Spelling	5	0
ER/Warner Bros.	8	0	The Steve Harvey Show/Brillstein-Grey	10	5
Frasier/Paramount	14	0			
Freaks & Geeks/Dreamworks	7	0	**UPN**		
Friends/Warner Bros.	12	0	Dilbert/Columbia-Tristar	3	0
Jesse/Warner Bros.	11	0	Grown Ups/Columbia-Tristar	12	1
Just Shoot Me/Brillstein-Grey	16	0	Malcolm & Eddie/Columbia-Tristar	8	3
Law & Order/Studios USA TV	6	0	Moesha/Big Ticket TV	9	8
Law & Order:SVU/Studios USA TV	5	0	The Parkers/Big Ticket TV	11	10
The Mike O'Malley Show/NBCS	16	0	7 Days/Paramount	10	0
The Pretender /20th TV	9	0	The Strip/Warner Bros.	6	1
Profiler/NBCS	4	0	Shasta McNasty/Columbia-Tristar	8	0
Providence/NBCS	6	0	Star Trek:Voyager/Paramount	5	0

WRITERS BY TELEVISION PRODUCTION

Production Company	Writers	African American Writers	Production Company	Writers	African American Writers
BIG TICKET TV	20	18 (all on UPN)	REGENCY TV	18	0
BRILLSTEIN-GREY	26	5 (5 on Steve Harvey)	RYSHER	6	0
CASTLE ROCK	6	0	SPELLING TV	23	0
CARSEY-WERNER	27	2 (2 on Cosby)	STUDIOS USA TV	11	0
CBS PRODUCTIONS	42	0	20TH TELEVISION	187	3
COLUMBIA/TRISTAR	101	5 (4 on black shows on UPN)	VIACOM TV	14	0
DISNEY	26	1	WARNER BROS. TV	142	14 (12 on black shows on The WB)
DREAMWORKS	31	0			
GREENBLATT-JAN.	21	5 (5 on The Hughleys)			
HBO-IP	10	0	Numbers were obtained through a telephone survey conduct-		
IMAGINE	14	0	ed by the Beverly Hills/Hollywood NAACP and the Coalition		
MIRAMAX TV	6	1	of African American Television Writers (CAATW).The Beverly		
NBC STUDIOS	42	0	Hills/Hollywood NAACP can be reached at (323) 464-7616.		
PARAMOUNT	52	0	CAATW is an organization made up of professional writers		
			who are members of the WGA.		

Figure 4.2 Ad taken by the Coalition of African American Television in *The Hollywood Reporter* Oct. 11, 1999. (Courtesy of David Wyatt.)

now, with such a public fight on its hands, the industry had to face the fact that is similar to every other business and must meet the challenge of diversity.

The Current State of Network Television

The three television networks started since 1986, Fox in that year, UPN and WB in 1995, have all taken advantage of two facts: African Americans watch more television than Whites and CBS, NBC, and ABC have never catered to the Black audience.[30] Zook has documented how Fox's targeting of Black viewership "inadvertently fostered a space for Black authorship in television."[31]

Even though some respondents worked on shows aired by Fox, WB, and UPN, many were critical of the "narrowcasting" to minorities. They witnessed a pattern: Once these networks established themselves by serving Black viewers, they dropped these shows and went with White-oriented programs. One writer said it was as if the networks say, "now it is time to bring on the real shows."

Sharon Johnson said the network strategy of airing and then dropping Black shows had a direct impact on her career. She explained that she broke into the business as a writers" assistant and then staff writer on two Black-oriented shows on Fox. Once Fox dropped all its Black shows she found it hard to get work. Johnson said, "I think that was the first time that I considered the racial aspects [of the business]." It helped her to recognize the impact of the industry's practice of funneling Black writers to primarily Black shows: When these shows were cancelled her chance of getting work diminished.

"The plantations" is how Frank Dawson described UPN and WB, the two networks that, in 1998, were still interested in Black-oriented material. As a producer committed to creating Black-themed shows, Dawson said these networks were the "only places that I can pretty much sell a Black show." For Dawson the problem was that these networks were uninterested in Black shows with any level of "sophistication." Dawson admitted that there are "stupid White shows." It is just harder for minority writers and producers to go beyond the "stupid Black shows." He said that some of the young Black writers he teaches in the USC program ask him for advice in getting "quality"

work on the air. Dawson explained their dilemma: since they have little chance to work on White shows and almost all the Black shows are
low-brow comedies, they have no opportunity to create shows with
any "level of sophistication" or that reflect "the experiences that your
life has really had." He advises these young writers to "distinguish
between what you write for commerce and what you write for yourself."

Felicia Henderson told me in 1998 that she saw market trends limiting her ability to pursue her interest in producing Black-oriented
work. Her agent had recently told her that if the ideas she was pitching weren't "multicultural" the networks were not interested; they
had no interest in any more primarily Black shows. The trend in the
late 1990s was shows that included both Black and White actors.
Henderson did not have a problem with shows with multiracial casts.
Her complaint was with the way television treated diversity:

> They don't want the series to talk about that these people are different .... [It
> is] as if you talk about it, you talk about the differences, you still can't be
> together .... You have to show those differences and the conflict, yet still be
> together .... No, we just want her to be Black in the White world.

What is depicted is a White version of diversity. Blacks and other
people of color exist only on White terms. Frank Dawson said while
the networks have determined that they want to show a "multicultural universe," these shows rarely explore what that means. He felt
that while having an interracial cast was positive, "the difference is
when you go home with a character on a show you don't go home
with the Black character." Dawson explained that these shows usually
don't fully develop the African American character's home life, their
family, let alone "their aspirations or dreams."

Despite the hopes of advocacy groups, minority writers, and many viewers little has changed in the years since the diversity agreements. A 2005 Writers Guild of American/West (WGA/West) report found that, "a large portion of the writers of color in television today are employed on African-American-themed situation comedies on UPN where script fees and other financial terms are contractually reduced."[32] The 2007 WGA/West report found that gains in employment and earnings noted in previous reports, "have either slowed in recent years or ground to a halt altogether."[33] Yet what change has come is of real value. People like Meg DeLoatch and Michael Ajakwe are glad to have a place that can serve as an outlet for their work. The industry as a whole can and should be criticized for limited opportunities but at least there is some space for African American workers and images.

Figure 4.3 Writer/Producer Michael Ajakwe (center) flanked by Bentely Kyle Evans, showrunner on *Martin* and *The Jamie Foxx Show*, and Stacey Evans Morgan, Writer/Producer on *The Parkers* and *Love That Girl*. Photo was taken at the inaugural Los Angeles Web Series Festival. Ajakwe is Executive Director of LAWEBFEST. (Photo by Ian Foxx of Foxx Photography, courtesy of Michael Ajakwe.)

Cable

"It's cable where some of the boldest moves have been made when it comes to minorities in evening entertainment series" asserted *Los Angeles Times* television critic Howard Rosenberg in the summer of 1999.[34] Some respondents also looked to cable as a potential avenue for producing programming that shows the diversity of African American life. One person cited HBO's *Laurel Avenue*, a 1992 Black family drama, as an example of how cable television has begun to explore the African American experience. Leonard R. Garner expressed hope that cable will open up new avenues of expression for creators but cautioned that the Black audience had to "be willing to see all facets of ourselves" for this potential to be realized.

Though cable might be open to more creative ideas, producing for cable is not as lucrative as broadcast television. Writers get much smaller residuals for shows on cable. Frank Dawson said the Family Channel had offered to finance the pilot for a show he co-wrote. He said, unfortunately, "they did not want to pay the kind of money so that we could actually do it right so we had to pass on it."

Martin Jones and Tim Reid's experience producing *Linc's* in the late 1990s for the Showtime cable network illustrates both cable's creative potential and the medium's fiscal constraints. Reid claimed that producing for cable was the most difficult episode of his career, given the disparity between the cable network's "vision" and the money they are willing to spend. He explained that he was able to produce a quality show for less money than it would have taken to produce a program for UPN, let alone CBS or NBC. But Showtime was still not happy. He attributed this to the inexperience of the people at the cable network. "You have people who don't have network television experience who are saying we want to do quality work. They don't even have the experience to even find out if you are doing anything wrong." Reid did say that if he had produced *Linc's* for network television "we would have made more money, we would have had less creative control, but we would have made more money and had less stress than doing this show."

Reid used the set design for *Linc's* as an example of the problems he encountered working with Showtime:

> That's not the bar I had in my mind, it's too bright, and the reason, they were so afraid of it being a drama they wanted to keep a comedy look so they chose bright. I remember the arguments, the production arguments we

had on just the wall paint. I wanted it to be green. I wanted it to look like a bar. Bars are long dark places. They're not bright.... I didn't want that... I lost that battle.

According to Reid, a friend who is an Emmy-winning director saw the show and asked Reid: "Blue? Who chooses blue [when depicting a bar set in a Black community]?"

Reid contrasted what cable and broadcast networks look for in a show:

> On Showtime they are telling you to say the "F" word more and can you get Pam [Grier] to show her breasts .... On the networks they are saying "Don't say anything about politics, stay away from any issue that may be human, and focus on the illusion of her breasts, and don't say the 'F' word."

Reid said producing the show for cable keeps his name alive as a producer and provider of material: "When you get reviewed in the *Wall Street Journal* people take notice. So I'm pitching to the networks and I figure within the next year I'll do a show on the networks."

A cable executive explained what cable networks look for in a show. She said her network, is a niche service, "very targeted, specifically adult women, cable viewers so we know they are probably higher education and income." Her network is not interested in attracting men or children. Advertisers buy the network's middle- and upper-income female audience. She compared this to broadcast networks, where the appeal was much wider:

> It's men and women, it's family, it's kids, it's a mix of people. So you have to sort of build up a coalition of viewers. Maybe you'll go for an action show, ... a broad base of men, a smaller number of women, and a lot of teenage boys and kids watching a certain kind of cartoonist sort of show. Or a show like a *Touched by an Angel* gets a broad base of women watching it primarily... more working class and blue collar.

Lifetime's niche market allowed it to air a program like *Any Day Now*, a show centered on a friendship between two women, one White and one Black. *Any Day Now* was set in the present, with flashbacks to the early 1960s. The executive explained the show's concept: "It's also about coming of age as women, about the civil rights movement, and about modern day race relations filtered through this friendship." She said the network wants the show to be "provocative." The goal of the producers and the network is to explore issues without relying on easy answers.

It's just boring if you are going to do another episode where, you know, Black church gets bombed, no one's for that. It's not the most interesting story to tell. Instead, Black-White adoption, there are really different views on this and thoughtful people can have opposing views on the subject.

The executive claimed her network's mandate to reach adult women allowed it to approach subject matter a bit differently than broadcast networks, which must attract a broader audience. They don't have the challenge of pleasing children or satisfying families. The cable network's research also shows its audience has a higher education level than the broadcast networks'. All these audience factors mean they can "try things that are a little more sophisticated." The executive described her network as an alternative to the broadcast networks, "so we are constantly coming up with things that are different, that are special."

Amanda Lotz's study of the production of *Any Day Now* explores how cable has made "possible textual content that would probably have been too controversial for the network ear."[35] The producers and writers explored both historical stories of the civil rights movement and contemporary issues of racism. Even though cable allows for greater creative freedom the producers and writers found their network interested in promoting stories of female friendship rather than more thoughtful, issue-oriented storylines. Lotz found that Miller "had to negotiate her desire to tell provocative stories about racism with Lifetime's desire to not alienate potential audience members who might be estranged by the show's uncompromising anti-racist position."[36]

Why would producers need to be concerned with how a show is promoted? If a network promotes only one aspect of a television series then audiences and advertisers may get turned off by unexpected issues-oriented programs. At the same time, without promotion of thoughtful and provocative episodes a series might never find an audience. As Lozt recounts, the producers used what power they had to force Lifetime's hand when producer Miller instructed her staff to "offer nothing soft to promote."[37] The need for producers to exercise the power they have—that is, the power of the script—is as evident on cable as it is on the networks. Miller's ability to control the show by controlling the one area within her power, the writing, is reminiscent of Tim Reid's recounting of the way Hugh Wilson left CBS little option in airing the *WKRP* episode on the Vietnam veteran 20 years earlier. It appears that neither time nor changes in distribution channels have changed the power dynamics of the creative process as dramatically as many think.

Conclusion

Race can play a defining role in the workplace for African Americans. Workers are often faced with situations where they are made to feel different: marginalized as simply filling affirmative action requirements with no opportunity for advancement, being called to account for the behavior of other African Americans such as O.J. Simpson, or feeling they have to speak out on racially offensive material. Workplace interactions influence what we see on television. When creators are open to discussing and exploring the vibrant diversity of Black life the result can be rich and successful shows like *A Different World*. Conversely, when workers are marked as "other" they may "go along to get along," not wanting to bring added attention to their race. Or, unwilling or unable to develop the thick skin required to immunize themselves to a workplace often fraught with gender and racial marking, some minority workers end up leaving the business altogether. That was certainly the case with a couple of the people I interviewed. Both former network executive Frank Dawson and writer Sharon Johnson, though still somewhat involved in the business, now primarily teach and work in higher education.[38] But either "going along" or leaving is a response that helps perpetuate a system of production that has created television's limited and/or stereotypical images of minorities.

The co-creation of identity, in this case through workplace interactions, combined with a politicization that can arise from being marked as "other," leads to the potential for multiple axes or bases of identity. This can occur, for example, when a minority writer points out that some material might be offensive to White audiences. In *The Souls of Black Folk* W. E. B. Du Bois spoke of the Blacks as being:

> gifted with second-sight in this American world—a world which yields him no true self consciousness, but only lets him see himself through the revelation of the other world. It is a peculiar sensation, this double-consciousness, this sense of always looking at one's self through the eyes of others, of measuring one's soul by the tape of a world that looks on in amused contempt and pity.[39]

According to this perspective, Blacks in American society not only "operate" as individual people, but they must also act in relationship to White's conceptions of Blacks. In some cases this might mean dealing with White racism, but more often it is having to function in relation to pre-conceived White notions of African Americans. In order to operate and survive in White-dominated society, Blacks must know and react to White culture. This knowledge of two cultures is also an asset in producing work (books, films, television series) that can appeal to both majority and minority audiences. One wonders how many Whites in Hollywood appreciate the significance of this skill. Most don't because they don't have to; they only recognize it when they need a "translator to make money."

Sociologists Joe Feagin and Melvin Sikes refer to the concept as a "second eye," where Blacks "look carefully at White-Black interaction through a distinctive lens colored by accumulating personal and group experience."[40] The term seems highly applicable here. While the people I spoke with rarely mentioned instances of overt racism, many said they often wonder if they were treated differently because of their race. For example, Leonard R. Garner questioned if his difficulties getting the kind of directing opportunities jobs he wanted hinged on race.

Tim Reid, Vida Spears, and Felicia D. Henderson provide evidence that African American creators are very willing to challenge the status quo. They also showed that in taking a stand on issues such as diversity and stereotyping they could make a difference in the workplace and on the television screen. Both Reid and Spears have been credited with creating work that reflects African American life.[41] Those workers who were hesitant to speak up, like Production Manager Kim Sizemore, seemed concerned with the repercussions. This may relate to her lower-status job. As director Leonard R. Garner explained, those "below the line" have less power and financial opportunities. Two studies of the television industry of the 1970s and 1980s found that media producers who want to maintain their current status or hope to move up in the system are averse to speaking out.[42] Both Tim Reid and Frank Dawson thought their willingness to take a stand had negatively affected their careers. This may have been true. As of the fall 2009 season, neither had a show on any of the broadcast networks.

The collaborative nature of the production process was most readily visible in the way some writers described their workplace. They argued, laughed, tossed ideas back and forth, all in an effort to come up with a new show each week. This open environment was also a place where conflict over race and gender differences occurred. Felicia Henderson used the term "work" to describe the extra effort required to explain Black life, challenge stereotypes, and cope with being made to feel different. She was articulating the sentiments of many of the people I interviewed. The constant reminder that they were marked as "other" was the primary reason some writers relished working on shows with primarily Black writing staffs. Henderson said that, even though she had only worked on Black-oriented programs, *Moesha* was very different. It was the first time she wrote for a show with African American executive producers. Henderson said this led to a more creative workplace because she no longer had to "work" to explain Black life or confront stereotypes.

While most of the Black people I spoke with had little problem working with Whites, most wanted a more diverse workplace—a place where they did not exist simply as tokens, representatives of their race, or people whose presence made Whites uneasy. The kind of emotional labor that FeliciaHenderson spoke of as draining her energy isn't required in a more integrated environment. But this means more than adding a few people of color to the workforce. What is needed for true diversity and creativity is an atmosphere of free communication and a willingness to talk and learn about our cultural identities without being defensive.

Tim Reid directly ties his work environment to the images he produces. He is inspired by both the diversity of the people around him and the treatment he's received working in Hollywood. His acting, writing, directing, producing, and now ownership of a production studio are inseparable from his attempts to produce a workplace and a body of work that reflect a world with a variety of races and ethnicities.

Few of these creators possess the energy or power to produce the kind of work environment that Reid requires. But many of them share similar interests. Vida Spears, Felicia D. Henderson, Oz Scott, and others have all attempted to create an atmosphere where the White male is not the norm. Their success in doing so can be found on *Moesha, Sister, Sister,* and other shows that were part of the emerging body of work by African Americans in the 1990s. These creators and their work helped lead the way for shows such as *Girlfriends* and *Soul Food* in the 2000s. It must also be noted that there were a few White-produced shows in the 1990s and early 2000s that depicted complex Black characters, the most important being *Homicide: Life on the Street* on NBC, and HBO's *The Wire*. The former was created by Barry Levinson and based on the book by David Simon who went on to create *The Wire*. Both shows, particularly *The Wire*, include a diverse group of creators and were filmed in Baltimore, a majority African American city.[43] In the DVD extras for the fourth season of *The Wire* David Simon cited the lack of recognition *Homicide*, *The Corner*, and *The Wire* have received for the diversity of the cast and the stories:

> So in some ways I think Hollywood is utterly ill equipped to address the idea of these voices. It's not an accident that this show is made in Baltimore. It's not an accident that it's made by people outside the television industry.[44]

Chapter five describes the world of the African American television writer, the struggle to obtain work, the often-limited options these writers face, and struggles to create work that reflects their lives. Special attention is paid to one creator who worked his way up from actor to writer and producer but who moved out of Hollywood in order to produce the kind of work that he could not do within that system.

The Central Role of African American Writers

Television is a producer's medium. That seems to be a given. Much of the literature on the production of entertainment television focuses on the television producer as central to the creative process.[1] Producers work with studios and networks in selling an idea for a show. They are involved in hiring the cast, writers, and directors. The executive producer has the final say on much of the work involved in producing a show. At the same time nearly all producers begin as writers and most television producers continue to write, helping to maintain the theme for their show in the process. Writing for television is the primary training ground for almost all television producers. In entertainment television a person who starts as a staff writer usually moves up to co-producer, then to supervising producer, and finally to executive producer. The executive producer is often the creator of the show and has the final word, in coordination with the production studio and the network, on each episode. The television producers interviewed for this book between 1998 and 2005 were still actively writing for TV, and all but one got their start in the business as writers. Many writers want to become producers for both the monetary rewards and the influence producers have in the creative process. Social expectations can also play a part in advancing within the system of production. As one writer explained: "The longer you stay in the business, they [peers and supervisors] almost force you to keep moving up and doing new things."

Actor Tim Reid started writing television scripts partly because he could not find the kind of non-stereotypical roles he was interested in. He knew that creating "characters of substance" was possible. He had seen this done by, among others, Hugh Wilson, the creator and executive producer of *WKRP*. Reid recalled how Wilson was able to develop his character into a multidimensional part on *WKRP*. Wilson had promised Reid each of the characters, including Venus Flytrap, would have an episode in which they were featured. But, as the first season neared the end Venus Flytrap had not yet been featured. Reid asked why not, and Wilson told him: "I wrote it a month ago but they [the network and production company] won't let me do it." The episode, *Who Is Gordon Sims?* revealed that Reid's character had deserted the Army during the Vietnam War. Wilson told him, "Everybody's afraid of it."

According to Reid, to get the episode made, Wilson had to use his power as executive producer to give the network very few options to work with. Wilson made sure he had only one script, the *Sims* episode, ready to produce for the final show of the season. The network's reaction was: "Oh my God, not this again. And by the way we are going to get rid of Tim next season; he's not Black enough." They agreed to the episode but were so uncomfortable about potential controversy that they invited a United States military advisor to the script reading. The network also asked that the advisor sit among the audience at the show's taping. The network was nervous "because this was the first show in the history of television, by the way, that was going to attempt to do anything on Vietnam. Nobody, *Lou Grant,* none of them had done anything on Vietnam, *WKRP* at that time did." The network had nothing to worry about, as the show was more than a success, Reid said:

> The night that we taped the show Mary Tyler Moore and Grant Tinker [at that time the owners of the MTM, *WKRP*'s production company were in the audience .... And [Moore] came up to me after the show and she said "I've got to tell you, I don't know when I've been moved by a half hour sitcom like you did and I want to thank you."

Reid said once it aired not only did the episode receive excellent reviews, it also helped establish his character. In fact, Venus Flytrap became one of the most popular characters on *WKRP* the following season. Reid added that the episode led to his first acting award, given by the Marine Corps because the *Who Is Gordon Sims?* episode portrayed a veteran with such dignity.

The experience taught Reid about convictions and to trust a person like Hugh Wilson, with whom Reid went on to co-create *Frank's Place.* It also helped Reid realize "the importance of creating and writing scripts." He saw the power that a successful writer/producer can wield—power to manipulate the system enough to create shows that address important social issues.

I interviewed staff writers, writers/producers, and producers, some of whom owned their own production companies. Their stories present a variety of experiences in and responses to television work. These narratives reveal a system that often imposes limits on the type of work that Black writers are allowed to do and the images they are permitted to create simply because they are African American. This chapter explores the way African American writers sometime struggle to create work that reflects their life experiences and how Whites often deny Black understanding of White life. At the same time, it tells the stories of writers who love their jobs and are proud of their work.

Obtaining Work

A "spec script" is a sample used by a writer to get a first writing job and progress to more popular and/or higher-quality shows. In order to get work, a person writes sample scripts of programs currently running on television. Spec scripts rarely, if ever, get produced. Conversely, they are offered as evidence that the writer has a clear understanding of the formulas and characters used on successful shows. One writer explained: "That was my license to be able to write in the business. You have to be able to do the spec scripts." He recalled that when his friend and fellow stand-up comedian was being courted by a network to star in a situation comedy, the writer gave the comic his spec scripts of *Fresh Prince*, *Roc*, and *Home Improvement*. The scripts confirmed the comedian's faith in the writer. In return for accepting the role, the comic demanded that the network hire his friend as the show's writer.

The writers I interviewed said that their spec scripts are almost always based on White shows. One writer/producer explained:

> In getting an agent and writing scripts you never write a Black spec script as a Black writer. You really don't want to reaffirm that "see, told you that they only could write for a Black show." We are put upon to make sure our writing is racially ... mainstream.

The hiring process in Hollywood in the late 1990s had not changed much from what media scholar Joseph Turow found more than 15 years earlier. Turow relates the advice that a literary agent gave to Black writers: "Sit down and write a good script that doesn't have a single Black in the damn thing. Make it a totally non-color-oriented experience."[2] Yet, even when Black writers downplayed their race by writing White spec scripts it was often not enough. One writer told me what she believes agents and producers say to themselves when they receive spec scripts from Black writers: "Oh this is good, this *Drew Carey* spec is great. Oh, [she is] a Black writer, let's see [she will fit on a new primarily Black show]." The writer added, "Then, still, you are not put on a White show. We have to be way up there as far as writing to be put on a White show."

Writer Sharon Johnson was frustrated that no matter how good her spec scripts for White shows such as *Murphy Brown* and *Mad About You* were, she was still only interviewed for African American–oriented shows. She was determined to find work on a show that would allow her to fully exploit her creative talents. But her experience working on a Black-oriented show led Johnson to conclude that quality work meant a White show. She explained her dilemma: "I am going to work on [a spec script of] *Frasier*, nail it, for nothing, because I'm [still] only going to get these horribly written Black shows. It took me that long to do the spec because I felt why [bother]. The futility." Her agent told Johnson the *Frasier* spec was a great job. Yet his next calls notified her of interviews at *The Jamie Fox Show, Sister, Sister,* and *The Parent'Hood,* all Black-oriented shows.

Johnson asked her agent why she was only getting interviews for Black shows. Instead of addressing her question, Johnson said, her agent "just blew up and started just cursing me out [saying], 'You don't know anything. I know more than you. You don't know anything about this industry. You're one of my lowest-level clients. I don't make a lot of money off of you but you are the biggest pain in the neck.'" Johnson said she started crying, struggling to find an explanation for the way her work was treated. She concluded that what she had tried to deny was in fact true: race was a determining factor in her career. Johnson recalled telling herself "All the things you keep saying, it seems that the industry does this. He's confirming it. It's coming from his mouth, it's not some paranoid Black person, some disgruntled Black person. He is personifying, he is literally saying, 'All the things you suspected are going on.'"

Johnson's skepticism about her ability to move to a higher-quality show, given that she had only worked on Black-oriented programs, was well founded. Her comments equating "higher quality" with a "White show" echoed those of producer and former network executive Frank Dawson, when he described the difficulties African American writers must confront:

> So, as a writer you write that kind of stuff and you are trying to get a job on another show but what do you have to send around? You send around that material and they go, "That's a nice *Wayans Brothers* script." Is that going to get you a job on a *Cheers*? That's not going to get you that job. It's not, but that's what you've got to show.

The problem is that these writers might not ever get the chance to work on a show like *Frasier*. According to the 1998 report of the Writers Guild of America, there were no minorities among the 11 writers employed during *Frasier*'s 1997–1998 season.[3]

Many African American writers worry that if they start working on a Black-oriented show they will never be able to progress to other types of work. The 1998 Writers Guild of America study found that "opportunities for minority writers are largely limited to specific sectors and genres,"[4] The Writers Guild employment figures showed that minority writers were much more likely to be found on shows at Fox, WB, and the UPN networks, not ABC, NBC, or CBS. In addition, the programs they wrote for were sitcoms that overwhelmingly featured "minority themes and characters."[5] The 2005 WGA report found "pockets of promise" but overall the "marginal gains primarily have been the product of employment on minority-themed situation comedies."[6] The fact that writers are often limited to the comedy genre is important. Television comedy is more formulaic than drama. Comedy writing often focuses on simple jokes with little opportunity for character development. Television dramas are more likely to address contemporary social or political issues. Of course there have been many topical sitcoms over the years, with *All in the Family* and *Roc* being good examples, but they are the exception, not the rule.

Sharon Johnson found herself immersed in a system that failed to recognize what she had to offer as a writer. An Ivy League–educated woman, she had succeeded in breaking into the television business, to the extent that she could work on certain types of shows. She has been a staff writer for several years on a variety of programs including *The Sinbad Show, Buddies,* and *Goode Behavior*. Yet Johnson's recollection of her career illustrates how an African American worker can be stymied when the production system treats her as "other." Her career was stuck in a catch-22 situation: If Johnson wanted steady work writing for television, she had to be willing to write for the kinds of shows for which she doesn't want to write. When Johnson saw her agent sending her work only to producers of Black shows, and always situation comedies, she knew she was being "earmarked as a Black writer."[7] Given the current production system, this limited her to certain types of work.

Johnson's dilemma was grounded in her being perceived as simply a Black writer. She was concerned how this might affect her career. Though she expressed some interest in portraying Black life, she had other interests as well. Johnson wondered aloud: "If what I have worked on are shows that never came back, and I have periods of unemployment, and they are all the same kind of show, as in a Black show ... [agents and producers will say] 'Why should we read 45 pages of her script when we can make an assessment based on this one page of resume.'"

To avoid being mired in a system she saw as limiting her creative opportunities, Johnson said, she "had to point blank tell my agent 'send me everywhere.'" She understood her demand might be useless because her agent would send her where he thought she had the best chance of getting work: Black shows. She explained her feelings: "It's me realizing [agents are] not looking at me, Sharon Johnson, individually, what my particular style is, and my tone. They're just looking at 'where can we get this person a job?'" No matter their level of work experience, many of the people I interviewed mentioned problems with the way agents treat the work of African Americans. Even when an African American writer has both a fair amount of success and a good relationship with her agent, the system is not necessarily easy to navigate. For example, producer/writer Felicia D. Henderson mentioned that she too has been limited to working on primarily Black shows. At the time of the 1998 interview, Henderson's show, *Sister, Sister,* had been on the air more than five years, was one of the more successful situation comedies on television, and had recently entered the lucrative syndication market. Henderson said, one of the reasons that she maintains her current agent[8] is "because he is very brutally honest." She explained: "Certainly he has been told 'We don't need that voice' and [her agent's response is] 'what, the voice of a smart woman who has a bachelor's degree in psychobiology, an MBA in corporate finance, who is now working on a Master's in film, you don't need that voice?'"[9] Henderson went on: "It's very interesting, it's like the voice is the color of your skin. And it's very frustrating."

The Quality of Color: Is White Better than Black?

One of writer Sharon Johnson's primary concerns with being sent to only Black shows had to do with her perception that the industry has lower expectations for Black programs. Johnson said, "The degree of success that is expected of a Black show is not as high as what's expected of a White show on a major network." Therefore, in her view, the networks did not try to ensure these shows had the best writing, the best talent, or the best publicity. While not all respondents shared this concern, some did mention differences in the way the industry treats primarily Black and primarily White shows. For example, Leonard R. Garner described some of the situation comedies he directed: "I have worked on some Black shows that I haven't really enjoyed because I don't feel the level of humor is what it should be." He said he was lucky to have the advantage of starting on high-caliber shows, among them *The Rockford Files* and *Streets of San Francisco*. "[They were] doing a certain level of show when I got in there and that helped [in his career]."

Garner's experience working in various genres gave him a perspective from which to assess the value those in the industry placed on Black and White shows. "I have actually had a harder time. I have gotten more, probably, negative reviews [from people in the industry] working on more Black shows than I have some White shows." He saw differences in the way networks[10] deal with Black shows: the attention these shows received, the expectations of ratings, and the quality standards, were often different for Black shows. Among the advantages in being known as someone who primarily works on White shows, Garner felt that, in the eyes of decision-makers, experience working on White shows gave him the expertise to work in a greater variety of programs.

Respondents defined the problem of lowered expectations for primarily Black shows in a variety of ways. Some described the lack of clever dialogue in the scripts, while others mentioned that almost all the shows targeted to African Americans were family-oriented comedies. Networks, they said, often use these shows to fill in their schedules rather than treating them as potential Emmy-winning programming. To other respondents "lower expectations" meant the networks treated Black shows as if they could not be major hits. This last point is ironic because the most successful show of the 1980s was *The Cosby Show*, a program with an African American cast and producer. Though few respondents felt as strongly as Johnson about differences in expectations, many worried that expectations would limit the kind of work for which they would be hired.

Some of these writers remarked that it is almost always White-oriented shows that receive high ratings and Emmy nominations. They often used *Frasier* as an example of the kind of "quality" show that many writers would like to work for. One of the most popular situation comedies of the 1990s, it received numerous Emmys.[11] Although *Frasier* has no African Americans in its regular cast, many minority writers expressed a desire to write for the show. For example, former network and studio executive Frank Dawson mentioned the aspirations of the students in a minority writing program he teaches at USC:

> Most of the students come in and the first thing they want to know is "will I get an opportunity to write on a *Frasier* or a *Spin City* or a show that can get nominated for an Emmy?" And my answer to them usually is "not as your first job." The reality is that the first job you get writing in this business is in a Black show. That's where Black writers get the opportunity. Is there something wrong with that? Yeah. Is it the reality? Yes, it is.

James Anderson, Senior Vice President for Publicity at Carsey-Werner,[12] explained that writers are not the only television professionals to face these constraints. He mentioned friends who, because they've worked on programs that are "perceived as Black shows," don't get called to work on shows with predominantly White casts. Though there are some who have certainly created or worked on shows with a diverse cast, he said African Americans encounter a system where they are only allowed to work on "Black shows." Anderson said the view is that when White agents and producers are placing workers on Black-oriented shows they ask themselves, "Where is that list of Black directors, that list of Black writers?" Anderson described the response to African Americans who object to this system:

> People perceive that as "you don't want to work," which is not the case at all. You just want to have options and given the opportunity to be considered for many different kinds of projects.

He pointed out that many Whites don't understand the problem, failing to recognize the potential career limitations once someone becomes "known as the Black writer who only writes on Black shows." Anderson compared minority writers' objections to those of an actor who says, "I don't want to play the drunk five times in a row because I get just pigeonholed. Or I don't want to always just get picked to play comedies, I want to do dramas."

Anderson has worked for the same "progressive," or liberal company for over ten years. As he advanced to his current position at Carsey-Werner he worked on a number of shows that the company produced, some primarily Black and some White. Anderson's diverse experience has widened his understanding of problems such as the limitations many minority workers face. He is able to acknowledge both the minority perspective and understand the inability of many Whites to comprehend the problems African American workers sometimes confront.

The obstacles faced by minority workers are due in large part to the conservative nature of the television industry. Network executives are risk averse. Vida Spears, co-creator and executive producer of *Moesha* and someone who has worked in Hollywood for a number of years, explained why the television production system tends to repeat the same types of shows:

> It is very easy to do certain kinds of shows that have been on the air since the '60s or '70s. But to switch over and do a show that is a little more sophisticated is a harder sell. And I think it is not that they can't be done, or anyone has expectations that are lower or maybe people think no one will want to watch them .... I think they go for the easier [producing the same type of show as was done before].

A network executive with experience in both broadcast and cable programming discussed the problems for African American writers in relation to gender and age prejudices:

> I definitely see Black writers being funneled on black shows and not being considered fully on White shows .... It's a strange irony that Harvard educated White writers can wind up on *The Simpsons* and wind up on the most high prestige *Frasier, Seinfeld* kind of shows. The equivalent Black Harvard writer doesn't get funneled into those shows. They're working on the *Wayans Brothers*. They're working on *Sister, Sister*. Those are perfectly fine, they are more kid oriented .... And part of the problem [is an] expectation of who can write what.

She compared the problem to women not getting considered for action dramas and older writers not being hired to write for young, hip shows. Some of that represents a bias concerning the type of show a person is capable of writing for. "That discrimination is part of kind of a broader pattern .... Black writers have not been singled out. It's a system." She mentioned that during the 1998 television season a thiety-year-old female writer passed as a nineteen-year old in order to get a job on the teen-oriented show *Felicity*. She thought it was an example of how "the marketplace [deals with] age, race, and gender," that in Hollywood women and Blacks are qualified to work only on shows about people like themselves. She added, "White men are presumed to sort of be the neutral element who can do everything."

The executive echoed a point made by other writer/producers: most Black-oriented shows are aimed at children and adolescents. They are family shows, a genre that often limits the issues writers can address. In a system that funnels African American writers to Black shows, the majority of which are intended for pre-teens, it is no wonder many writers would rather work on White shows such as *Frasier*, one of the more adult-oriented situation comedies on television at the turn of the millennium.

Filling a Role—Generic Black Writer

Various factors may help explain why African Americans are steered to Black programs. One is the role that Black writers often play in the production process: filling a specific and limited need. For example, in discussing incidents of discrimination, one writer/producer not only cited the problem of funneling Black writers, but also explained how some of the system's needs are defined and filled:

> Basically the call goes out to your agent from a Black show and it says "They need some Black writers over at *Moesha*, they need some Black writers over at *Sister, Sister*." When they need writers at *Friends* they don't say "we need some White writers at *Friends*, we just need some writers."

What ends up happening is that some agents "don't even send or submit Black writers to any shows but black shows." As far as agents sending scripts by Black writers to White shows, she said, "In their mind that's just a waste of paper."

Why are Black writers almost always limited to Black-oriented shows? One writer, whose sole staff writing experience was as one of two African Americans on an otherwise all-White staff writing for a primarily Black show, had a caustic view of why the system needs Black writers on Black shows:

On a TV show they don't really want your input. They just want your body so if anybody walks in the room and looks around they see some Black bodies on this Black show. But they really don't want you to be there at all because you remind them that they don't know what the hell they are doing.

Artistic goals may also explain the funneling of African American writers to Black shows. A writer/producer described the creative advantages of having African American writers on a Black show:

A major flaw in network programming is they get a Black show and they put all White writers on it. They put a staff writer on it who is too intimidated to argue the sensibilities that are being put out for the show. And I think that is why you get a limited focal point. I think television ... does an injustice to the viewers.

He went on to illustrate the limitations of a creative process that excludes diversity:

It's just like I couldn't bring an all-Black staff to write a Jewish show. I could write a funny show, but it's going to get goofy at a certain point because I am losing the sensibility, the credibility of what the Jewish community expects from that particular show.

A related and even more practical explanation for calls for Black writers on primarily Black shows is the practice of using Black writers to explain Black life to White writers and producers, what one person called being a "Black dictionary." Director Leonard R. Garner described the experience:

That happens all the time. I feel that all African Americans are at any given time called upon to represent the race. That's the greatest burden we all share .... "How do you think people will react? Do you think this will offend somebody?" That happens a lot. "Do you think this would offend somebody?"

Garner touched on another major reason for hiring Blacks to work on Black shows: White producers and writers don't know enough about African Americans to understand what might be offensive. One writer told me that White producers ask these questions on a regular basis: "Every showrunner always goes 'Am I being out of line? Would a Black person say this?' or 'Do we need to be hip at this point?' And often times you don't want to be a Black dictionary."

One of the only times Sharon Johnson's agent suggested she interview for a writing job on a primarily White show, *The Single Guy* on NBC, he indicated they were looking for someone to help write the part of "an ethnic woman friend." The agent said the work "would kind of assist you in what you want to do," in other words getting a job on a primarily White show. While this was a goal of Johnson's, she was nevertheless offended. Her race seemed to be the main reason she was being sent on the interview. She felt that every potential job was somehow related to her being Black. In this case, Johnson met with a staffer for *The Single Guy* but the producers had already hired another Black woman.

Interviewees' responses to their role in explaining Black life and attitudes to Whites seemed to relate to how much power they had in the production system. Staff writers had the most complaints. A staff writer is at the lowest level of seniority in the writing hierarchy and usually has little impact on the overall direction of a show. A lack of power may have affected their view of their roles in the production. Being asked to explain Black life seemed to be one of the few reasons that Sharon Johnson was writing for *Goode Behavior*. Johnson explained: "In the room, I had to tell them 'I am not pitching anymore slang.' I had pitched them other things, [such as] structure and it's perceived as criticism. But as soon as they want "the Black way" to say something [it's] 'Sharon?'" Another staff writer described her role in the writing for one show: "What they kept trying to do was make us give them slang for the Black characters. That's all that we were really there for was to give them slang." Her experience echoed that of Vernon Winslow, the African American DJ refused on-air work by White radio owners in the 1950s, who ended up being hired to teach White DJs how to impersonate the hipness of the Black man.[13]

Leonard R. Garner said that being asked his opinion as an African American was a fact of life in Hollywood. Martin Jones, the General Manager of New Millennium Studios at the time of our interview in 1998, expressed similar resignation in describing the role that African Americans often play in the creative process:

> Initially you get sort of pissed off about it, but on the flip side you say [to yourself] "well, they are better asking me than somebody else, or not asking anybody at all." I guess we, especially in this business, whether we like it or not, we are guides, teachers.

Jones explained that Whites are usually interested in cursory information, not any real understanding of African American culture. He added these "pupils aren't necessarily that apt to want to get down and dirty and learn that much."

Vida Spears described how her views have changed concerning the practice of translating minority groups' cultures. Spears worked her way up in the production system as a writer on shows like *Family Matters* to co-creator and executive producer of *Moesha,* a show where almost all the writers were Black. She said she had dealt with Whites' questions concerning Black culture such as "What would you think?" and "How would you say this?" Since working on *Moesha* Spears said these kinds of questions were now a distant memory. She added that explaining different cultures is sometimes just a part of the cross-cultural production environment:

> It is sort of interesting because we have a Latino writer on the show and I find myself in certain instances [asking questions regarding Latino culture]. So now I do understand it to a certain extent, because I want to be sensitive. I don't want to put something in that is stereotypical and I can't say I completely know the Latino culture.

Spears acknowledged that the problem with requests to explain one's culture is that they are often communicated in offensive ways. Yet, her experience in trying to portray the vibrant diversity of minority life on *Moesha* has helped her to see positive aspects of the exchange: "Sometimes, if you give [information] to me, I can represent characters better."

Understanding the White World — Du Bois' Double Consciousness: Revisited

The frustrations resulting from not being allowed to write for White shows are exacerbated by the fact that Black writers, by nature of their education and work experience, have a deep understanding of White culture. These African American creators must understand the dominant culture in order to survive in it, yet they are given few outlets to express their perceptions. The people I interviewed said they are given little credit for their grasp of White culture.

One writer discussed the dilemma as she recalled trying to explain Black life to a White producer:

> It's so weird because all these years Whites have written for Black shows but we haven't written for White shows. But if anybody's been inundated with anybody's culture, that's all we knew growing up. You saw [White culture] in magazines, in television. We knew more about the White experience ... because we were seeing it. You couldn't see the Black experience because we

weren't seen anywhere. We knew because how else could a lot of us have gotten this far without [understanding White culture]. Yet, we're not allowed to write.

The writer pointed out the irony of the dilemma faced by African Americans in Hollywood:

If you were on a *Frasier* and say "I want to bring on this Black writer" they say "Why? What could a Black person do?" Because in some people's minds the only reason a Black person is around is to add flavor, to give that "What would a Black person say? I need something Black right here. OK that's where you come in."

Felicia D. Henderson also raised the issue of minority understanding of the White world when describing how limited some of the writing can be on primarily Black sitcoms:

For instance, some of the joke areas that are starting to really wear on my nerves that are distinctly Black show joke areas …. It's not the way that I want to write any longer. As a person who has grown up in White-dominated America, my experience is pretty White-dominated America.

A production environment hesitant to deal with issues involving race frustrated Henderson. The problem she sees is that some White people feel threatened by talking about race: "I want to talk about what it's like to have that double consciousness, to have to live in both worlds, in a humorous way, but it scares people." She felt that White people often avoid questions, such as why Black students tend to congregate together, because exploring these areas may raise issues that Whites are uncomfortable discussing. Henderson touches on a central aspect of American life—the reluctance, particularly among Whites, to openly discuss race. I have found that many African Americans are much more open to exploring racial issues, this research being a prime example.

Martin Jones related White failure to acknowledge the multiple perspectives held by African Americans to the life experiences of many Whites:

The thing I learned, inside of Hollywood, is that as enlightened as you would think these people are, they're very unenlightened. I mean [they] really have no experience with Black people whereas I [have] hundreds of acquaintances and friends in the business and not in the business who are White … In all honesty, I think White people are very isolated and insulated from people of color.

Jones tied the situation to life in Los Angeles:

> They [Whites] are living in a city where they are the minority, if not quickly becoming [one] …. For the most part [they] have no real clue, very afraid of the ghetto, and very afraid of the barrios, and very afraid of a lot of things.

When I interviewed one writer in 2004 in a Starbucks in a primarily African American middle-class area of Los Angeles he pointed to the environment and asked me, "How often you see this on television?" My answer was *Girlfriends*, a sitcom produced by African Americans.

Without a racially diverse group of neighbors, friends, or co-workers, many majority group members cannot begin to understand the life experiences of African Americans. Or even worse, they often view Blacks as having a very limited perspective. One writer described White people's surprise when he explains the concept of double consciousness:

> I have been in many situations where I have said that [the idea of having to understand the White world] to them and you see people that look at you like you would think you took their skull off and poured water on it. It's like "Wow, I never really thought about it."

One writer's sense of working in Hollywood summed up the sentiments of many of the people I interviewed:

> If White writers can write on Black shows why can't Black writers write on White shows? Why not? We are told a lot of times … that we don't have anything to bring into a White show. Well excuse me, we [work] in a White world and we go home to a Black world.

One of the few people I spoke with who had experience writing for a primarily White show, *Eve* executive producer Meg DeLoatch, recounted how she got a job on the Bette Midler show on CBS, *Bette*, in 2000:

> I've heard stories that Bette really wanted a Black woman. The way I got my job though was that I went out for another show, *The David Allen Grier Show*. And the show runners really wanted to hire me but ABC wanted them to hire a White man. So they were so disappointed that they gave my script to the showrunner of *Bette* and said, "You've got to read this one." And he loved my script. That's how I got my job.

DeLoatch recalled what it was like to work on a staff where all the other writers were White.

> I don't necessarily get to do that with a lot of the other shows I've worked. It was a good experience. I didn't feel isolated. You are definitely going to feel sometimes you are the "only." But with comedy sometimes it's coming from a common place. People speaking the same language that jokes come from. And sometimes if people don't intimately know your culture, your world, sometimes they don't get you. But then there are a lot of other things that are universal that you have in common.

She said that *Bette* was the only primarily White show on her resume. That was not unusual. Figures show that for the fall 1999 season, of the fifty-five African American writers employed, eighty-three percent worked on Black-themed shows.[14] Only one White-themed show, *The Practice*, employed more than one African American.

It's Not Black Enough

Ironically, while the production system often denies Black interpretations of White culture and bars African Americans from creating White images, some White producers apparently believe they have a great understanding of Black life. I heard a number of stories of White producers and writers telling Black creators that an African American character wasn't "Black enough" or that a theme was or was not "Black." Former network executive and producer Frank Dawson described the frustration of trying to pitch show ideas to the networks: "The projects [shows] my partner and I tend to develop are, 'Oh, it's really good, but it's not funny enough, it's not really a Black show. These aren't really Black characters.'" Dawson explained the dilemma:

> Because of the level of the sophistication in the material, it's like "These are not really Black characters so Black audiences won't like it and White people just won't be interested because it's a Black show." So it's a Black show but it's not a Black show? Black people won't think it's a Black show and White people will think it's a Black show.

These White network executives are the writer/producer's audience in the early stages of production. Their approval is required before anything goes into full production for eventual broadcast. According to Dawson, for any kind of success, producers often have to meet the demands of executives for more obvious or even stereotypical portrayals of Blacks. Felicia D. Henderson blamed the media for White executives' inability to understand Black creators: "For the most part the people making these decisions, what they know of black people is what they have seen on television."

People with the longest tenure in the business were most likely to recall being told by Whites that something was "not Black." For example, actor, writer, director, and producer Tim Reid described the reaction from agents and producers to some of his first scripts (work he did even before his acting on *WKRP*): "People would look at them and say, 'This is not quite Black enough... a White guy could play this.'"

Some of Reid's acting received the same discouraging reception as his scripts. He called auditioning in 1978 for the part of Venus Flytrap, the Black disc jockey on *WKRP*, "the strangest audition anybody had ever seen." Reid said he was chagrined by "what was written to be a very stereotypical, broad, buffoonish character." He told producers Hugh Wilson, Grant Tinker, and Jay Sandrich that he didn't really think he wanted the part. Wilson asked Reid how he saw the character. Reid replied that he knew Black DJs and they were not one-dimensional. He was interested in playing a character with "a human side ... some substance." Wilson agreed with Reid and promised that as the show progressed, Wilson would write scripts that would develop the character. Reid said some of the other producers had strong objections to his taking the part because he would not act like a stereotypical Black DJ. He recalled, "they sent a guy down from the network to teach me how to be more Black, to shuck and jive."

Vida Spears, whose experience in Hollywood goes back to working for Norman Lear when Lear was producing *The Jeffersons*, claimed that she rarely has to face these kinds of reactions from White people in her current work:

> Luckily I haven't heard too much of that lately. I used to hear it all the time. I would be amazed. "Could you make this more Black? That's not Black. Is this streetwise? Could we have a streetwise character here?" ....

Spears' point is important. This seems to be an issue that African Americans working in television in the 1970s and 1980s dealt with often. The people I spoke with who have entered the system after 1990 did not mention this problem. This may be due to the increased diversity of the workplace. Over the past fifteen years Whites have become more familiar with Blacks through work. Or it could be that Whites today are afraid to make these kinds of comments because of the reaction they might elicit.

Creating African American Images

"It's important to turn on the TV and go, 'that girl looks like me ....
And she's beautiful. The way she's shaped. The way she's wears her
hair. She's beautiful. She is worthy of love ....' Those things are really
important. And they're the unspoken things we do with these
programs." More often than ever before African Americans like *Eve*
showrunner Meg DeLoatch are creating African American–centered
programming. A number of writers and producers expressed pride in
producing programs that dealt with African American issues and
images.

While working on *Sister, Sister* in 1998, a program with a primarily pre-adolescent audience, writer/producer Felicia D. Henderson
had a specific commitment to creating images that carried a positive
message concerning African Americans, given the impact these images can have on young people. Henderson explained why she
wanted the college experience depicted on *Sister, Sister* to look a certain way:

> All universities are basically all-White, unless they are historically black.
> That we put four [African Americans] there; that is a little odd. In all my
> classes in college I was usually the only Black one there. At UCLA I was. But
> I put four Blacks in this [calculus class scene] because, my bigger concern
> becomes, I have to show otherBlack kids that there are Black kids in college,
> even if I am now distorting reality a little bit.

Henderson said she felt a responsibility to create these positive representations. She related her concern to the youthful audience that
Sister, Sister attracted:

> I am always thinking of Black kids first and then kids in general. That won't
> happen when I am writing adult shows. I'm like, you can either watch it or
> not. I know how it [media portrayals of African Americans] affects me
> because I also speak at schools all the time and I hear them tell me ... some
> of it breaks your heart and some of it inspires me. But in every word I write
> I am thinking about what I am saying to ten million people who watch
> every week.

Some *Sister, Sister* episodes overtly addressed issues of race. Henderson mentioned an upcoming episode (which had not yet aired at
the time of the interview) in which one of the sisters will "pass" for
White, thus providing an opportunity to deal with the issue of discrimination in the United States. She also mentioned an episode from

the 1997–1998 season in which one of the sisters, who was supposed to be studying for a history test, dreams about meeting famous figures from Black history. In describing the program Henderson discussed her creative goals:

> We did a Black history episode here last year that we tried to do in a way that ... wasn't preachy. Tamera basically was studying for an exam, getting stressed out about it and went to sleep and dreamt about meeting all these people.... I purposely used my will, forced my will upon the writer to say "Let's not do all the typical," we'll do a Martin Luther King and Harriet Tubman but we'll also do a C. J. Walker, who people don't know. Gee, the first female millionaire was a Black woman ....

She emphasized the importance not only of reminding audiences about important African Americans they may be somewhat familiar with, but also of using the show to broaden their knowledge.

Henderson explained how the show came to include rarely portrayed historical figures. She was able to use her position as supervising producer to prod the writer of that episode, another African American. Together, in an open and collaborative process they created a show that addressed issues not usually explored in a sitcom aimed at teenagers. This process, so successful in creating the episode of *Sister, Sister* illustrates the impact of involving a number of African Americans in production—a fresh view of African American life emerged.

Carsey-Werner executive James Anderson compared two programs Cosby and Carsey-Werner produced, *A Different World* and *The Cosby Show* simultaneously in the 1980s. He said they "were two different shows and had two different missions," as *A Different World* dealt more directly with societal issues. Anderson contended that *A Different World* avoided moralizing and instead encouraged audiences to think for themselves about the issues it raised. Media scholars including Michael Dyson and Sut Jhally have criticized *The Cosby Show*.[15] Media scholar Herman Gray commented that *The Cosby Show* "often failed to even comment on the economic and social disparities and constraints facing millions of African American outside the middle class."[16] Anderson knows that some complained that by concentrating on an upper-middle-class family *The Cosby Show* unrealistically portrayed Black life in America. But he thinks the criticism was unfair, arguing that there were Black families such as the Huxtables and that some didn't give Bill Cosby credit for the way *The Cosby Show* proved that such a show with these portrayals could be successful. He also pointed out that *A Different World*, with a timeslot directly after *The Cosby Show*, built upon that program's success. In television, scheduling is a key to a program's success. Bill Cosby was able to use the power of *The Cosby Show* to create a lead-in for *A Different World*, a show that Anderson believed explored the differences among African Americans from various "socio-economic backgrounds and ... different hues." It was the first diversified intraracial group of young Black adults on television

One network executive connected the greater variety of African American images on television to the numerical increase in minority characters and programs over the past thirty years. She explained:

> For many years, because there were so few African Americans portrayed on television, the actual image was really, really important because this was all people had. It had to sort of represent a broader spectrum. And for the broad group of Americans who might not have as much contact [with Blacks], they learned things from what was seen on television.

She has observed attitude change in the minority creators she deals with:

> I do think there is a younger generation that, yes, is concerned about images, but I think is a little bit more open to a broad range ... that each Black character doesn't have to represent Black people.

The executive used the example of *Any Day Now*, a Lifetime original program that ran on that cable network from 1998 to 2002. The series was centered on the Black–White female friendship of two childhood friends who reunite after a long estrangement. She said producers originally wanted to set the show in the early 1960s. The network rejected that idea and asked the producers to bring the relationship up-to-date and use flashbacks to the early 1960s. "We want the show to feel more provocative .... We try to do the race issues in the present because the issues are more gray, cloudier. It's more interesting if you can do "it's not right or wrong." The executive believes that portraying Black–White relationships at a somewhat complex level helps to create more interesting television. In its first season alone *Any Day Now* dealt with such racial issues as "passing" and reparations for African Americans. This helped push some of the boundaries of the typical show about female friendships.

Amanda Lotz's study of *Any Day Now* finds that one of the goals of the White creators of the show was to expand "social discussions about ethnic difference and racism."[17] Lotz recounts some of the dissatisfaction the producers had with Lifetime's promotion of the show, promotion that often ignored any mention of the show's "provocative stories about racism." Networks, even those on cable, seem to operate on the assumption that viewers will shy any from any discussion of race.

According to Felicia D. Henderson it can be difficult to incorporate issues of cultural identity into a television series that is perceived as having a Black viewpoint. She claimed *Moesha* was recognized in the industry as having a "distinctive African American perspective" and therefore increased scrutiny from network executives. Henderson described one script where Moesha was to visit Africa. UPN executives questioned if Moesha's family could afford the trip. Henderson wondered if writers on a White show would get the same treatment in sending a teenage character on a European trip. She contrasted this treatment to her work on *Sister, Sister:* "We don't get that here because it's a much safer show and because the perspective isn't African American, even though the characters are." That made addressing topics such as Black history easier on *Sister, Sister.*

Moesha starred the singer Brandy, who is popular among pre- and young adolescents. Henderson, who had been a staff writer on *Moesha,* spoke openly about the racial aspects of a show that depicted such African American–centered topics as the Harlem Renaissance. She mentioned the criticism the show received one season when the main character transferred from a mostly Black public high school to a primarily White private one. Vida Spears, one of the two creators and executive producers of *Moesha* was somewhat reluctant to tackle some of the issues that Henderson raised. Still, Spears did express her goal to create more realistic images:

> I do feel that responsibility, and I also feel really good when people come up to me and tell me how much they like the show and how happy they are to see a show without stereotypes. That we have a strong family, that the father is not buffoonish. It's a real family that they can relate to.

Spears claimed audience feedback showed that viewers appreciated how the show portrayed Moesha's father, a car salesman, achieving his dream of owning a car dealership.

Moesha's significance as a family show with realistic and positive Black images was highlighted during the fall 1998 Emmy awards special anniversary broadcast. One clip, part of a series highlighting important shows in television history that ran throughout the Emmy program, featured an African American viewer praising *Moesha* as one of the first television programs she could relate to. This viewer contrasted the program's portrayals with the stereotypical images of the television programs that she watched growing up in the 1950s.

Figure 5.1 Writer/producer Felicia D. Henderson. Creator and showrunner of *Soul Food*. (Courtesy of Felicia D. Henderson.)

With *Soul Food* Felicia D. Henderson had a unique opportunity for an African American writer/producer: the chance to help create and be the showrunning executive producer of an African American-centered drama. Henderson recounted that Jerry Offsay, President of Programming for Showtime Network, used to say the show was "ninety percent the same as other American shows, 10% different." To Henderson that ten percent meant creating work that rarely, if ever makes it to the television screen. She gave the example of an episode about a riot:

Seeing that riot from an inside perspective and trying to answer the question so many of my White friends asked me after the Rodney King riots: "Why are they burning down their own neighborhoods?" To try and answer that question from the perspective of the people as opposed to those on the outside looking in. To do stories like that but from that perspective was wonderful.

Henderson also used the opportunity to explore interpersonal relationships.

To show very healthy sexuality amongst Black people was very rewarding because you don't ever see it [on television]. And then you are also on cable so you can really go there. But to show Black people making love is huge. To show a family that is like most Black families that I know. Where you have everything from the very well-educated attorney to the guy who's done time.

Creating Images

Though producers and particularly writer/producers are central to what we see on the television screen, organizational structures are as important a factor as any in the creation of the television image. Negotiating through corporate, marketplace, and audience considerations is essential for any creator looking to get to the broad audience that television gives. The writers, producers, directors, and actors interviewed here described some of the barriers and opportunities in creating a fuller picture of African American life. Some recalled how they met resistance from networks or production studios when they tried to create images that portrayed the variety of Black experiences. For example, Felicia Henderson described working on an episode of *Moesha*, in which a school class traveled to Africa. Henderson said a network executive questioned: "'Well why, wouldn't they be going to Europe?' and 'Where is she [Moesha] getting the money for that?'" She said the executive person had no idea how racist these kinds of questions were. Henderson said that executives would not challenge a show about White people sending their children on a trip to Europe for the summer. "But this Black girl who is going to Africa, something is wrong with that," she said sarcastically.

Director Leonard R. Garner said that whenever an opportunity arose to add minor characters on *Just Shoot Me*, a primarily White show, often his first instinct was to use an African American. The problem he confronted was the producer's sensitivity to any racial aspects in the way the main characters treat people. Therefore, when Garner suggested that an African American play the part of a delivery person on one episode, the producer balked on the basis of political correctness. He did not want one of the main characters to hit an African American on the back of the head, as the script called for.

Director Oz Scott said he's worked with White producers who were interested in exploring racial differences. For example, in an episode of the ABC drama *The Practice* that he directed, an African American lawyer became embroiled in a dispute with an Asian American dry cleaner. There was no simple conclusion to the conflict, but each character learned a little about the other. Scott credited David Kelly, the executive producer of *The Practice*, for creating programming that sometimes explore cultural differences.

On the other hand, even as an executive in the 1980s, Frank Dawson faced difficulties when he tried to get his studio (Universal) to produce shows featuring African Americans. Dawson used the example of the genesis of the successful situation comedy *227*. When he was at Universal he went to see Marla Gibbs, then starring as a maid on *The Jeffersons*, in a play being performed in Los Angeles. Dawson thought the play's first act could form the basis of a situation comedy. According to Dawson, Universal was unwilling to pay Gibbs money comparable to what she was paid on *The Jeffersons*. The deal fell apart at Universal and *227* ended up being produced by Norman Lear's company. Dawson explained: "Clearly, when you talk about racism and the differences of dealing in the industry, we lost that show because [Universal] could not see paying a black woman that amount of money at that time."

A small but poignant example of what it can take to bring a more realistic minority character from the writer's page to the screen can be found in Daphane Maxwell Reid's story of a role she had on a 2004 episode of *Crossing Jordan*. A crime drama set in Boston, the show centers on a female medical examiner. The episode Maxwell Reid guest starred on, *Justice Delayed*, depicted an unsolved 1964 murder in the Deep South. Maxwell Reid played the widow of the murdered man. She recalled reading the script, "What impressed me was the dignity of the way they handled it." Maxwell Reid said the writer of the episode was an older White woman, "I think she was from Mississippi or Alabama. She was from the South but she was a rebel and she understood what was going on in her life and knew that there were two sides to that story." She added that the director was an African American woman. But Maxwell Reid brought her own ideas to the portrayal.

> The role called for a sixty-seven-year-old woman. I am fifty-six. And I try to look young, most of the time. But when I went to that audition I did not attempt to look like I was sixty-seven. I knew that I had a 33-year-old child. It was not a stretch to make it a forty-year-old child. It didn't make me decrepit. I didn't want to play an old Black woman. There was no need because sixty-seven is not old. And that image needed to be changed and thank goodness the director thought the same way I did. The people that I auditioned with went in with mammy looking long skirts and wigs. And I was going, "No, you never know what sixty-seven looks like and I don't have to propagate an image that is untrue and is stereotypical. And the director, who was a Black woman, said "I wanted also not to do something stereotypical." I was very proud of that.

Tim Reid: Actor/Writer/Director/Producer

This chapter began with the story of actor Tim Reid realizing the impact that a writer can have to create images that better reflect his world. "I began to understand that if I was going to be successful I was going to have to think more as a creative being and create opportunities for myself," recalled Reid. He was explaining how, as an actor, he started on a career path that led to writing, directing, and producing television and film. Tim Reid exemplifies a person who has dealt with the constraints and challenges imposed by the production system in order to create work that reflects the diversity and complexity of African American life. His work also illustrates media scholar James Ettema's finding that television programs are "the result of the complex organizational process in which the creative activity of the executive producer was activated and energized by problems or puzzles arising from the production routines and conflicts within the organization in which he labored."[18]

Though Reid is most recognized by television viewers as a star on *WKRP* and *Sister, Sister,* his most critically acclaimed work was as co-creator and co-executive producer of *Frank's Place.* The show ran for only twenty-two episodes during the 1987 season. Reid said in 1998 that he is amazed that people still discuss and study the show. He found this ironic in an industry with little institutional memory. "I can't remember what was on last year on most of the network stations, let alone ten or eleven years ago."

Reid remembered that the production of *Frank's Place* was a "very creative venture" that allowed him to explore characters and stories of "substance." His complaint was with the way the network handled the show. For instance, CBS did not seem to understand its audience. The network moved the program around its schedule, never letting it build any ratings. It then cancelled the show after only one year on the air. As an executive at CBS when *Frank's Place* was cancelled, explained that it was not unusual for a network to move a program around its schedule in the hope it would find an audience. She said the decision to cancel the show "had nothing to do with race" but then added that *Frank's Place* was not an easy fit for CBS, a network that "didn't have a big Black viewership."

A second issue for Reid was the way the industry labeled the show: "Some ignoramus, because he did not have the creative intelligence to see what we were doing, couldn't classify as a comedy or a drama …. He labeled these things dramadies." The executive who had been at CBS when the show was canceled explained that programs like *Frank's Place*, those that are produced "single camera, half-hour, and no laugh track," are rarely hits. She said a similar, critically acclaimed show produced around the same time, *Molly Dodd* lasted only a couple of years on NBC before moving to cable. She pointed out that the only program of that genre that succeeded was *The Wonder Years*. The success of that 1988–1993 show was due in many ways to baby boom nostalgia for the era that program depicted so expertly. Reid said the problem was that people have continued to associate him with the dramedy label. "It hurt my career because I became known as this guy who wants to do sort of these dramadies quality shows." He said that when he pitched the idea for his show, *Linc's*, to network television, "the first thing they say is 'we don't want any more of these dramadies, nobody watches them.'" When Reid sold the idea for *Linc's* to the Showtime cable network the first thing they said was "[we] know it's a dramadey but …," expressing their hesitancy to produce a show in a genre with a poor track record.[19]

Yet, Reid admitted that his track record for producing quality television has also benefited his career. He said the support of television critics has helped draw attention to his work. In a 1998 interview at his office at New Millennium Studios in Virginia Reid pointed out two large volumes of newspaper clippings—all reviews from the premiere week of *Linc's*. He said the program was the cover story on the television sections of 16 newspapers across the country including the *New York Times*. According to Reid the theme of many of the articles was "co-creator of *Frank's Place* takes another shot" at a television series:

> So the good news is … people are interested to see what I am coming up with …. One day those people and the audience are going to click on the same plane and I am going to have a major hit.

Reid tried to explain his methods for getting "quality" work to the airwaves. He said he tries to write scripts that are "rich in character and rich in potential." His problem is getting the quality writing on the air. Reid mentioned that *Linc's* was not the program that he and his co-creator, Susan Fales-Hill had envisioned because Showtime requested so many changes. Yet, because Reid and Fales-Hill wrote scripts with "layers and layers of story and character within one premise" he was able to make *Linc's* a "quality" show.

Reid accuses the newest generation of creators of lacking the skills to write complex characters, or to create shows that are more than a series of jokes. He said good writing "has become a lost art. People don't know how to layer enough character and story and the premises." Reid added that when writers fail to layer a script, "after the networks gets to it, what you are looking at is basically a sex joke."

Reid said that every now and then he thinks of resurrecting *Frank's Place*. He wrote some feature scripts based on the show that he said will probably never get made as a film. He has even considered doing *Frank's Place* as a stage play. Reid thought if cable had been the force ten years ago that it is today a channel like HBO or Showtime would have aired *Frank's Place*. Reid added that the lost potential of such a quality show is "something that just tears at you." When I interviewed Reid in 1998 he compared the cancellation of *Frank's Place* to the state of his latest television project, *Linc's*, a program he was awaiting word on from Showtime concerning its return for a second season.[20] "It will be a loss of what could be but I don't think it will strike me like the loss of *Frank's Place*," he said. Reid claimed that a cancellation of *Linc's* would be another lost opportunity to show the complexity of African American life. He explained:

> We have a problem in this country that nobody will really face and that is accepting the truth. And the truth of the matter is that the dominant culture, the people who have ruled the television and motion picture business for so long, doesn't have any interest in showing the multifaceted, politically diverse, non-myopic Black community ….

Reid said one reason network executives have no interest in depicting the complexity of African American life is that they believe the White audiences will not watch these shows. But Reid saw the popularity of the work of a playwright's such as August Wilson as evidence that there are White and Black audiences for this kind of work. That audience did get addressed, starting in 1993 *Homicide: Life on the Street* followed by *Oz* in 1997 and *The Wire* in 2002. But those programs were never hits, with *Homicide* perennially on the verge of cancellation during its seven seasons and *Oz* and *The Wire* gaining plaudits from the critics and a small and loyal cable audience.

Conclusion

It is not difficult for some African Americans to feel marginalized by a system that channels many of them towards specific types of programs: situation comedies with minority themes and characters. In some respects this is simply part of the industry's long-running practice of using talent with proven track records. Media scholars James Ettema and Joseph Turow have shown that reliance on people with a demonstrable record is an essential part of the Hollywood system.[21] Such experience often encompasses television genres. Writers and producers of comedies rarely work in drama and vice versa. A successful comedy or dramatic writer is given little incentive by production studios and networks to pursue different avenues, aside from the rare exceptions, such as that of Steven Bochco who was able to use the clout he gained from the success of the drama series *Hill Street Blues* to create the sitcom *Doogie Howser, M. D.* and the drama/musical hybrid *Cop Rock*.

For African Americans the industry's reliance on track records can result in the narrow label "minority writer" along with very limited job options. As Fredrick McKissack in *The Progressive* terms it, "Black people are often hired as writers just to make sure the jive is right."[22] This expectation seems to be so pervasive in the industry that one Black writer, Harvard-educated David Wyatt, said the joke is that some Black writers have to read the hip-hop magazine *Vibe* to "keep up on what's the latest slang."[23] Black writers confront a system where, because some Whites are uncomfortable in depicting Black life, they ask Black writers to supply street lingo, but never allow these writers to contribute work that portrays the complexity of African American life.

But the dilemma faced by African American creators is that if they do not fill this role then Whites will be the ones creating the images — Black life as slang and youth culture. Television writer David Wyatt expresses a view that some of the writers I interviewed also articulated:

> Other times you get White writers who actually do attempt to write slang or do attempt to re-create Black culture the way they think it is, but it's usually just a re-creation of what's been seen on television or a small aspect of it that you get from hip-hop culture.[24]

The positive aspects of the role that Black creators play in supplying information and therefore in depicting Black life need to be acknowledged. As the writers I talked with explained, if they were not involved, these shows would be even less realistic and more stereotypical. In fact, one of the primary justifications that African Americans offer for their involvement in production is to paint more realistic pictures of Black life. For example, producer/director Charles Dutton explained why he wanted more African Americans on the crew of the HBO mini-series *The Corner*: "Hey, we're making a movie about these Black people and *we're* the experts."[25]

Nevertheless, the Writers Guild of America sees a system of "typecasting," where minority writers are provided "with very few opportunities outside this genre."[26] For example, the 1998 Writers Guild Report found that during the 1997–1998 television season the three most popular shows, *Law & Order, Frasier,* and *Ally McBeal,* used no minority writers.[27] This is the same system that Joseph Turow found in his study of the television industry of the early 1990s: "Having paid their dues in that area and developed track records for writing about Blacks, the writers are then pigeonholed by artist-sponsors, talent agents, and production firm selectors."[28] As the 1990s progressed minority writers also found themselves limited to shows on certain networks. The 1998 Writers Guild report shows minority writers accounting for just three percent of the writing credits on ABC, CBS, and NBC. Being limited to work on the newer and less popular networks, Fox, WB, and UPN, can be especially troubling. By the end of the 1990s Fox, WB, and UPN, to one degree or another, shifted their focus away from serving a minority audience.[29] As a result of this cutback in Black-oriented programs, African American writers ended the decade with fewer opportunities for work. In a *New York Times* article profiling the state of television for Black writers and producers during the 2000 television season, *Moesha* producer Sara Finney claims, "When an African American show goes down ... there's no work."[30] In the middle of the last decade the dilemma intensified as UPN the one network that still targeted African American viewers joined with WB to form the CW. The industry professionals I spoke with saw this as setback for African American creators as UPN was a prime source of minority employment. A 2008 NAACP report on the entertainment industry confirmed those opinions, finding that the merger of the two networks decreased minority representation and employment.[31]

Enormous variety marks the responses of African American writers to an industry that limits their creative opportunities. For example, Sharon Johnson initially questioned her own abilities, until interactions with her agent helped Johnson realize that it was the system that was the problem. Applying Sandra Harding's feminist analysis of institutions suggests the value of seeing the Hollywood social order as "crazy," not Johnson. Harding contends, "Feminism teaches women (and men) to see male supremacy and the dominant forms of gender expectations and social relations as the bizarre beliefs and practices of a social order that is 'other to us.'"[32] Johnson began to understand how the social relations in Hollywood marginalize African American writers. Her realization afforded Johnson a standpoint from which to analyze how the television production system treats Blacks. In writing about this system for industry publications, Johnson began to share her views in the hope of changing the system.

Though cognizant of how their work was sometimes mistreated some writers took advantage of their opportunities to work on Black-oriented shows. Felicia D. Henderson looked to create images that might have a positive influence on the audience, knowing from her interactions with young people that television has an impact on how people think about race. Henderson, like media scholar Marcia Wallace, recognized that media images play a part in children's self-perceptions.[33] Similarly, other writers reported seeing television's influence on both the White people who control the industry and the young African Americans they interact with in their everyday life. Henderson worked with other writers on *Sister, Sister* to create stories that portray a more complete picture of African American life to their young audience. In a small way they were helping expand the ways television constructs society's image of African Americans.

The notion that Black-oriented shows are of lower quality than White shows, voiced by some of the people I interviewed, does not find much support in the scholarly literature. That may be because these African American–oriented shows, often shown on the newer networks, are a relatively new phenomenon. Only the recent books by Krystal Brent Zook and Donald Bogle begin to even touch on the subject.[34] Nevertheless, the perception that the industry treats most Black shows as having less merit was expressed by several of the interviewees, particularly those new to the industry, workers with little power. For the most part the greatest complaint was a lack of true creative opportunity. Staff writers who work on shows where they were treated as "others," whose exclusive role was to speak as the African American, are bound to get frustrated. Creators such as Felicia D. Henderson, who had the advantage of working in an environment where their co-workers were also interested in communicating diverse images, were less likely to let these barriers frustrate them. Writers at the executive producer level like Vida Spears and Tim Reid were more likely to talk about their role in creating shows. Their complaints concerning the treatment of their writing were mostly expressed in the past tense. Most of their current frustrations centered on their role as a producer, with responsibilities that included dealing with networks and selling show ideas.

What was most clear from these African American writers is that they must deal with situations that few White writers in Hollywood ever face. As one network executive said, White men are presumed to set the norm, to be able to do "everything." This means that anyone else is viewed and treated as "different." Too often in American society, "different" has been interpreted to mean "not as good." Their stories reveal that these writers have responded by creating images that reflect their own lives, writing scripts that show the variety of Black experiences, and even taking a stand in an attempt to change the system.

Being marked as "other" seemed to motivate Sharon Johnson and Meg DeLoatch to confront the way the industry treats African American writers. After her unsuccessful effort to push the Writers Guild to intercede on her behalf, Johnson began to take a stand on both a personal and public level. First she started to decline writing jobs that she felt would continue to limit her long-term career options. For example, she refused an offer to write for *The Parent'Hood*. Johnson also increased her efforts to find work on higher-quality programs. When interviewing for a position at a primarily Black television program she asked the producers about the possibility of writing for a White show that the company also produced. More and more Johnson seemed to see her situation through the prism of race. She compared her frustrations to the success of a White writer she knew:

> Another writer, who was no higher than I was on the learning step level, she got on *Friends* ... for a number of years, and now she's got a deal to develop her own shows. Is she a better writer than me necessarily? No. But something about her seemed more appropriate for *Friends* than something about me. Even though we are both from New York, are both the same age, both single, we both went to the same Ivy League school. So what is the deciding factor? It's race.

Johnson was also inspired to help publicize the plight of minority television workers. Her efforts have included writing articles focusing on race and television production for magazines and trade journals. One, in *Emmy* magazine, concerned color-blind casting. Another was an opinion piece on the situation of African American writers for *Written By*, the journal of the Writers Guild of America/West.[35] In each she quotes minority actors and writers describing both their progress and their frustrations in television production. In the *Emmy* article she calls for Black writers to candidly share their myriad experiences with the creative community:

> By not reducing ourselves to mere "paycheck players" and stepping forward as skilled writers with a long-term commitment to our craft. By bravely refusing to be coconspirators in our own degradation. By addressing any false representations and questionable practices firmly, intelligently, diplomatically, and publicly, if necessary. By becoming active and visible, and changing the face of industry organizations.[36]

Johnson also became Chair of the Committee of Black Writers at the Writers Guild of America, West. In this position she hosted a forum in 1999, *Where Do We Go from Here? Black Writers in the New Millennium.*[37] The roundtable discussion focused on the state of Black writers in the entertainment industry. Johnson's efforts have assisted the Writers Guild as it tries to increase diversity in the television workplace.[38]

Meg DeLoatch was motivated to get involved with the African American Writers, a group that researched minority employment figures and published the results in a full-page ad in *Daily Variety* and *The Hollywood Reporter*. These efforts helped increase the pressure on the studios and network and played a part in the diversity initiatives signed by the networks early in 2000.

The door to the writers' room was pried open in 2002 as Amaani Lyle, a writers' assistant on *Friends*, sued Warner Brothers Television Productions for sexual harassment. Lyle claimed she was discriminated against on the basis of race and gender because she was exposed to lewd and bigoted jokes during the writing process. The case made headlines in the trades and fodder on the opinion page of the *Los Angeles Times*.[39] One executive told me that people in the industry showed great interest in the case. Many were afraid that if the court found for the plaintiff, writers, producers, and executives would not know how to deal with the common interactions of the writers' room.

The industry let out a collective sigh of relief in April 2006 as the California Supreme Court overturned a lower court ruling and found in favor of Warner Brothers. The decision sheds light on how the court interpreted the unique nature of the television workplace. Although Lyle admitted that she had been told during the interview for the job that the "the humor could get a little lowbrow in the writers' room," she said the warning severely underestimated the reality of the workplace.[40] Lyle described the *Friends'* writers' room like "like being in a junior high locker room."[41] Words like "cunt" and "bitches" were common, although Lyle never claimed they were directed at her.

The Court's decision emphasized the creative aspects of the television workplace. It cited the *Friends'* writers' room as a place that "focused on generating scripts for an adult-oriented comedy show featuring sexual themes." As such, "these types of sexual discussions and jokes (especially those relating to the writers' personal experiences) did in fact provide material for actual scripts."[42] In a concurring opinion Justice Ming W. Chin reiterated that the First Amendment protects creativity, "Lawsuits like this one, directed at restricting the creative process in a workplace *whose very business is speech related*, present a clear and present danger to fundamental free speech rights."[43]

In legal briefs supporting Warner Brothers Television as the plaintiff, both Steven Bochco and Norman Lear stressed the importance of a work environment where writers are free to say whatever they wished. Lear, the person responsible more than any other single individual for bringing relevant social issues to entertainment television, explained the relationship between the television workplace and what the audience eventually saw on *All in the Family*: "There were things we said we would never print. That's true of racism or any touchy subject. That's what it takes to make a great show: smart people sitting in a room, going wherever they want."[44] Lear found it impossible to imagine "how writers, directors, and actors could work together if they had to worry about doing only what was 'creatively necessary' in order not to offend a worker on the set."[45] The Court's decision cited Bochco for pointing out both the danger of lawsuits such as Lyles, and the drawbacks to even talking about what goes on in the writers' room where a "certain level of intimacy is required to do the work at its best, and so there is an implicit contract among the writers: what is said in the room, stays in the room."[46]

So what is the answer for women and minorities working in this environment? One is for the industry to encourage mentoring. The people I interviewed who were most successful navigating the often-hostile domain of the writers room were those who had mentors they could go to for advice and guidance. Most of those who had no support system eventually left the television business. Networks and studios should structure mentoring and networking programs that help women and minority writers prepare for and cope with a creative environment where jokes and comments may mark them as "other."

Today more African Americans are writing and producing television programs. There are many reasons for this trend: workers building on the legacies of those who came before; the increased interest in minority-themed programming to attract underserved audiences; and pressure from advocacy groups. These factors have combined to create a growing creative atmosphere in television where diversity is more evident both in front of and behind the camera.

The following chapter explores three writer/producers working in the mainstream Hollywood television system. These women have created work reflective of their cultural identity, two cases in sitcoms, and one in hour-long drama. Their experiences show that in the first decade of the twenty-first century there are spaces where, through networking, talent and the use of the storytelling conventions these African American women have produced successful shows.

CHAPTER SIX

Three Showrunners

The opening credits on a television show often list producer, supervising producer, and executive producer, some of these with "Co-" in front and sometimes multiples of each title. The one title not listed is the most important: showrunner. That person is the executive producer responsible for overseeing all aspects of a show. The showrunner is often, but not always, a writer/producer and often, but not always the creator of the show.[1] He/she supervises the writers, the other producers, casting, and hiring. The showrunner also deals with the demands of the network, production studio, and actors. Their responsibilities and power mean the show is more their vision than any other single person involved in production. For most of television history no showrunners were African American. That's changed over the last twenty years as Blacks have created and run sitcoms and in a just a couple of cases one-hour dramas. One result of the increase in African American showrunners is that viewers now have a greater chance to view programs that begin to reflect minority life experiences. The stories of three African American showrunners and their successful television shows illustrate the unique issues minority creators sometimes face, how they are able to create programming that reflects their lives and interests, and as a result produce television programs that help to show the variety of African American life.

African American Drama — *Soul Food* on Showtime

After working on *Moesha* and *Sister, Sister* Felicia Henderson was interested in writing drama. She did not want to abandon situation comedies but she was interested in exploring more serious issues, work that she could not do in the limited confines of the sitcom, especially those of African American sitcoms. In 1999 Henderson wrote a script for a film drama and gave it to Rose Catherine Pinkney to get her opinion. Pinkney was Vice President of Comedy Development at Paramount. Henderson was not looking for any kind of professional connection, she simply wanted feedback from a good friend and industry professional. But Pinkney was so impressed with Henderson's script that she gave it to a colleague in drama at Paramount, telling him, "I know you think she is a comedy writer but she can absolutely do drama." Pinkney knew that the producers working to bring *Soul Food* to television were looking to involve Black writers, but she also knew that few executives were "going to look outside the box, at somebody who had primarily worked on comedies."

Hollywood's habit of encouraging creators to continue writing and producing the same kinds of shows was familiar to Henderson. She was looking for a new direction after working on the family-themed sitcom *Sister, Sister*. "People in Hollywood, no matter who you are, they want you to keep doing what you've done. So I had a hard time [making a] transition to anything else." After leaving *Sister, Sister* and not getting the kind of creative work she was interested in Henderson decided to return to school to get her MFA at UCLA. She wanted to study directing and hone her writing skills. Henderson recalled that she had been "telling stories in twenty-two minutes for six years." The UCLA film program allowed her to write a screenplay for a film, creating a three-act feature structure. In addition to getting advice and constructive criticism on the script from the faculty at UCLA Henderson was interested in getting feedback from a studio executive. She gave her dramatic film script to Pinkney as a friend, never expecting that she would show it to anyone else. Henderson's first reaction when Pinkney told her that she had shown it to others: "I was ballistic. I said, "You've done what? It's not ready! And I gave it to you as a friend who knows my writing to see how you thought how good I was at this and to get your notes." As soon as Pinkney told her that the people looking to develop *Soul Food* loved it Henderson took a 180-degree turn. She laughed recalling how she told Pinkney "Oh, you're the best friend I've ever had." A friendship had opened the door to the most important opportunity of Henderson's career.

Henderson then met with the production company Edmonds Entertainment and Paramount. She said she told the executives "Here's what I think the series is. They were, "That's exactly what it is, let's go to Showtime." And Showtime said, "That's exactly what it is, go write." So the deal was made very quickly. Henderson says this was one of those "right place — right time" occurrences, but it is more than that. The fact was an African American writer and producer with a successful track record in television sitcoms could turn to an African American studio executive for her opinion on her script. Moreover, that executive could use her contacts to open doors that could lead to the creation of one of the most successful African American–centered dramas in television history. Henderson's experience in getting the opportunity to produce *Soul Food* is evidence of how contacts, networking, and friendships can lead to opportunities for African Americans in Hollywood.

Although Henderson had experience as a producer, she had never been a showrunner on an hour-long drama. As a result, the production company brought in a veteran drama showrunner, Kevin Arkadie, to run the show during its first season. Henderson said that not being technically "in charge" was difficult. Nonetheless, she added, "It was still my vision." Arkadie is African American so the reservations about Henderson's ability to run the show should not be seen as an issue of race. In fact, as with most things in television it can be looked at as an issue of money. Producing a television show involves the investment of millions of dollars and studios can be reluctant to turn that responsibility over to someone without the relevant experience. One example of that can be found in the production of one of the most successful television franchises of the new century: *CSI*. The brainchild of Anthony Zuiker, the tremendous hit *CSI* spawned *CSI: Miami* and *CSI: New York*. But Zuiker was a newcomer to network television production. He needed to gain experience before the studio and network would sign-off on his running a show. So it was on the third series, *CSI: New York* where Zuiker finally got the opportunity to be a showrunner.[2] In Henderson's case it took only one season for the "Co-" to be dropped from executive producer. She was fully in charge of *Soul Food* in its second year.

Henderson's initial production challenge was Paramount's decision to film in Canada. One of the most significant developments in film and television production over the last ten years, Canadian production can cut production costs by ten to fifteen percent or more through tax incentives and rebates for hiring Canadian workers. According to Henderson Paramount originally planned to film the show in Los Angeles; the show was already in pre-production when it was decided to film in Canada to save money. For Henderson, someone committed to having a diverse workplace, this presented a challenge:

> Shooting in Toronto, if there was a disappointment, it was that I had this dream in my head of all of the Black people I was going to be able to hire when I thought I was shooting here [in the U.S.]. And then I was sent there. And suddenly everyone was White. And I was struggling with the line producer saying, "There are no African Canadians. Please help me." And he really tried. We were bringing people and none of them were well trained because nobody made that request before in Toronto.

Henderson said, "The hardest lesson I learned from that was no one had asked that question before." (The question being: Why aren't there more Blacks on the crew?) So in a time when more television and film work is made in Canada, Henderson found that producers had not made hiring a diverse crew a priority. This did not stop Henderson from trying:

> So as much as I wanted to have a diverse crew, as much as I wanted people who looked like me, they weren't ready and nobody had trained them to be ready. And so they weren't at the same level because no one had made that request before. And so there you were, seeing them fall by the wayside because they couldn't do it. And you have to go back to the experts, which is what you were hoping you were doing but it didn't look like me.

Even with this problem Henderson said she still hired more minority directors than any other drama showrunner. She citied hiring experienced directors like Oz Scott and LeVar Burton as well as people who were getting their first break directing an hour-long drama. One person I spoke to referred to Henderson as the "Spike Lee of television" for hiring so many people of color behind the camera. Even though she was proud of her efforts, especially in hiring minority directors, Henderson was disappointed she could not have done more: "everyday crew, that's where your heart is kind of broken."

With *Soul Food* Henderson was able to explore issues such as sexuality, social ills, and family dynamics. Henderson explained that part of her passion for the show was the fact that it was about a large family: "That's my family. That's most families I know." One of her goals was to "show all that exists in one family," the good and the bad. Henderson remarked that people sometimes are surprised to hear about problems of some of her relatives because Henderson herself is "so accomplished":

That has noting to do with me. It has nothing to do with their life choices and it has to do with the way the system sees and treats a Black man than it does a Black woman. So there are more opportunities for him to get in trouble that have nothing to do with him.

Henderson was able to portray a family that included among others, a successful lawyer, an ex-convict, and a father trying to run a small business. She was also able "to normalize higher education among African Americans." One of the show's central characters, Teri Joseph, is a successful lawyer. Having a show where week after week an African American woman can be seen as smart and accomplished within a family of multi-dimensional characters allowed Henderson and the show's writers to normalize middle-class Black success. Henderson wanted to portray intelligent and hard working African Americans as common in the American society, not as what she called "a crazy anomaly."

Henderson told me of her dedication to the show, stating that each of the characters on the *Soul Food*, "all the way down to little Ahmad [the boy who narrates each episode] was a part of me." She tied her success in portraying her vision to the support from the production company, Edmonds Entertainment/State Street and Showtime. "Support meaning they just stayed away and let me do [what I wanted to do]. That's support as well. They believed that I knew what I was doing. And the audience was watching so it must be OK."

Henderson's story of getting the show off the ground and then overseeing its successful run gives some idea of what is involved in being an executive producer. One of her goals for the show was to give it the look and feel of a high-quality production, something not always easy on cable. Henderson insisted that the show be shot on 35-mm film giving a look reminiscent of shows like *LA Law* and *The Practice*. This is evident in the establishing and transition shots of the show's Chicago locale. The visual style lends the show a look that says broadcast network quality, not run-of-the-mill cable. But Henderson constantly struggled with the limited budgets inevitable in producing for cable. She said she never had enough money to produce the show the way she envisioned. For example, Henderson did not always have the money to acquire the music release rights to use a song on the show. But she did not let that stop her, "I made some deal, or begged enough to some record company. That was huge."

Part of *Soul Food*'s success can be credited to the fact that people working on the show knew they were creating an African American drama. Early on, Henderson said, everyone, from the production assistants on up the ladder, people knew they were doing something special: "We knew what we are doing hadn't been done before. And it was palatable, in the air. Everybody was on the same page about why we had to work so hard. Why there was no room for error, if you will. Why you couldn't slack off." Once *Soul Food* was established and became a hit Henderson saw the show fitting the pattern of many successful shows: the power struggles and actors and actresses who now see themselves as stars who can "call the shots." She said that by the fourth season it wasn't as much fun, one reason Henderson decided not to return for the show's fifth and final season.[3]

Henderson can be credited for hiring many African Americans while producing *Soul Food*, getting them into unions, giving them experience directing one-hour shows, or writing drama. In the summer of 2004 she expressed her frustration that this success had yet to lead to a great amount of work on other shows for these individuals. "We did this really groundbreaking historic show that was also very successful and a ratings hit for the network. The top ratings hit for the network. Yet it hasn't been sort of a tent pole for all of our careers the way those shows, that kind of success usually is. Where almost the entire writing staff is offered deals around town and everybody's hot. That did not happen for us." For Henderson, seeing writers that you hire go on to other shows would have meant *Soul Food* was even more of a success. Henderson did not include herself on this list. She told me that she turned down work because she wanted some time off.

As far as monetary success, Henderson had reason for complaint. When *Soul Food* went into syndication in 2004, Paramount, as a part of the Viacom conglomerate, sold the syndication rights for the show to BET. This hindered the chances of Henderson's making any money off of what for most producers is the most lucrative part of their work: syndication deals. The trend toward vertical integration in media benefits giant media conglomerates but not the individual producers in the creative end of the business.

Henderson tied both the success of *Soul Food* and the pride she takes in the show to the audience:

> What that show did for the audience ... how people still come up to me and say, once they know who I am, "Can't you do anything to bring it back?" That obsession. Some people cry and say, "Thank you so much for showing me my life for real on TV for the first time." I had a woman come and cry

when I was sitting on a panel ... it was so moving. "To thank you for the first time. Our lives are not just sitcoms. We're only represented in sitcoms."

For most of its history television dramas included either no African Americans, a few people of color peppered throughout a cast, or one African American to represent all. Henderson's goal with *Soul Food* was to have Blacks portrayed "as full human beings." She added, "The audience was really taken in and that is a beautiful thing."[4]

Meg DeLoatch — A Romantic Comedy

For a writer, to write something and then see it a couple of weeks later on screen is always amazing. Meg DeLoatch gets to see her version of a modern day romantic comedy each week on *Eve*. But it is her vision filtered through the process of television production with its network notes, studio feedback, and relations and input from cast and co-workers.

Eve began as DeLoatch's project in the Cosby writing program at USC. She used her love of romantic comedies to write a sitcom pilot she called *Together*. DeLoatch pitched it to the production company, which apparently loved it. She then took it to UPN. Aware the network was interested in moving beyond its role as network targeted primarily to African Americans, she said she wrote the script "color blind." "In my mind because I knew UPN was supposedly opening up, race wise I thought, I bet they will go with someone White." It was ironic that the production ended up casting the African American rap star Eve as the lead. Delaotch recounted her initial phone conversation with Eve after finding that she might star in the show:

> I [told her] I am a Black woman, don't worry I can totally slant this character so that she has more the feel of a Black woman. She [said], "I thought you wrote it for a Black woman. I love it." Which really thrilled me. That I didn't have to sort of Blacken up my script.

Conceptions of race can be much more complex than what we are so often quick to read into them. In writing a "color-blind" script DeLoatch thought that readers of that script would see the main character as White. She expected that Eve "was going to read it and think that the language of Shelly didn't fit her voice." Yet Eve saw her as Black, evidence that we can often overlook that much of our constructions are of common sets of traits rather than differences.

DeLoatch said that Eve has brought her own experience and style to the title role, making the character her own without any need for slang or street language. DeLoatch said that she and the writers "only use incorrect grammar for emphasis, usually to punch a joke. If you are going to hear an 'uhs' or a double negative it's because we are trying to be funny with it." Her concept is to have a show whose characters are educated and articulate. She used the example of the character Nick:

> Depending upon who's viewing it, some people feel like he might be more of a stereotypical Black man. I tend to disagree. He's an educated Black man who is only 26–27 years old who is having a good time and is "into" women. But he has no interest in a commitment. But I want him to speak well. He works for the IRS, wears a suit to work, and I don't think he should sound like one of the [guys] out on the corner. He needs to sound intelligent. And that's important. But at the same time it's a comedy. It's an accessible show. We want to be relaxed. We don't have a problem speaking slang in it. But when the time comes for the characters to be in a professional situation we absolutely want them to sound intelligent.

Figure 6.1 *Eve* creator and showrunner Meg DeLoatch (second from left) flanked by stars Ali Landry (left), Eve, and Natalie Desselle. (Courtesy of Meg DeLoatch.)

In what can be seen as a type of color-blind casting, DeLoatch ended up changing some of the characters on the show from Black to White. She originally wrote Rita as "a bitter Black woman," but when the actress Ali Landry did such a great "read" for the part DeLoatch said, "I guess Rita is a White woman now." DeLoatch said UPN wanted an integrated comedy. She was glad to supply it because she knew that a romantic comedy with a multiracial cast was missing from mainstream television. DeLoatch pointed out that *Friends,* although it was set in New York City, was not an integrated show until the producers added a Black character near the end of that show's run. She added:

> What I really like about [*Eve*] is that I believe these people are friends. The there's no reason why you can't do it and buy that there are Black people and White people that are genuinely friends. Especially in the generation that is coming into being now. That's just more fluid race-wise. And that's the way it should be.

While stressing that *Eve* is a comedy that does not deal with "heavy" issues, DeLoatch still said she believes with a show like hers, "you can take anything and you can bring comedy to it in a respectful way." An example is how in one episode she and the writers used the issue of some Black women's resentment of White women dating African Americans. On the episode Eve breaks up with boyfriend JT Hunter. Word gets around through a series of telephone calls, including a call where a gay man shows interest. The sequence ends with a White woman running into Eve's fashion store:

> And the last beat of it is, a blond woman comes busting in to Diva Style [Eve's fashion store], where Shelly, Rita, and Janey are, and she says, "O my god have you heard? JT Hunter is single and he is looking for a White girl!" And then she realizes, oh my god I am talking to these Black women. And Alie's character Rita screams to her "Run." And Janey and Shelly pretend like they are going to chase her and they laugh.

DeLoatch explained that this was a lighthearted way to deal with the fact, "OK we know that we have some issues going on within our culture. We know that Black women feel that White women take away their men. Yet not all of us are angry about it."

In bringing *Eve* to the small screen, DeLoatch helped create what she called "the most diverse writing staff that I've ever been on." She stressed that all writers brought their own experience; her job was to help bring those experiences to the camera. In order to do that she encouraged open discussions in the writers' room on items ranging from the typical sitcom jokes to how and when to bring issues of cultural difference to the show. A small item such as a writers' discussion of food where someone says, "I've never had that before," might be incorporated into the show. But romantic relationships are central to *Eve*. When the writers discuss if and when they are going to bring cultural difference into a relationship DeLoatch looks to "find another way to come at it" rather than just Black–White.

DeLoatch told me that the writers had several discussions of what type of person Eve should end up dating on the show once she has broken up with JT. Although an interracial relationship had been pitched at number of story meetings, her feeling was "it's been done." She said:

> There's nothing special about doing this interracial thing. Its sort of all been explored. It's certainly been done on all the UPN shows. That to me is not the interesting thing to do. Now we have to find something new. Whether, not being a race thing. At one point we toyed with the idea of him being physically handicapped. It could be that he's just kind of a computer geek. The kind of man that you'd never see with this woman, who you think is so cool, and [looks beautiful]. We are a comedy, we haven't had to really deal with any heavy issues per se, other than romantic ones.

In handling the responsibility of being a showrunner DeLoatch said she not only looked to the modeling behavior of someone like African American Yvette Lee Bowser, but was able to turn to her old boss when she was a writer on *Family Matters*, the White male, David Duclon. "It was a really cool thing when I've got my own show, to turn to one of my mentors and say, hey, I would really like you here by my side to sort of guide me through show running. And he took the job. And it was sort of a wonderful opportunity for the both of us, for him to sort of see the mentoring all the way through." DeLoatch also hired one of her friends and former colleague, Michael Ajakwe. Ajakwe recalled that he and DeLoatch had made a pact years earlier that whoever became a showrunner would hire the other. He said their friendship helps make for a stronger yet relaxed working relationship on the show. This was something I observed in the pre-production and taping of an episode of *Eve* in 2004. Ajakwe had written that episode. In watching the run-through, DeLoatch and Ajakwe listened closely to what was working and what they saw could be improved, adding an old-style African American term, "boo-boo the fool," to one of the exchanges between the three female characters.

DeLoatch is well aware of the limitations of the sitcom genre, always having to look to the joke, sometimes sacrificing moments or ideas because the goal is to make people laugh. She also admitted how hard it is to produce her vision of a modern day romantic comedy, a show that reflected her cultural identity:

You get your own show and you realize how many compromises are involved. You never necessarily get 100 percent where you get to bring your vision to the masses. But in general it has been a really positive experience. I am really proud of the show. You could say it's a Black answer to a show like *Friends*, but it has its own sort of tempo and speed to it.

Girlfriends — Eight Seasons Sitcom

"It is not often that you get adult, mature, sophisticated Black women on television in an ensemble. So what are you going to do with it?" Mara Brock Akil is an African American woman whose success is unprecedented in television history. She has created and run a situation comedy for eight seasons. *Girlfriends* is more than a successful sitcom, it is a show about four African American women, their problems, successes, and most of all their friendship. Each episode first shoots for the laughs. Sometimes that is all the writers go for. But *Girlfriends* also reflects Black female life. Akil based these women on her life experience: "It is certainly people I know. It is a lot of me in there: the single me; the trying to figure my life out me. There are a lot of Black women that are close to me that are in this series." The story of how *Girlfriends* came to be and the way that Akil has been able to address issues important to her and to African American women, exemplifies how the television industry may finally be breaking free of the cycle of progress where there is a period with an increase in the number of African American images and creators followed by a retreat to the status quo of a few Black shows.

Akil did not use the term "responsibility" in describing how she has used the show to explore women's health issues. She simply said that it is "important to me to do issues that are important to Black women." In *Girlfriends'* first season she addressed fibroids, which are "benign tumors found in smooth muscle tissue, including the uterus." Black women are three to nine times more likely to develop fibroids than White women, and fibroids in Black women tend to be larger and grow more quickly, according to a study supported in part by the Agency for Health Care Policy and Research.[5] Akil tied the issue to her own life and relationships:

At the time that I did this I think every single one of my girlfriends had fibroids, some worse than others. Some actually threatening their reproductive capabilities. So that scared me so I wanted to do something about it, just to bring some attention.

Akil explained that health issues that get attention in the media, even on a fictional show, might get more research dollars "in the real world."

Figure 6.2 Writer/producer Mara Brock Akil. She is the creator and showrunner of *Girlfriends* and *The Game*. (Courtesy of Mara Brock Akil.)

While contending that she did not want to do a "disease every year," Akil said that as the show's third season approached she considered addressing sickle cell anemia, another condition more prevalent among African Americans than Whites. But she also read that HIV/AIDS was making a resurgence, particularly among African American heterosexual women. While debating which health concern to address, a memo from Viacom, the parent company of both Paramount and UPN, crossed her desk. Viacom and the Kaiser Family Foundation were teaming up on public service announcements, billboards, AIDS-related themes woven into Viacom-produced entertainment series in a media campaign to eradicate ignorance about

HIV/AIDS.[6] Akil explained, "And the business woman in me said, here is an opportunity to not only take advantage of it but to actually exploit it in a really good way for us." She said the studio and the network gave her full support in her four-episode story-arch on this major health issue. Akil said she was able to "do it my way ... and push the envelope" for a sitcom, giving the example of having "a woman cut herself with a knife" in one of the episodes. Akil and her staff approached the topic of HIV/AIDS both directly and creatively. One character contracted AIDS from unprotected sex with an in-denial gay boyfriend. One of the main characters, Lynn, made a documentary about women living with HIV/AIDS. The latter theme played on the fact that for the length of *Girlfriends'* six seasons Lynn had bounced from one career to another, never finding something to do for the longterm. Even with her inability to make a commitment to a career Lynn managed to create a touching documentary about these women. In the final scene of the four-story arch the show moves from Lynn's fictional documentary to images of real women living with HIV/AIDS. It was a rare moment for a sitcom and was due not only to the efforts of Viacom and the Kaiser Family Foundation but to Akil, who used her years of experience in entertainment television to take advantage of that creative opportunity.[7]

Learning the System— Taking Advantage of Opportunities

Mara Brock Akil's background working her way through the system, gaining valuable mentors and friendships, and moving up the ladder in television production enabled her to create this successful African American female-centered sitcom. The contacts she made and the knowledge she gained helped her to take advantage of the television system to create programming that reflects her life and interests. Starting as a production assistant on the sitcom *Sinbad*, she became a writer trainee on *South Central* through a Writers Guild of America Program.[8] The work and relationships she made there led to positions as staff writer, story editor, and finally producer. Akil explained that *Moesha's* executive producers Ralph Fraquhar, Sara Finney, and Vida Spears communicated the attitude "that if I took the initiative they would expose me to everything." So she worked on casting, sound mix, and observing editing sessions. This type of mentoring enabled her to move up the system and leave what she referred to as the "nest" of working on *Moesha* to become supervising producer on *The Jamie Foxx Show*. Her deal there gave Warner Brothers "first look" on any show ideas she was pitching, all of which the studio was not interested in.

Even though Akil advanced through the system in a fairly typical fashion for most television showrunners, her show's development was far from routine. She explained that *Girlfriends* was developed in the reverse order, with the idea for the show initiated by the network. UPN heard that she was pitching ideas for different shows, and they came to her with a need for an adult-oriented situation comedy. The network had a new hit with the sitcom *The Parkers* and wanted "a companion piece" to build that show's African American female audience. Akil recalled that *Sex and the City* was becoming a big hit on cable and UPN saw a need for an ensemble show about Black women. "I plucked a few characters from other shows I was pitching ... and wrapped it into *Girlfriends*." Instead of following the usual routine of pitching a concept to a production company, which then sells the idea to a studio, which then pitches the show to a network, Akil had to develop the sitcom in reverse order. Her first step was to find a studio. This was no easy task, given that the word in the industry in 1999 was that UPN was in trouble and might not survive. Since Paramount was part of the same conglomerate the studio was open to working with UPN. Akil then worked with Paramount executive Rose Catherine Pinkney to find a production company. Akil ended up with Gramnet, Kelsey Grammer's production company. She said he was still an important name in the industry, which she knew could be helpful in getting a pilot into a series.

Having a program on the air for eight seasons is rare in television, especially today.[9] For Akil one of the keys to the show's success was her ability to work though the early nervousness that everyone, the network, the studio, the cast and crew has in the early days of a show. Networks are quick to drop a show after just a few episodes if the audience is not there or negative feedback comes from critics. Akil recalls:

> I was able to keep the show's creative focus during that first crazy six to nine episodes. And though it's important to fight for your vision, it's also important to keep the support of the network and studio. There are plenty of situations where shows are on the air but the executives and the producers are at odds and the show suffers more because of that conflict. I

don't want that for my show and as a result found a way to balance it all
and the result was that we had immense support for the show.

Her only frustration was lack of promotional support from the network. Akil knows that marketing can make a new show and build
audience for an existing one. An advertising campaign can also get
attention that can lead to Emmy nominations and other awards.
While *Girlfriends* has been nominated five times for NAACP Image
Awards only Tracee Ellis Ross, in 2007 and 2009 for outstanding actress in a comedy series, and Reggie Hayes, who plays William Dent,
Joan's best friend and former colleague as well as the "honorary girlfriend," in 2005 and 2006, for outstanding supporting actor in a comedy series have been honored.[10] Akil takes great pride in the success
of the series, pointing out that the program was the number one
scripted show on UPN in the February 2006 sweeps period while noting that another new UPN show, *Everybody Hates Chris,* was launched
with a $13 million-ad campaign. Yet she takes this in stride, under-
standing that when her show launched UPN was on the brink of col-
lapse. She is grateful for the support that she consistently received
from the network despite a number of changes in the network hierarchy in the eight seasons of *Girlfriends.*

The final episodes of the 2006 season included the back-door pilot
for her latest project, a sitcom about football players called *The Game.*
Being able to spin-off a project like this is a perk that comes with a
successful show. From *The Andy Griffith Show* starting as an episode of
The Danny Thomas Show to *The Cosby Show* spinning off *A Different
World,* production companies and networks often launch new shows
by building on the audience of current hits. Akil is taking advantage
of that system.

Akil is working to build a successful production company with
plans for a number of shows. She used Steven Bochco and Carsey-
Werner, two of the most important production companies of the past
twenty years, as models. These people and their companies have not
only had a number of successful shows, they have a legacy of excel-
lence, which is what she looks to leave. Akil ties her goals directly to
her minority identity: "That our images are complex and fully fleshed
out. Telling our stories and try to reshape some of the lasting images
that are about us as a people."

Conclusion

These three African American women and their work are real life illustrations of Stuart Hall's circuit of culture. They are not simply creators of successful television programs they are producers of cultural representations that build on the shows that they consumed as fans of television. Henderson, DeLoatch, and Akil have created programs that succeed in an industry that treats ratings numbers and audience demographics as the primary definition of success. Yet their work also succeeds as a reflection of their life experiences. Their shows have filled representational voids, from the absence of Black family life, to the joys and problems in the pursuit of love and friendships among African American women.

Henderson, DeLoatch, and Akil have received enough viewer feedback to know they are contributing to the meaning audiences make from television viewing. Akil apparently goes to the Web to see what the show's devotees are saying. She's found that some of these online comments have continued the discussion of health issues that her program has precipitated. Igniting those discussions may be the best that a sitcom can do, and that role should be acknowledged. Henderson understands that her drama is speaking to an audience that has looked for this type of work, but rarely found it. The audience has told her how important it is to see stories that reflect their lives on the television screen.

These three showrunners are aware of their heritage and reflect that in their work. This can be found in their diverse workplaces. It can also be found in small ways on the screen, such as the casting of Melvin Van Peebles, one of the forefathers of modern Black media, in two episodes in the sixth season of *Girlfriends*. Akil said:

> Casting Mr. Van Peebles on the show was a milestone moment for me. He is our legacy. He was one of the few who found a way to present our people as the complex and interesting people that we are. Having him on the show was a small way to honor him, and a selfish way to meet him and thank him.

Henderson, DeLoatch, and Akil's legacies will be that their cultural representations are now are part of that circuit of culture that audiences will use in forming meaning and that future producers may use as the basis of their own work.

The primary issue in television today now is that what many have predicted for years, the end of broadcast network television is now in sight. The creators and audiences, like the U.S. population as a whole, are increasingly multicultural. But the industry structures, from production through scheduling and promotion are changing in the face of more niche audiences, new delivery systems, and smaller audiences for network shows resulting in fewer advertising dollars to produce high-cost programs. The final chapter addresses how the industry, advocacy groups, and creators face these challenges.

The New Television World

"Fifty percent of the American population lives between New York and San Diego." When Ron Taylor told me that in 2006 I had to remind myself that I was talking with a television executive, someone who tends to think demographically rather than geographically. Nielsen Media Research shows that half the television households in the United States are in the top twenty-five television markets, those designated market areas listed from New York to San Diego.[1] Taylor explained these are metropolitan areas that research shows are not only multicultural, but contain young audiences who see diversity as "normal life." That fact, as much as any other, may drive the future of minorities in television. According to Taylor, "We are beginning to no longer talk about diversity as a sort of desirable social goal, a way of balancing inequities and so forth. That era has kind of passed. What we are now talking about is the reality of the new multicultural American."

Taylor, Vice President of Diversity Development at Fox, has been around long enough to be familiar with the cyclical nature to the television industry's interest in diversity. An ABC Standards and Practices representative on *Roots* in the 1970s, a production studio executive and a writer in the 1980s, and one of the main programming executives involved in the creation of UPN in the mid-1990s, Taylor has seen the interest in minority images and minority employment come and go. His current position is due directly to the threat of boycotts and the diversity initiatives signed by the networks and advocacy groups in 1999 as networks created offices dedicated to carrying out diversity programs.

Part of Taylor's job involves educating producers that programming with a diverse audience in mind can be key in making a show a hit. He recounted a recent presentation his department hosted for the showrunners on all of Fox's programs. The group was shown statistics indicating that the television audience in the United States is now approximately thirty-four percent non-White. Programmers who only appeal to White audiences have less than seventy percent of the population to recruit from. Taylor explained that during the presentation Peter Ligouri, President of Fox Entertainment, made a key point: a show that increases its audience by as little as one-tenth of a rating point from 3.3 to 3.4, for example, has increased its worth to Fox by millions of dollars. According to Taylor, the message Fox was sending to the showrunners was that this small increase, recruiting another 103,000 viewers, provides more incentive for the network to renew the show, thereby increasing the chance to get to the eighty to one-hundred episodes essential for the lucrative syndication market. "This can be the make-or -reak factor for their success."

The Changing Marketplace

Changes in the demographics of the American audience may be a key factor in influencing what gets on the television, but it is far from the only recent development impacting diversity. Showrunner Felicia D. Henderson found global financing, distribution, and foreign production affecting her work in guiding *Soul Food* from pre-production in Los Angeles through its successful run on Showtime. It was not simply Canadian production incentives, with their cost-saving tax rebates and labor practices that impacted Henderson's plans for staffing the show. An additional motivating factor in the move to Canada was the loss of "foreign money" as a German corporation slated to help the studio finance the production dropped out late in the show's pre-production stage. "So suddenly Paramount had to pick up a bigger part of the deficit than they normally do for shows."[2] The quickest way for the studio to cut costs was to move production to Canada, impacting the potential for a multicultural workplace.

International considerations can also play a role in syndication, a key factor in the financial success of most entertainment television programming. As Timothy Havens documents in his research on the effect of cultural differences in the international television trade, pro-gram distributors and buyers often bring many of their own biases into the business.[3] Havens found that buyers and sellers have precon-ceptions regarding what will sell internationally. For example, many in the international television trade believe that only "mainstream"

African American television show such as *The Cosby Show* will appeal to audiences in other countries. There was a strong sense, "that if a show is too tied to Black American experience then it won't work internationally."[4] This attitude was prevalent throughout most of the business, although some international buyers, especially those in non-European areas, saw the potential crossover appeal of African American–centered shows, particularly among younger audiences. The popularity of African American music and hip-hop culture throughout the world will most probably increase the likelihood that African American–themed television shows will find a more welcoming home. Much like the United States, audiences in other countries are becoming more comfortable with diversity. But that cannot be taken as a given. Changes in both industry practices and attitudes among the people involved in the international television trade need to be tracked and Havens' important work needs to get wider attention. His findings and Felicia Henderson's experience confirm that international considerations are becoming more central to what kind of programs are produced and how and where that work is produced.

Syndication usually defines financial success for producers in entertainment television, and it too is subject to the changing marketplace. It is often seen as the pot of gold at the end of the television rainbow in television. Fresh from syndicating *The Cosby Show*, Bill Cosby had enough money to consider purchasing NBC in the early 1990s. But syndication dollars are growing smaller every year. With broadcast and cable audiences diminishing as they scatter to the Internet, video games, and other entertainment venues, the kind of money that could be made in syndication is no longer there. That is not to say that it is still not a lucrative area. With the end of the Fin-Syn rules, syndication rights are an important revenue source for the broadcast networks.[5] For production studios syndication is often the place not only to recoup the money lost in producing at a deficit, but also to make a healthy profit with a mega-hit show like *Seinfeld*. Syndication can spell lifetime financial security for individual producers. It can also provide the resources to finance and grow their own production companies.

Yet when *Soul Food* went into syndication, Felicia Henderson was faced with the reality of the new media marketplace. *Soul Food* was a program produced by Paramount, aired on UPN, and then syndicated on BET, all Viacom properties—a perfect example of vertical integration. Here the advantage is to the giant corporation, not the small producer. By syndicating the show to BET, another part of the Viacom conglomerate, revenue remained in house. "Making sure I never see a penny worth of profit." Henderson found this, "very frustrating." The realities of the ever-more-global marketplace and multinational media conglomerate are proof that the more multicultural American audience will not in and of itself continue the trend of diversity on the screen and behind the camera.

Figure 7.1 The 2002 NAACP Image Awards. Left to right Rockmond Dunbar, Vanessa Williams, Aaron Meeks, Nichole Ari Parker, Malinda Williams, Darrin Dewitt Henson, Kenneth "Babyface" Edmonds, Tracey E. Edmonds, Felicia D. Henderson, Boris Kodjoe. This was the first of three times that *Soul Food* recived the NAACP Image Award for Best Drama. (Courtesy of Felicia D. Henderson)

In 2006, the CBS and Times Warner media conglomerates combined two of their broadcast networks leading to the end of the one network, UPN, that had aired the most African American–centered programs. UPN and WB became the CW, with the new network dropping UPN shows such as *Eve* and *Half & Half*. This did not bode well for African American employment either, as the Writers Guild of America/West report showed that UPN's parent company had the most African American employees in 2005 and predicted that those numbers would fall with the end of that network.[6] The fall 2007 CW schedule included only one night of African American–themed shows. Vic Bullock, executive director of the NAACP's Hollywood chapter, said his organization was tracking these changes, "It's one that has caused concern among people in our community, from showrunners to craft services."[7]

Advocating Diversity

The rapid rate of change in the television industry and the global marketplace of the twenty-first century are two reasons that those who advocate for diversity should remain vigilant. It was not some natural progression in attitudes regarding diversity that brought structural change at the turn of the century. What motivated the networks to address racial inequities were the threat of boycotts by the National Association for the Advancement of Colored People (NAACP) and other civil rights organizations, the media coverage of the problems faced by minority creators, and the statistical studies undertaken by the Writers Guild of America (WGA) and the Coalition of African American Writers. The diversity agreements signed early in 2000 were a major step forward. The resultant diversity offices are keeping the issue alive from within these corporations.[8]

The most immediate effect of this attention has been the efforts to rebut one myth widely accepted in the television industry: that there are not enough qualified and talented African Americans to fill creative positions. Former television executive Frank Dawson said that, over the years, network executives and producers have often told him, "the talent just isn't out there." This myth is often raised whenever there is any question as to why more African Americans are not working in the industry.[9] In his 1999 book *The Showrunners*, David Wild quotes one television agent explaining why the people who write and produce television are primarily White and male: "If I could find a bunch of black female TV writers, I'd be one very happy guy."[10] This counterfactual claim that there is not a pool of candidates places the burden on African Americans: it is Blacks' fault for not being qualified. This stance also deflects criticism from White agents and producers who are responsible for industry hiring practices. The myth also helps to reinforce racist attitudes in the television industry — it is easier not to hire minorities if Whites believe that none are qualified. That is why the current structural efforts, over the long term, may have an important impact. Network diversity offices hosting talent showcases publicizing the fact that there are qualified minorities is not a solution, but it is an effort to counter the long-held myth. One of the more substantive efforts is a program coordinated by the Directors Guild of America and Touchstone TV/ABC. Initiated in 2004, the program places women and minority directors on both half-hour sitcoms and hour-long dramas.[11] Showrunners are given real incentive to work with DGA program participants because their salaries are paid by Disney and not deducted from a show's budget. Participants also are paired with veteran executives who help mentor them through the maze of landing a job. Stephen McPherson, President of ABC Primetime Entertainment explained to *The Hollywood Reporter* that the program acknowledges the industry reality of personal networking: "Producers told us when we did our initial sessions that when they get a list of 45 names of directors at a mixer, they're not going to hire any of them—but if they get a list of two people, on a personal recommendation from someone they know in the industry, there's a 100% better chance that they're going to hire one of them."[12]

Since many of the people involved in the network diversity efforts are industry veterans the emerging talent can be schooled in the reality of what it is like to work in the business. For instance, helping new writers to understand that they have to develop a "thick skin" concerning the interplay that can occur in the writers' room may better prepare minority talent for the sometimes rough and tumble world of television production. It is not a coincidence that many of the most successful creators interviewed for this book had been informally mentored into what to expect and how to move ahead in the business. This kind of work needs to be part of the structure of fostering diversity in the television workplace.

Taylor of Fox's Diversity office told me that much of his work is "getting people jobs." He described one program that Fox initiated and that other networks are now following:

> Showrunners like most bosses in our business, like certainly most bosses in life, hire their friends. And once they finish staffing their show with their friends and so forth, we obviously encourage them to hire diverse writers who are more experienced, perhaps at the mid or upper levels in our business, although again there are relatively few of those still. But once that is done we say to them, now we are going to offer you for free, a diverse staff writer because the company will absorb that cost. It will not be against your budget. You know we have a handful of showrunners who resist that but the vast majority totally get it. All we are offering them is a very smart,

very capable, often young person who can only help their show. Can't hurt their show and if they don't work out fine .... A number of people have gotten started that way in the last three years. In one or two instances they have remained on successful shows or more commonly have worked on shows that didn't succeed, since most don't, and have gone on to other shows. [They] have been able to through these relationships and through their beginning reputation, get connected on a new series. And that is what we are trying to do. Help people build careers, get them longevity.

This work gives hope that the current diversity efforts, built on a strong knowledge of how the business typically operates, may translate into long-term change for the industry.

Yet there is also the danger that if the media and advocacy groups don't continue to pay attention to the issue of diversity the industry will lose interest. That attention is essential, not just in keeping the new industry programs alive but in communicating to creators that they will face heat if they ignore the issue. The *New York Times* account of the production of the 2000 HBO mini-series *The Corner* illustrates that White producers are often aware that if African Americans are not involved in producing Black-themed programs they will risk pressure from outside groups. That was one of the reasons that HBO brought African American writer David Mills and director Charles Dutton into the project. *Times* reporter Janny Scott explained, "HBO needed African-Americans involved for two reasons, Mr. Albrecht [president for original programming at HBO] said: for creative reasons and for public relations."[13] The network anticipated that a series about the inner-city drug culture would attract criticism and even protests. Hiring an African American writer and a director who had first-hand knowledge of that street culture would help protect HBO. Even the expectation of pressure from outside the industry can effect change. The potential downside to this practice is that African Americans who are hired simply to fend off criticism may have little input into the final product. But that is not inevitable, as shown by the *New York Times* account of *The Corner* where both Mills' writing and Dutton's direction helped construct the show's more realistic portrait of inner-city life.

There were three constants among the people I interviewed concerning the diversity initiatives signed in 1999–2000 and the resultant creation of diversity departments by the networks. The first was skepticism. Some people saw the latest push for more minorities in front of and behind the camera as another example of the thirty-year cycle in the television industry: there is attention to the issue of lack of minority workers, then the creation of programs to address the problem, and eventually a loss of interest leading to no long-term solutions. A related sentiment was that attention and pressure from advocacy groups must be long term. The issue of minority representation will only be solved with extended training and employment programs, networking and mentoring. The third sentiment was that real progress will finally be made when an African American has the power to greenlight a television program. The power to make the final determination that a show gets produced and aired is a responsibility that an African American has never possessed. For many of the people interviewed, only when that occurs will the industry be able to say it has made real strides in showing that minorities have the same opportunities as Whites. African Americans will be able to bring their experiences and their perspectives to one of the most powerful positions in television. The television industry will be able to say that it was open enough and confident enough to share that power.

One industry veteran told me that for an African American to attain that position of power they simply have to be "picked" early in their career. From what he has observed, the individuals who've reached the level to greenlight a project were simply picked as rising stars with great potential. They were not more intelligent or dynamic than other young executives. This helped explain a question that I had after interviewing the people for this book: why didn't one of these intelligent, creative, dynamic people go all the way to the top of the industry? The best answer may be the simplest: an industry centered on duplicating successful ideas and using track-record talent is not structured for risky decisions like "picking" an African American as a future head of a television network.

What Are You Going to Do with It?

This book started with the question of responsibility. It seems clear that many African American creators feel a responsibility concerning television—a responsibility to create a more multicultural workplace, more diverse images, and to acknowledge the work of those who came before. In the 2006 TV Land three-part program *That's What I'm Talking About*, Harry Belafonte gave a description of responsibility befitting his stature in the industry:

Just being an actor is not enough. If you are at the top of the game you have the capacity to make an impact. The question is when Black people achieve, as any person who is a minority ... there is an expectation from the tribe somehow you got where you are because somebody paid the price to get you there .... Then when you have access and a voice and the capacity to influence... reach back into the plantation and reach back into the suffering of our group and lift it up. It's what you do with power.[14]

Mara Brock Akil put it simply when discussing producing a show about African Americans: "so what are you going to do with it?" There are enough African Americans working in television today to know that there are numerous answers to this question. This book presented some of those answers. Many more responses can be found in the programs on the television screen and in the stories of their creators.

The creative legacy of earlier generations of Black television workers has allowed today's writers and producers to, in most cases, move beyond issues of positive and negative stereotypes. Audiences have told today's creators that they see people like themselves on the screen. Unlike the first twenty-five years of its history, issues important to African American life do appear on television, and it is often Black creators who make them possible. Cultural diversity is contributing to the best of what we see on today's television. The presence of race and ethnic difference are what have made some of the newest television shows, such as *Lost* and *Grey's Anatomy* so interesting and appealing. For entertainment television to remain relevant the industry must not only acknowledge the increasingly diverse audience, it must enable and encourage minority producers to bring their perspective to the creative workplace. Is the variety of perspectives within and among minority creators acknowledged by the White community that dominates Hollywood? That is a question for another text. The stories of the creators interviewed for this book and the multiplicity of their experiences and viewpoints cannot be denied. The lived experiences of these writers, producers, and executives relate to the work they produce. And in listening to their stories one can both acknowledge the social history of African Americans in television while also emphasizing individual experience.

Historian Annette Gordon-Reed writes of the dilemma that for African Americans group experience determines how people view individual lives while White peoples' lives are written from the inside out.

If anything, the history of African Americans working in television emphasizes that individual African Americans used their lived experiences to create work that told their own stories and helped paint the multidimensional and multiplicity of stories of Blacks in America. But to do so required the power to tell that story. It was Bill Cosby, who wielding his power as one of the most successful comedians of the 1960s and 1970s, set out to tell a Black story. Yes, it was an upper-middle-class family but it was the story Bill Cosby wanted to tell, and tell with such a sense of responsibility that he hired Psychiarist and Harvard Medical School Professor Dr. Alvin Poussaint. Bill Cosby also used the power he acquired with the success of *The Cosby Show* to tell other African American stories through *A Different World*, and helped insure the success of that show in NBC scheduling it after the smash hit *The Cosby Show*. Twenty-five years ago no one could have predicted that *The Cosby Show* would be give credit for paving the way for America's first Black president. Novelist Alisa Valdes-Rodriguez coined the term "Huxtable effect" for the way that show impacted America's racial views as the children who grew up watching *The Cosby Show* voted in overwhelming numbers for Barack Obama.[15] But there could be no "Huxtable effect" without a Bill Cosby to create that image and tell that story. It was Felicia Henderson who, wielding track-record talent and industry connections, was able to tell stories of African Americans over a number of seasons in *Soul Food*.

There are many stories yet to be told. An industry in the midst of tremendous upheaval, as the television industry is today makes it hard to predict what those stories will be. But we should continue to listen to those stories of African Americans and other minority creators.

Since this book began with a call from one of the elders, Ossie Davis, it may be appropriate to cite the tribute writer/producer Tina Andrews wrote to another groundbreaker, Judi Ann Mason, who died in the summer of 2009. Mason's work went all the way back to *Good Times* in 1978:

So I honor her, as I do all of the writers—regardless of background—who have opened doors despite great odds to make it easier for the next generation of scribes. To illustrate the importance of such legacies, I have taken the now famous quote from former Congressman Cleo Fields about the decades-long link between Rosa Parks sitting on a bus to Barack Obama becoming president: Back in 1953 the first black WGA member in history, Helen Thompson, crawled so that a Judi Ann Mason could walk, so that an Yvette Lee Bowser could run, so that Shondra Rhimes, Sara Finney-Johnson, Vida Spears, and Mara Brock Akil can fly.[16]

Show Summaries

Any Day Now (Lifetime: August 18, 1998–March 10, 2002)
This show told the story of a friendship between two successful women, one Black and one White, in Birmingham, Alabama. Through flashbacks in each episode, we see how their characters and their friendship developed in the wake of the Civil Rights Movement of the 1960s.

Buddies (ABC: March 5, 1996–April 3, 1996)
This was a short-lived sitcom starring Dave Chappelle.

The Corner (HBO: April 16, 2000–May 21, 2000)
Based on the nonfiction book *The Corner: A Year in the Life of an Inner-City Neighborhood,* by journalists David Simon and Edward Burns, this show conveys the world of select Baltimore streets using real names and real events. The show is based on the story of men, women, drug pushers, and children living among the open-air drug markets of West Baltimore.

The Cosby Show (NBC: September 30, 1984–April 30, 1992)
Dr. Heathcliff Huxtable (Bill Cosby) was a prominent OB-GYN and his wife Clair (Felicia Rashaud) was a successful attorney. Set in Brooklyn, New York, the story lines focused on raising their five children: helping them deal with dating, school, marriage, and everyday life. One of the most popular shows in TV history, when it ran, it helped turn NBC into a #1 network.

Cosby (CBS: September 16, 1996–April 28, 2000)
Based on the British sitcom *One Foot in the Grave,* Bill Cosby portrayed Brooklynite Hilton Lucas, a grumpy man forced into retirement. His wife was played by Felicia Rashaud. Madeline Kahn portrayed her neighbor until her death in 1999.

A Different World (NBC: September 24, 1987–July 9, 1993)
As a spin-off series from *The Cosby Show,* this show centered on the life of students at Hilman College, a fictional HBCU in Virginia. *A Different World* addressed many issues such as racism, class relations, fraternity pledging, and on-campus romances.

The District (CBS: October 7, 2000–May 1, 2004)
Set in the nation's capitol, *The District* followed a justice-seeking cop and his team that were determined to reduce crime and make the streets safer for everyone.

Eve (UPN: September 15, 2003–May 11, 2006)
Grammy Award–winning hip-hop artist, Eve starred in *Eve* as Shelly, an attractive, feisty, and intelligent modern woman of twenty-first century. Based in Los Angeles, the sitcom revolved around the relationships with her outgoing friends and situations of love, career and romance.

Everybody Hates Chris (CW: September 22, 2005–still running)
Motivated by his childhood, Emmy Award–winner/actor/comedian Chris Rock, narrates this funny and heartfelt story of a teenager growing up as the oldest of three children in Brooklyn, during the early 1980s. Many of the show episodes center around Chris being the only Black student in his middle school, his very cheap father, and strict but loving mother.

Family Matters (ABC: Septmeber 22, 1989–July 17, 1998)
This upbeat sitcom was about a hardworking middle-class family and the inventive nerd Steve Urkel. Steve unexpectedly barged into their home, which was unsettling at first, but eventually he made a lasting impact in their hearts. Often times, his crazy situations that he inevitably pulled them into, made the family re-examine themselves and their bond with each other.

Frank's Place (CBS: September 14, 1987–March 22, 1988)
This show gave us a portrayal of life of African Americans. However, CBS changed time slots so many times that it failed to find a larger audience; therefore it was canceled after only one season.

Frasier (NBC: September 16, 1993–May 13, 2004)

Dr. Frasier Crane was the insecure, pretentious psychiatrist who hosted a Seattle radio advice show at KACL. The twice-divorced doctor's serene home life of excellent cigars and expensive cuisine was crushed when his crotchety, ex-cop father, Martin, was injured in the line of duty and is forced to move in with Frasier. His snobbish brother Nile is also a regular annoyance in Frasier's life.

The Fresh Prince of Bel Air (NBC: September 10, 1990–May 20, 1996)
Produced by Quincy Jones, the focal point of this comedy was a wealthy African American family living in Bel Air, California, that reluctantly opens their doors to their relative, Will. He was a street smart teenager from the West Side of Philly. When the Banks family opened their home to the Fresh Prince, they both learned that there is more to life than their egos, and the bonds that tie family together are unbreakable.

Friends (NBC: September 22, 1994–May 6, 2004)
This show focused on six friends in New York as they find their way through life and mature as they all approach their thirties.

Girlfriends (CW: September 11, 2000–February 11, 2008)
Girlfriends, one of the most successful sitcoms with an entire African American cast, followed the friendship of four African American women from different walks of life. They explored the many trials and tribulations of relationships, family, and career.

Goode Behavior (UPN: August 26, 1996–May 19, 1997)
A newly paroled convicted con artist came to live with his successful estranged son and his family, unannounced. To satisfy the requirements of his probation, he must live at his son's house, under house arrest.

He's the Mayor (ABC: January 10, 1986–March 21, 1986)
A twenty-five-year-old man decided that he can repair his town's problems if he is the mayor. After winning the election he soon learned that finding solutions to these problems isn't as easy as he thought. He often asked his father for advice and guidance. His father was a janitor at city hall.

Homeboys in Outer Space (UPN: August 27, 1996–May 13, 1997)

In the twenty-third century, two easygoing, gregarious freelancers were under pressure to make something of themselves. The young men spent their days hopping galaxy to galaxy in their Space Hoopty. Along the way, Ty and Morris picked up odd jobs, met hot space babes, and struggled for a way to make ends meet.

Homicide: Life on the Street (NBC: January 31, 1993–May 21, 1999)
Based on *Homicide: A Year on the Killing Streets,* by David Simon, a writer who spent a year with the members of Baltimore's homicide unit, this series was a reality-based police drama. To contribute to the authenticity of the show, it was shot entirely with handheld cameras on location in the Fells Point community of Baltimore, Maryland.

I Spy (NBC: September 15, 1965–April 15, 1968)
A pair of American operatives worked undercover as a tennis pro, Bill Cosby, and his trainer, played by Robert Culp. This was the first popular drama with a Black lead character.

The Jeffersons (CBS: January 18, 1975–July 23, 1985)
Originally, a spinoff of *All in the Family* in which the Jeffersons were Archie and Edith Bunker's next-door neighbors, the family "moved on up" when George found success in the dry cleaning business. This allowed them to move into a lush, spacious high-rise apartment. The nucleus of the show was the ties that bound the family together and their lively and humorous relationships with their neighbors.

Just Shoot Me (NBC: March 3, 1997–August 16, 2003)
Just Shoot Me was an ensemble comedy set in the New York editorial offices of the fictional fashion magazine Blush. *Just Shoot Me* was centered on the lives of Blush's diverse, witty, and electric staff.

Linc's (Showtime: August 1, 1998–February 15, 1968)
Created by Tim Reid, this fresh, short-lived comedy was about Linc, a politically conservative proprietor who catered to a diverse crowd in a bar in Washington, DC.

Living Single (FOX: August 29, 1993–January 1, 1998)
Living Single was a situation comedy. The show spotlighted the lives of a group of six African American friends living in a Brooklyn

brownstone as well as the professional and personal lives of each character.

Moesha. (UPN: January 23, 1996–May 14, 2001)
The series featured Grammy Award winning artist Brandy Norwood in a series that displayed what life was really like in Leimert Park, Los Angeles, California. Moesha Mitchell was a teenager who becomes an adult. She dealt with various issues of love, sex, family, womanhood, and relationships.

One on One (UPN: September 1, 2001–May 16, 2006)
Set in Baltimore, this show revolved around the relationship between an outspoken teenager and her sportscaster dad. Flex adored his only daughter and provided advice in her times of need. The story lines are heavily centered around Breanna and her high school sweetheart, as well as the many ladies in Flex's life.

The Parent 'Hood (WB: January 11, 1995–July 25, 1999)
The series was about the Peterson's, an upper-middle-class Black family living in Harlem. Robert Peterson was a college professor and his wife was a law student. They balanced their personal lives, their work, and their four children simultaneously. Robert stands out as a parent as he constantly tried to solve his family's problems, with untraditional solutions.

The Practice (ABC: March 4, 1997–May 16, 2004)
Set in Boston, the show centered on a firm of fervent attorneys that believed every case was significant and every client was worth fighting for until the end. The quest for justice remained the first priority until the final verdict was announced.

Roc (FOX: August 25, 1991–May 10, 1994)
Roc Emerson was a city garbage collector from Baltimore. In each episode, he genuinely tried to balance the demands of work with the daily pressures of family life in an attempt to do what he thinks is best for his family. This show dealt with issues such as gang violence, drugs, community politics, and sexually transmitted diseases.

The Rockford Files (NBC: March 27, 1974–January 1, 1980)

Jim Rockford was an ex-convict turned private investigator who lived and worked from his trailer in Malibu, Los Angeles. Rocky, Jim's father a retired truck driver, frequently pressured his son to leave the private investigator business and apply for honest, secure work.

The Secret Diary of Desmond Pfeiffer (UPN: August 5, 1998–August 26, 1998)
This short-lived and controversial sitcom followed the diary of Desmond Pfeiffer, a butler in the White House during the Lincoln administration.

Sex and the City (HBO: June 6, 1998–February 22, 2004)
Based on the bestselling book by Candace Bushnell, *Sex and the City* revolved around the lives of four young professional women in search of the perfect relationship. In each episode, it is evident that the undeniable friendship among all of them was the staple of the show.

The Sinbad Show (FOX: September 16, 1993–July 28, 1994)
Comedian Sinbad played a happy-go-lucky bachelor who is also the foster parent of two siblings.

Sister, Sister (WB: April 1, 1994–May 23, 1999)
Tia and Tamera are twin girls separated at birth, who suddenly found each other after 14 years. Tia was studious and focused and Tamera was wild and boy-crazy. After their unanticipated encounter in a department store, Ray, Tamera's adopted father, reluctantly allowed Tia and her adopted mother, Lisa to move into his home for the benefit of the girls.

Soul Food (Showtime: June 28, 2000–May 26, 2004)
Soul Food explored traditional family life through the ups and downs of a close African American family living in Chicago.

South Central (FOX: April 5, 1994–June 7, 1994)
South Central was about the trials of a family residing in South Central, Los Angeles. An independent-minded single mother had to find a way to make ends meet while keeping a close watch on her teenage children. She also took in a five-year-old foster child with special needs.

The Wayans Bros. (WB: January 11, 1995–May 20, 1999)
Comedians Shawn and Marlon Wayans starred as Shawn and Marlon
Williams as brothers in this sitcom. They're both affable, but Marlon
is the one who is more immature and loves to party. They shared a
one-bedroom brownstone in New York City and always seemed to be
disagreeing over most issues, big and small.

WKRP in Cincinnati (CBS: September 18, 1978–April 21, 1982)
This show was about the comical situations of a struggling staff of a
disorganized fictional radio station in Cincinnati, Ohio.

Interviewees [1]

Mike Ajakwe Jr.—Writer/Producer, *Martin, Sister, Sister, Eve, Brothers Garcia, Between Brothers, Built to Last, Soul Food, The Parkers, Moesha, Love That Girl*. Degree from University of Redlands. Interviewed June 2005, Los Angeles, CA.

Mara Brock Akil—Executive Producer *Girlfriends, The Game*. Degree from Northwestern University. Phone interview March 2006.

James L. Anderson—Senior Vice President Publicity/Public Relations Carsey-Werner; Production Assistant *A Different World*. B. A., Denison University. Interviewed August 1998, Los Angeles, CA.

Frank Dawson—Executive Producer and founding partner in Nu House Flix; Associate Professor of Communications at Santa Monica College. Network executive CBS Television Network. Director of Comedy Development, Universal Television. A.B., Cornell; Masters in Television and Radio, Newhouse School, Syracuse University. Interviewed August 1998 and August 2004, Los Angeles, CA.

Meg DeLoatch—Creator, Executive Producer and Writer *Eve*; Writer *One on One, Bette, Living Single, Family Matters*. Interviewed August 2004, Los Angeles, CA.

Leonard R. Garner—Director *Wings, Just Shoot Me, Lateline, Suddenly Susan, King of Queens, Girlfriends*; Assistant Director *Rockford Files*; Second Assistant Director, *The Blues Brothers*; Assistant Director, *Miami Vice*; B. A. Drama, Syracuse University. Interviewed August 1998 and August 2004, Los Angeles, CA.

Felicia D. Henderson— Executive Producer, *Soul Food*; Supervising Producer *Sister, Sister*; Staff Writer, *Fresh Prince of Bel Air, Family Matters, Moesha*. B. A. Psychobiology, UCLA; MBA University of Georgia;

---

1 Interviewees are listed with the job they held at the time of the interview listed first. This is followed by a chronological list of jobs, education, and month and place of the interview.

working on Masters in Film, UCLA. Interviewed August 1998 and August 2004, Los Angeles, CA.

Sharon Johnson—Freelance writer. Writers Assistant *Living Single;* Staff Writer *Sinbad, Buddies, Goode Behavior.* A. B. Program in the Arts, Barnard/Columbia University; Masters in Media Studies from New School for Social Research. Interviewed August 1998 and August 2004, Los Angeles, CA.

Martin Jones—General Manager, New Millennium Studios, B. A., Denison University. Interviewed November 1998, Petersburg, V.A.

Rose Catherine Pinkney—Senior Vice President, Comedy Development Paramount Communications at the time of the interview. A. B., Princeton; MBA, UCLA. Interviewed August 2004, Los Angeles, CA.

Oz Scott—Freelance television director. Television Director *The Jeffersons, Hill Street Blues, 227, Northern Exposure, Picket Fences, The Practice, Any Day Now;* Film Director *Bustin' Loose.* Degree in film and theater from New York University. Interviewed August 1998 and August 2004, Los Angeles, CA.

Kim Sizemore—Stage Manager (Assistant Director) *The Parent'Hood;* Production Assistant on numerous films; Production Assistant *He's the Mayor;* various production positions on *Head of the Class, A Different World, Fresh Prince of Bel Air.* Degree from Manhattanville College. Interviewed August 1998, Los Angeles, CA.

Shirley Salomon—Director of Production Development, Black Entertainment Television. Production Manager, MTV. Production Assistant on various network shows including the soap operas *All My Children* and *One Life to Live, Cosby.* While in college interned at NBC News, and NBC soap operas and *Saturday Night Live.* B. S., College of Staten Island/CUNY. Interviewed May 1998, Staten Island, NY, and November 2005, New York, NY.

Daphne Maxwell Reid—Actress, Co-Founder, New Millennium Studios. Interviewed March, 2005, Petersburg, VA.

Tim Reid—Executive Producer and Co-Creator *Linc's;* Co-Founder and Owner, New Millennium Studios, Writer, Producer, Director, *Frank's Place, Snoops;* Director and Producer of film *Once Upon a Time When We Were Colored.* Degree, Norfolk State University. Interviewed November 1998, Petersburg, VA.

Vida Spears—Executive Producer/Co-Creator *Moesha;* Writer/Producer, *Family Matters;* Executive Producer/Co-Creator *The Parkers.* Degree from Michigan State University. Interviewed August 1998, Los Angeles, CA; phone interview July 2009.

Ron Taylor—Vice President, Diversity Development Fox Entertainment Group. Degree from Yale University. Phone interview February 2006.

Notes

Chapter One Introduction

1   Foxx Tribute to Charles' Legacy BBC News Monday, 28 February 2005 http://news.bbc.co.uk/1/hi/entertainment/film/4303547.stm

2   Michelle Hilmes, "Invisible men: Amos 'n' Andy and the roots of broadcast discourse," *Critical Studies in Mass Communication*, 10, no. 4, (1993) 301–321; Bishetta D. Merritt, "Illusive reflections: African American women on primetime television," In *Our Voices: Essays in Culture, Ethnicity and Communication*, eds. Alberto Gonzalez, Marsha Houston, and Victoria Chen (Los Angeles: Roxbury Publishing, 1994), 48–53.

3 Larry Gross, "Out of the mainstream," In *Gender, Race and Class in Media*, eds. Gail Dines and Jean M. Humez (Thousand Oaks, CA: Sage, 1995), 61–69; Douglas Kellner, *Media Culture*, (New York: Routledge. 1995); Kerner Commission, *Report of the National Advisory Commission on Civil Disorders* (New York: E. P. Dutton, 1968); Bishetta D. Merritt, "Illusive reflections: African American women on primetime television," In *Our Voices: Essays in Culture, Ethnicity and Communication*, eds. Alberto Gonzalez, Marsha Houston, and Victoria Chen (Los Angeles: Roxbury Publishing, 1994), 48–53; Jane Rhodes, "The visibility of race and media history" *Critical Studies in Mass Communication*, 10, no. 2, (1993) 184–189.

4 Todd Gitlin Inside Prime Time (New York: Pantheon, 1983) 13.

5 Muriel Cantor, *The Hollywood TV Producer* (New York: Basic Books, 1971); Todd Gitlin *Inside Prime Time* (New York: Pantheon, 1983); Horace Newcomb and Robert S. Alley, *The Producer's Medium* (New York: Oxford University Press, 1983); Joseph Turow, *Learning to Portray Power: The Socialization of Creators in Mass Media Organizations* (Beverly Hills, CA: Sage, 1985).

6 Newcomb and Alley, *The Producer's Medium*, xvii.

7 Jennette L. Dates, "Commercial television," In *Split Image: African Americans in the Mass Media*, eds. Jennette L. Dates and William Barlow (Washington, DC: Howard University Press 1993), 267–328; Jim Hillier, *The New Hollywood* (New York: Continuum, 1992); Darnell Hunt, *Channeling Blackness* (New York: Oxford University Press, 2005); J. Fred MacDonald, *Blacks and White TV* (Chicago: Nelson-Hall,1992); Judith Mayerle, "Roseanne—How did you get inside my house?: A case study of a hit blue-collar situation comedy," In *Television: The Critical View*, ed. Horace Newcomb (New York: Oxford University Press, 1994,) 101–116; Krystal B. Zook, *Color by Fox: The Fox Network and the Revolution in Black Television* (New York: Oxford University Press, 1999).

8 Larry Gross, "Out of the mainstream," In *Gender, Race and Class in Media*, eds. Gail Dines and Jean M. Humez (Thousand Oaks, CA: Sage, 1995), 68.

9 Stuart Hall, "Cultural identity and diaspora," In *Identity, Community, Culture, Difference*, ed. Jonathan Rutherford (London: Lawrence & Wishart, 1990), 236.

10 Zook, *Color by Fox*.

11 Stuart Hall, *Representation: Cultural Representations and Signifying Practices* (Thousand Oaks, CA: Sage, 1997).

12 http://www.census.gov/prod/www/statistical-abstract-03.html

13 Jimmie L. Reeves and Richard Campbell, "Misplacing *Frank's Place*: Do you know what it means to miss New Orleans?," *Television Quarterly*, 24, no. 1, (1989) 48.

14 Robert Stam and Ella Shohat, "Contested histories: Eurocentrism, multiculturalism, and the media," In *Multiculturalism: A Critical Reader*, ed. David Theo Goldberg (Cambridge: Blackwell, 1994); Newcomb and Alley, *The Producer's Medium*.

15 Stuart Hall, "The whites of their eyes," In *Gender, Race and Class in Media*, eds. Gail Dines and Jean M. Humez (Thousand Oaks, CA: Sage, 1995), 20.

16 Herman Gray, *Watching Race* (Minneapolis: University of Minnesota Press, 1995), 10.

17 Ibid.

18 Gray, *Watching Race*; Sut Jhally and Justin Lewis, *Enlightened Racism: The Cosby Show, Audiences and the Myth of the American Dream* (Boulder: Westview, 1992).

19 Robert J. Thompson and Gary Burns, *Making Television: Authorship and the Production Process* (New York: Praeger, 1990).

20 Zook, *Color by Fox*.

21 Cornell West, "The new cultural politics of difference," In *Out There: Marginalization and Contemporary Cultures*, eds. Russell Ferguson, Trinh T. Minh-Ha, Martha Gever (New York: The New Museum of Contemporary Art, 1990), 27.

22 Gray, *Watching Race*.

23 Newcomb and Alley, *The Producer's Medium*.

24 MacDonald, *Blacks and White TV*, 124.

25 Gray, *Watching Race*.

26 Jhally and Lewis, *Enlightened Racism*.

27 Joe R. Feagin and Melvin P. Sikes, *Living with Racism: The Black Middle-Class Experience* (Boston: Beacon Press, 1994), 29.

28 Nichelle Nichols, *Beyond Uhura: Star Trek and Other Memories* (New York: Putnam, 1994).

30 Ibid., 164.

31 Trinidad-born pianist and singer Hazel Scott also had a musical program on television in the early 1950s. Though critically acclaimed, the show was cancelled after only a few months. Scott's name had appeared in the anti-Communist publication *Red Channels*, which named supposed Communist sympathizers. *The Hazel Scott Show* found itself without a sponsor. Bogle, Donald, *Primetime Blues:*

African Americans on Network Television (New York, Farrar, Straus and Giroux, 2001), 520.

32 Zook, *Color by Fox*.

33 William T. Bielby and Denise D. Bielby, *Telling All Our Stories: The 1998 Hollywood Writers' Report* (Los Angeles, Writers Guild of America, West, 1998); Darnell P. Hunt, *The 2005 Hollywood Writers Report: Catching Up with a Changing America?* (Los Angeles, Writers Guild of America, West, 2005).

34 "As We Head Into the Next Millennium, Shamefully, Hollywood Still Looks Like Pleasantville," *Daily Variety* Oct. 8, 1999; "1964: RCA Introduces Color TV. 1999: Most Writers' Rooms Still Cast in White," *The Hollywood Reporter* Oct. 11, 1999.

35 Darnell Hunt, *Channeling Blackness*. Hunt finds both white and black Americans overrepresented, accounting for a combined 81% of the nation's population and 92% of all prime-time television characters.

36 Ibid.

37 Darnell Hunt, *UCLAlumni* September 2003.

38 Muriel G. Cantor and Joel M. Cantor, *Prime-Time Television: Content and Control* (Newbury Park, CA: Sage, 1992); Newcomb and Alley, *The Producer's Medium.*; James Ettema, D. Charles Whitney, and Daniel Wackman, "Professional mass communicators," In *Individuals in Mass Media Organizations*, eds. James Ettema and D. Charles Whitney (Newbury Park, CA: Sage, 1982).

39 All interviewees named in this book signed releases for the interviews to be used for publication. In two cases subjects did not sign a release. Therefore the names and positions are not included and direct reference to the shows these people worked on is not included.

40 Philomena Essed, *Understanding Everyday Racism* (Newbury Park, CA: Sage, 1991).

41 Newcomb and Alley, *The Producer's Medium*, 71.

42 Cornel West lecture at Rutgers, New Brunswick, NJ, 1995.

43 W. E. B. Du Bois, *The Souls of Black Folk* (New York: Signet, 1982), 3.

44 Todd Gitlin, *Inside Prime Time* (New York: Pantheon, 1983), 13.

45 bell hooks, *Black Looks: Race and Representation* (Boston: South End Press, 1992).

46 Linda Brodkey, "Writing Critical Ethnographic Narratives," *Anthropology & Education Quarterly*, 18, no. 2, (1987), 74.

Chapter Two: Getting In — Staying In

1 Joseph Turow, *Media Systems in Society* (New York: Longman, 1992).

2 Horace Newcomb and Robert S. Alley, *The Producer's Medium* (New York: Oxford University Press, 1983).

3 Turow, *Media Systems in Society*, 168.

4 "On April 19, 1969, Black students occupied Willard Straight during Parents' Weekend as a continuing form of protest about racial issues on campus. Citing the university's racist attitudes and irrelevant curriculum, the students occupied the building for thirty-six hours. The takeover received national attention as thousands of Black and White students became involved, which engaged the community in broad discussion about race relations and educational matters." http://www.library.cornell.edu/africana/guides/wsh.html

5 At the time of this interview Ms. Salomon was Production Manager at MTV. In August 2005, she took a position as Director of Production Development at BET.

6 Ajakwe emphasized that Bruce McAllister is also a well-known science fiction author. They have recently collaborated on a film script based on McAllister's novel *Dream Baby*.

7 Joseph Turow, *Media Industries* (New York: Longman, 1984).

8 Herbert Schiller, *Information Inequality* (New York: Routledge, 1996).

9 NBC currently sponsors a writing fellowship at UCLA in conjunction with the NAACP, (http://newsroom.ucla.edu/portal/ucla/NAACP-NBC-Fellowship-in -Screenwriting-8064.aspx NBC also a staffing initiative) NBC Diversity Initiative for Writers, and a writers program, NBC Writers on the Verge (http://www.wga.org/content/default.aspx?id=1042).

10 I explore Dawson's experience with the CBS Black employees association in the next chapter.

11 CETA was the Comprehensive Employment and Training Act, a U.S. government program enacted in 1973. It was designed to assist economically disadvantaged, unemployed, or underemployed persons (Concise Columbia Electronic Encyclopedia).

12 This is from the 1998 interview with Henderson.

13 http://www-cntv.usc.edu/cosby/

14 Joseph Turow, "Learning to portray power: The socialization of creators in mass media organizations," In *Organizational Communication: Traditional Themes and New Directions*, eds. Phillip Tompkins and Robert D. McPhee (Beverly Hills, CA: Sage, 1986), 231.

15 Joe R. Feagin and Melvin P. Sikes, *Living with Racism: The Black Middle-Class Experience* (Boston: Beacon Press, 1994), 29.

16 This was a show aired on CBS in the mid-1990s not *The Cosby Show* mentioned elsewhere.

17 Feagin and Sikes, *Living with Racism*, 154.

18 Newcomb and Alley, *The Producer's Medium*.

Chapter Three: Workplace Culture

1 CBS became a part of Viacom in 2000. As of 2005 Viacom properties included CBS, Paramount Studios, UPN, MTV, and Showtime Networks.

2 Lynn Hirschberg, "Giving Them What They Want," *New York Times*, Septermber 4, 2005.

3 Fredrick McKissack, "The problem of black T.V.," *The Progressive*, 16, no. 2, (February 1997), 38.

4 *Mediaweek*, December 6, 1999. Retrieved from http://www.allbusiness.com/ services/business-services-miscellaneous-business/4807693-1.html

Chapter Four: Culture of Production

1 Muriel G. Cantor and Joel M. Cantor, *Prime-Time Television: Content and Control* (Newbury Park: Sage, 1992).

2 Todd Gitlin, *Inside Prime Time* (New York: Pantheon, 1983) 13.

3 W. E. B. Du Bois, *The Souls of Black Folk* (New York: Signet, 1982).

4 Darnell Hunt, *Channeling Blackness* (New York: Oxford University Press, 2005), 17

5 Ibid.

6 This is the actress's full name.

7 Kamille Gentles, "The Construction of Black female Bodies in Amos 'n' Andy: A Case for Hybridity" (2004, May), p. 16, Paper presented at the annual meeting of the International Communication Association, New Orleans Sheraton, New Orleans, LA Online <.PDF> Retrieved June 28, 2008. http://www.allacademic. com/meta/p_mla_apa_research_citation/1/1/3/2/2/p113228_index.html

8 Elizabeth Hadley Freydberg, "Sapphires, spitfires, sluts, and superbitches: Aframericans and Latinas in contemporary American film," In *Critical Readings: Media and Gender*, eds. Cynthia Carter and Linda Steiner (Maidenhead, UK: Open University Press, 2004), 277.

9 Henderson's work on *Soul Food* is discussed in greater detail in chapter seven.

10 In June and July of 2000 the *New York Times* published a series of reports entitled How Race Is Lived in America." The series is based on the premise that "Race relations are being defined less by political action than by daily experience, in schools, in sports arenas, in pop culture and at worship, and especially in the workplace." (http://www.nytimes.com/library/national/race) In addition to the published reports, the *New York Times* web page included additional forums with expanded information on each article and feedback from readers. The fourth article in the series, "Who Gets to Tell a Black Story?" profiled the production of the HBO mini-series *The Corner*.

11 http://www.nytimes.com/library/national/race/discuss-dutton.html#one

12 Janny Scott, "Who Gets to Tell a Black Story?: Forum," *New York Times* (June 11, 2000), 1, 22.

13 Ibid.

14 Ibid.

15 Michael E. Dyson, "Essentialism and the complexities of racial identity," In *Multiculturalism: A Critical Reader*, ed. David T. Goldberg (Cambridge: Blackwell, 1994), 218.

16 My interview with this writer occurred after I talked with Leonard R. Garner. I never had an opportunity to follow up on this issue with him.

17 *Goode Behavior* was a short-lived show on UPN in 1996.

18 The 1995 trial of former football player and actor O. J. Simpson for the murder of his wife was called "the trial of the century" with unprecedented television coverage. The trial had racial implications as the defense was said to play "the race card" in using the racist history of the Los Angeles Police Department to win its case.

19 James Ettema, "The organizational context of creativity: A case study from public television," In *Individuals in Mass Media Organizations*, eds. James Ettema and D. Charles Whitney (Newbury Park, CA: Sage, 1982); Joseph Turow, *Media Systems in Society* (New York: Longman, 1992).

20 Turow, *Media Systems in Society*; Krystal B. Zook, *Color by Fox: The Fox Network and the Revolution in Black Television* (New York: Oxford University Press, 1999).

21 William T. Bielby and Denise D. Bielby, *Telling All Our Stories: The 1998 Hollywood Writers' Report* (Los Angeles: Writers Guild of America, West, 1998), 3.

22 Ibid.

23 Darnell P. Hunt, *The 2005 Hollywood Writers Report: Catching Up with a Changing America?* (Los Angeles: Writers Guild of America, West, 2005).

24 Bernard Weinraub, "Stung by Criticism of Fall Shows TV Networks Add Minority Roles," *New York Times* (September 20, 1999), 1, 14.. 1.

25 Greg Braxton and Brian Lowry, "Small Screen, Big Picture," *Los Angeles Times* (July 23, 1999), F 1.

26 *Daily Variety* ad is titled "As We Head into the Next Millennium, Shamefully, Hollywood Still Looks Like Pleasantville." (October 8, 1999).

27 Michael Schneider and Peter Bernstein. "NAACP, NBC Reach Pact ABC Expected to Follow Suit." *Variety*, Jan. 6, 2000, 1.

28 Eleizabeth Jensen, Greg Braxton, and Dana Calvo, "NBC, NAACP in Pact to Boost Minorities in TV Diversity," *Los Angeles Times* (January 6, 2000) F 1, 1.

29 Alex Kuczynski, "Following NBC's Lead, ABC Outlines Minority Hiring Plan," *New York Times*, January 8, 2000 A, 8

30 Donald Bogle, *Primetime Blues: African Americans on Network Television* (New York: Farrar, Straus and Giroux, 2001); Zook, *Color by Fox*.

31 Zook, *Color by Fox*, 4.

32 Hunt, *The 2005 Hollywood Writers Report*.

33 Darnell Hunt *Whose Stores Are We Telling? The 2007 Hollywood Writers Report* (Los Angeles: Writers Guild of America, West, 2007) p. 16.

34 Howard Rosenberg, "The Invisible Man, Alive and Well," *Los Angeles Times* (July 25, 1999), F 1.

35 Amanda D. Lotz, "Textual (im)possibilities in the U.S. post-network era: Negotiating production and the promotion process on Lifetime's *Any Day Now*," *Critical Studies in Media Communication*, 21, no. 1 (2001), 23.

36 Ibid., 34.

37 Ibid., 36.

38 One person I interviewed ended up suing the studio the person worked for. The settlement did not allow this person to talk about the suit. That was the reason this individual gave me for not allowing our interview to be quoted in this book.

39 Du Bois *The Souls of Black Folk,* 45

40 Joe R. Feagin and Melvin P. Sikes, *Living with Racism: The Black Middle-Class Experience* (Boston: Beacon Press, 1994), 25.

41 Braxton, 1999; Perkins, 1998; Rosenberg, *Los Angeles Times*.

42 Muriel Cantor, *The Hollywood TV Producer* (New York: Basic Books, 1971); Joseph Turow, *Learning to Portray Power: The Socialization of Creators in Mass Media Organizations* (Beverly Hills, CA: Sage, 1985).

43 Though most of the writers and producers on *The Wire* were White, the show has a number of African American directors including Ernest R. Dickerson and Clark Johnson. No television drama series has had as many African American actors.

44 "All the Pieces Matter," DVD Season 4 of *The Wire*.

Chapter Five: The Central Role of African American Writers

1 Robert S. Alley and Irby B. Brown. *Murphy Brown: Anatomy of a Sitcom* (New York: Dell, 1990); Horace Newcomb and Robert S. Alley, *The Producer's Medium* (New York: Oxford University Press, 1983); Robert J. Thompson and Gary Burns, *Making Television: Authorship and the Production Process* (New York: Praeger, 1990).

2 Joseph Turow, "Learning to portray power: The socialization of creators in mass media organizations," In *Organizational Communication: Traditional Themes and New Directions*, eds. Phillip Tompkins and Robert D. McPhee (Beverly Hills,CA: Sage. 1985), 232.

3 William T. Bielby and Denise D. Bielby, *Telling All Our Stories: The 1998 Hollywood Writers' Report* (Los Angeles: Writers Guild of America, west, 1998), 45.

4 Ibid., 37.

5 Ibid.

6 Darnell P. Hunt, *The 2005 Hollywood Writers Report: Catching Up with a Changing America?* (Los Angeles: Writers Guild of America, west, 2005).

7 I did not ask about the race of her agent. While respondents did not specifically mention the ethnicity of agents, the way they talked led me to believe that these agents were all White. There is nothing in the literature on the race of agents.

8 Henderson did not mention her agent's race, but the way she talked led me to believe that he was White.

9 Since this interview in 1998 Henderson has completed her MFA and started on a Ph.D. at UCLA.

10 Garner is referring to the major broadcast networks, not cable.

11 http://www.emmyonline.org/

12 Carsey-Werner is one of the most successful television production companies. Among the shows it has produced is *The Cosby Show, Roseanne, A Different World, 3rd Rock from the Sun* and *That '70s Show.*

13 Baptiste, Bala. "Vernon Winslow: The innovative art teacher whose radio personality, Dr. Daddy-O, changed the sound New Orleans Radio," Paper presented at the annual meeting of the Association for the Study of African American Life and History, Atlanta Hilton, Charlotte, NC, Oct 02, 2007 Retrieved December 19, 2008 from http://www.allacademic.com/meta/p207158_index.html; William Barlow, *Voice Over: The Making of Black Radio.* (Philadelphia: Temple University Press, 1999).

14 *Daily Variety,* October 8, 1999.

15 Michael E. Dyson, "Essentialism and the complexities of racial identity," In *Multiculturalism: A Critical Reader,* ed., David T. Goldberg (Cambridge: Blackwell, 1994); Sut Jhally, and Justin Lewis, *Enlightened Racism: The Cosby Show, Audiences and the Myth of the American Dream* (Boulder: Westview, 1992).

16 Herman Gray, *Watching Race* (Minneapolis: University of Minnesota Press 1995), 81.

17 Amanda D. Lotz, "Textual (im)possibilities in the U.S. post-network era: Negotiating production and the promotion process on Lifetime's *Any Day Now,*" *Critical Studies in Media Communication,* 21, no. 1 (2001), 23.

18 James Ettema, "The organizational context of creativity: A case study from public television," In *Individuals in Mass Media Organizations,* eds. James Ettema and D. Charles Whitney (Newbury Park: Sage, 1982), 91.

19 Dramadies gained popularity in the mid-1990s with the success of *Ally McBeal* and continued into the next decade with shows such as *Scrubs* and *The Office.*

20 Showtime did renew *Linc's* for the 1999–2000 season. It cancelled the show in 2000, after its second season. It ran for a total of 37 episodes.

21 James Ettema, *Individuals in Mass Media Organizations*; Joseph Turow, *Media Systems in Society* (New York: Longman, 1992).

22 Fredrick McKissack, "The problem of black T.V.," *The Progressive,* 16, no. 2 (February 1997), 39.

23 Marsha Scarbrough, "Writing with jive: Forget Harvard Law. Study *Vibe* magazine," *Written By* (September 2000b), http://www.wga.org/writtenby/writtenby.aspx

24 Ibid.

25 Janny Scott, "Who Gets to Tell a BlackStory?: Forum," *New York Times* (June 11, 2000), 1, 22.

26 Bielby and Bielby, *Telling All Our Stories,* 11.

27 The WGA classifies all African Americans, Latinos, Asian Americans, and Native Americans, male and female as minorities.

28 Turow, *Media Systems in Society,* 172.

29 James Stengold, "A Racial Divide Widens on Network TV," *The New York Times* (December 29, 1998), 1, 12; Krystal B. Zook, *Color by Fox: The Fox Network and the Revolution in Black Television* (New York: Oxford University Press, 1999).

30 Robert F. Moss, "The Shrinking Life Span of the Black Sitcom," *New York Times* (February 25, 2001), 35.

31 "Out of focus: Out of sync Take 4," NAACP Report December, 2008 http://www.naacp.org/news/press/2008-12-18/NAACP_OFOS_Take4.pdf

32 Sandra Harding, *Whose Science? Whose Knowledge? Thinking from Women's Lives* (Ithaca: Cornell University Press, 1991), 125.

33 Marcia Wallace, "Modernism, postmodernism and the problem of the visual in Afro-American culture," In *Out There: Marginalization and Contemporary Cultures,* eds. Russell Ferguson, Trinh T. Minh-Ha, and Martha Gever (New York: The New Museum of Contemporary Art, 1990), 19–36.

34 Zook, *Color by Fox.*; Donald Bogle, *Primetime Blues: African Americans on Network Television* (New York: Farrar, Straus and Giroux, 2001).

35 *Emmy* (October, 1998); *Written By* (July, 1998).

36 *Emmy* Johnson, 1998, p. 17.

37 http://www.wga.org

38 Chapters six and seven explore the Writers Guild's work in this area.

39 Catharine A. MacKinnon, "Smut's insidious threat," *Los Angeles Times* (March 20, 2005), http://www.latimes.com/news/printedition/suncommentary/la-op-discrimination20mar20,1,2183704.story?coll=la-headlines-suncomment

40 Lyle, Plaintiff and Appellant, *v.* Warner Brothers Television Productions et al., Defendants and Respondents, S125171 Ct.App. 2/7 160528 Los Angeles County Super. Ct. No. BC239047, 24.

41 Ibid., 27

42 Ibid., 6

43 Lyle, Plaintiff and Appellant, *v.* Warner Brothers Television Productions et al. Defendants and Respondents S125171 Ct.App. 2/7 160528 Los Angeles County Super. Ct. No. BC239047. Concurring opinion by Chin, J., 3.

44 Ibid., 6

45 Ibid.

46 Ibid., 4

Chapter Six: Three Showrunners

1 Showrunner is not a formal title. It should also be noted that programs may have multiple executive producers one of whom will be the showrunner.

2 Broadcast Education Association Panel, April 2004.

3 Henderson also mentioned some family responsibilities, which made it hard to be out of the country producing a show in Canada.

4 *Soul Food* was one of the most popular programs in the history of Showtime, holding that network's record for most viewers, 1.21 million for a 2004 broadcast. That audience level was not eclipsed until late 2007. http://www.zap2it.com/tv/ news/zap-dexterratingsrecord,0,1166160.story

5 http://www.ahrq.gov/research/fibroid/fibreg.htm

6 http://www.knowhivaids.org/utility_campaign.html

7 I do not want to discount the efforts of other television producers in the effort to educate viewers about HIV/AIDS. It should be noted that *The District* (CBS), *Queer as Folk* (Showtime), and *Eve* (UPN) among others have all created episodes as a part of the Viacom–Kaiser Foundation. More information can be found at http://www.knowhivaids.org/learn_tv.html#2003

8 The Writers Guild of America (WGA) program, established in 1988, is designed to provide opportunities for "ethnic minorities, women, people with disabilities, writers who are gay or lesbian, and writers who are 40 years of age or older." The program allows a production company to hire a writer at below union scale. There are limits and stipulations regarding these hires. http://www.wga.org/subpage_writingtools.aspx?id=933

9 In a personal e-mail in July 2009, Akil informed me that *Girlfriends* was cancelled after 172 episodes as a result of the 2007–2008 writers strike.

10 *Girlfriends* received one Emmy nomination in 2003 for outstanding cinematography in a multicamera comedy series.

Chapter Seven: The New Television World

1 http://www.nielsenmedia.com/DMAs.html

2 The fees paid to production studios by networks or cable outlets only cover part of the costs of producing a television show. Studios, with help from other corporations, have to cover the rest of the costs. The production studio will cover the rest of the costs and a healthy profit with a successful show in syndication.

3 Timothy Havens, "'It's still a white world out there': The interplay of culture and economics in international television trade," *Critical Studies in Media Communication,* 19, no. 4 (December 2002), 377–397.

4 Ibid.

5 The FCC was concerned by the power of companies that could control both the production and distribution of television programming and in 1970 implemented rules preventing this practice. In the face of political pressure and the arguments that these rules were outdated in the new media marketplace of new networks and cable outlets, the FCC relaxed these rules in 1991 and then eliminated them in 1995 as a result of court rulings.

6 Darnell M. Hunt, *Whose Stories Are We Telling? The 2007 Hollywood Writers Report* (Los Angeles: Writers Guild of America, west, 2007), http://www.wga.org/uploadedFiles/who_we_are/HWR07.pdf

7 Michael Schenider, "Skein Scene Hinges on a New CW Net's Exex Promise to Maintain Penchant for Diversity," *Variety,* February 23, 2006. http://www.variety.com/index.asp?layout=awardcentral&jump=news&id=naacp&articleid=VR1117938777

8 NBC established a Diversity Council in 2000 leading to internships, pipline programs for jobs, and supplier diversity initiative. NBC's efforts are cited on its web site. http://www.nbcuni.com/ About_NBC_Universal/Diversity/

9 Greg Braxton and Brian Lowry, "Small Screen, Big Picture," *Los Angeles Times* (July 23, 1999), F 1.

10 David Wild, *The Showrunners* (New York: Harper Collins, 1999), 5.

11 Michael Schenider, "Diversity directive: Touchstone, ABC, DGA tout hiring effort," *Variety,* March 30, 2004. http://www.variety.com/article/VR1117902641?categoryid=14&cs=1&nid=2616

12 Stephen McPherson, "ABC Primetime Entertainment," *The Hollywood Reporter,* November 15, 2004. http://www.hollywoodreporter.com/thr/interviews/article_display.jsp?vnu_content_id=1000719360

13 Janny Scott, "Who Gets to Tell a BlackStory?: Forum," *New York Times* (June 11, 2000), 22.

14 "That's What I'm Talking About," *TV Land,* February 2006. http://www.tvland.com/originals/twita/

15 Tim Arango, "Before Barack Obama, There Was Bill Cosby," *New York Times* (November 7, 2008). http://www.nytimes.com/2008/11/08/arts/television/08cosb.htm

16 Tina Andrews, "Tribute … and the people shall know thy name," *Written By* (August–September 2009), 11.

Bibliography

Alley, Robert S., and Irby B. Brown. *Murphy Brown: Anatomy of a Sitcom.* New York: Dell, 1990.

Andrews, Tina. "Tribute ... and the People Shall Know Thy Name." *Written By,* Aug.--Sep. 2009.

Arango, Tim. "Before Barack Obama, There Was Bill Cosby." *New York Times.* Nov. 7, 2008.

"As We Head into the Next Millennium, Shamefully Hollywood Still Looks Like Pleasantville." *Daily Variety,* Oct. 8, 1999.

Barlow, William. *Voice Over: The Making of Black Radio.* Philadelphia: Temple University Press, 1998.

Baptiste, Bala. "Vernon Winslow: The Innovative Art Teacher Whose Radio Personality, Dr. Daddy-O, Changed the Sound of New Orleans radio." Paper presented at the annual meeting of the Association for the Study of African American Life and History, Atlanta Hilton, Charlotte, NC, Oct. 2, 2007.

BBC News. "Foxx Tribute to Charles' Legacy" BBC.Com. Retrieved on Mar. 2, 2008, from http://news.bbc.co.uk/1/hi/entertainment/film/4303547.stm

Bielby, William T., and Denise D. Bielby. *Telling All Our Stories: The 1998 Hollywood Writers Report.* Los Angeles: Writers Guild of America, West, 1998.

Bogle, Donald. *Primetime Blues: African Americans on Network Television.* New York: Farrar, Straus and Giroux, 2001.

Braxton Greg and Brian Lowry. "Small Screen, Big Picture." *Los Angeles Times,* F 1. July 23, 1999.

Brodkey, Linda. "Writing Critical Ehnographic Narratives." *Anthropology & Education Quarterly,* 18, 2, (1987): 74.

Cantor, Muriel. *The Hollywood TV Producer.* New York: Basic Books, 1971.

Cantor, Muriel G., and Joel M. Cantor. *Prime-time Television: Content and Control.* Newbury Park, CA: Sage, 1992.

Dates, Jeanette L. "Commercial television." In *Split Image: Africa Americans in the Mass Media,* eds. Jeanette L. Dates and William Barlow. Washington, DC: Howard University Press, 1993, 267--328.

Davis, Ossie. "Where are the black image makers hiding?" In *Black Families and the Medium of Television,* ed. Anthony Jackson. New Haven, CT: Bush Program in Child Development & Social Policy, 1982, 61--70.

Du Bois, W. E. B. *The Souls of Black Folk.* New York: Signet, 1982.

Dyson, Michael E. "Essentialism and the complexities of racial identity." In

Multiculturalism: A Critical Reader, ed., David T. Goldberg. Cambridge: Blackwell, 1994.

Essed, Philomena. *Understanding Everyday Racism.* Newbury Park, CA: Sage, 1991.

Ettema, James, D. Charles Whitney, and Daniel Wackman, "Professional mass communicators." In *Individuals in Mass Media Organizations,* eds. James Ettema and D. Charles Whitney. Newbury Park: Sage, 1982.

Ettema, James. "The organizational context of creativity: A case study from public television." In *Individuals in Mass Media Organizations,* eds. James Ettema and D. Charles Whitney. Newbury Park, CA: Sage, 1982.

Feagin, Joe R., and Melvin P. Sikes, *Living with Racism: The Black Middle-Class Experience.* Boston: Beacon Press, 1994.

Gentles, Kamille. "The Construction of Black Female Bodies in *Amos 'n' Andy:* A case for Hybridity" p. 16, Paper presented at the annual meeting of the International Communication Association, New Orleans Sheraton, New Orleans, LA, May 2004, p. 16. Retrieved on June 28, 2008, from http://www.allacademic.com/meta/p_mla_apa_research_citation/1/1/3/2/2/p113228_index.html

Gitlin, Todd. *Inside Prime Time.* Berkeley: University of California Press, 2000.

Gray, Herman. "Television, black Americans, and the American dream." *Critical Studies in Mass Communication,* 6, (1989): 376–386.

————.*Watching Race.* Minneapolis: University of Minnesota Press, 1995.

Gross, Larry. "Out of the mainstream." In *Gender, Race and Class in Media,* eds. Gail Dines and Jean M. Humez. Thousand Oaks, CA: Sage, 1995, 61–69.

Hall, Stuart. "Cultural identity and diaspora." In *Identity, Community, Culture, Difference,* ed. Jonathan Rutherford. London: Lawrence & Wishart, 1990, 236.

————."New ethnicities." In *"Race," Culture & Difference,* eds., J. Donald and A. Rattansi. Newbury Park, CA: Sage. 1992.

————."The whites of their eyes," In *Gender, Race and Class in Media,* eds. Gail Dines and Jean M. Humez. Thousand Oaks, CA: Sage, 1995, 20.

———— . *Representation: Cultural Representations and Signifying Practices.* Thousand Oaks, CA: Sage, 1997.

Harding, Sandra. *Whose Science? Whose Knowledge?* Ithaca, NY: Cornell University Press, 1991.

Hardley Freydberg, Elizabeth. "Sapphires, spitfires, sluts, and superbitches: Aframericans and Latinas in contemporary American film." In *Critical Readings: Media and Gender,* eds. Cynthia Carter and Linda Steiner. Maidenhead, UK: Open University Press, 2004, 277.

Hass, Nancy. "A New TV Generation is Seeing Beyond Color." *New York Times,* 1, 38. Feb. 22, 1998.

Havens, Timothy. "'It's still a white world out there': The interplay of culture and economics in international television trade." *Critical Studies in Media Communication,* 19, 4, (2002): 377–397.

Hilmes, Michelle "Invisible men: Amos 'n' Andy and the roots of broadcast discourse." *Critical Studies in Mass Communication,* 10, 4, (1993): 301–321.

hooks, bell. *Black Looks: Race and Representation.* Boston: South End Press, 1992.

Hunt, Darnell P. *Channeling Blackness: Studies on Television and Race in America*. New York: Oxford University Press, 2004.

———.*The 2005 Hollywood Writers Report: Catching Up with a Changing America?* Los Angeles: Writers Guild of America, West, 2005.

———.*2009 Hollywood Writers Report*. Los Angeles: Writers Guild of America, West. http://www.wga.org/subpage_whoweare.aspx?id=922 (accessed Jan. 11, 2010).

Itzkoff, Dave. "Spinning off into Uncharted Cartoon Territory." *New York Times*, 1. Aug. 30, 2009.

Jensen, Elizabeth, Greg Braxton, and Dana Calvo "NBC, NAACP in Pact to Boost Minorities in TV Diversity." *Los Angeles Times*, F 1.: 1. Jan. 6, 2000.

Jhally, Sut, and Justin Lewis. *Enlightened Racism: The Cosby Show, Audiences and the Myth of the American Dream*. Boulder: Westview, 1992.

Johnson, Sharon S. "The Writing on the Wall." *Written By*, July, 1998.

———."True colors: TV Dramas Are Doing Better at Color-blind Casting, But Sitcoms Lag Behind." *Emmy*, Oct., 1998.

Kellner, Douglas. *Media Culture*. New York: Routledge, 1995.

Kerner Commission. *Report of the National Advisory Commission on Civil Disorders*. New York: E. P. Dutton, 1968.

Kuczynski, Alex, "Following NBC's Lead, ABC Outlines Minority Hiring Plan," *New York Times*, January 8, 2000 A, 8

Lee, Tonya "That's What I'm Talking About," *TV Land*, Feb. 2006. http://www.tvland.com/originals/twita/ (accessed February 27, 2006).

Lotz, Amanda D. "Textual (im)possibilities in the U.S. post-network era: Negotiating production and the promotion process on Lifetime's *Any Day Now*." *Critical Studies in Media Communication*, 21, 1, (2004): 22–43.

MacDonald, J. Fred. *Blacks and White TV*. Chicago: Nelson-Hall, 1992.

Mayerle, Judith. "*Roseanne*—How did you get inside my house?: A case study of a hit blue-collar situation comedy." In *Television: The Critical View*, ed. Horace Newcomb. New York: Oxford University Press, 1994, 101–116.

McKissack, Fredrick. "The Problem of Black T.V." *The Progressive*, Feb., 1997.

McNary, Dave. "Little Diversity Among Writers." *Variety*, Nov. 17, 2009.

Merritt, Bishetta D. "Illusive reflections: African American women on primetime television." In *Our Voices: Essays in Culture, Ethnicity and Communication*, eds. Alberto Gonzalez, Marsha Houston, and Victoria Chen. Los Angeles: Roxbury, 1994, 48–53.

Moss, Robert F. "The Shrinking Life Span of the Black Sitcom." *New York Times*, 19, 35. Feb. 25, 2001.

Newcomb, Horace, and Robert S. Alley. *The Producer's Medium*. London: Oxford University Press, 1983.

Nichols, Nichelle. *Beyond Uhura: Star Trek and Other Memories*. New York: Putnam Pub Group, 1994.

"Out of focus: Out of sync take 4," NAACP Report, Dec., 2008. http://www.naacp.org/news/press/2008-12-18/NAACP_OFOS_Take4.pdf (accessed January 4, 2010).

Reeves, Jimmie L., and Richard Campbell, "Misplacing *Frank's Place*: Do You Know What It Means to Miss New Orleans?" *Television Quarterly*, 24, 1, (1989): 48.

Rhodes, Jane. "The visibility of race and media history." *Critical Studies in Mass Communication*, 10, 2, (1993): 184–189.

Riggs, Marlon. *Color Adjustment*. VHS. Directed by Marlon Riggs. San Francisco: Resolution Inc. California Newsreel, 1991.

Rosenberg, Howard. "The Invisible Man, Alive and Well." *Los Angeles Times*, F 1. July 25, 1999.

Scarbrough, Marsha. "Any Way Now: Where Diversity Is a Reality." *Written By*, Sep., 2000a. http://www.wga.org/WrittenBy/index.html (accessed March 12, 2004).

———."Writing with Jive: Forget Harvard Law. Study *Vibe* Magazine," *Written By*, Sep., 2000a. http://www.wga.org/WrittenBy/index.html (accessed March 12, 2004).

Schiller, Herbert. *Information Inequality*. New York: Routledge, 1996.

Schneider, Michael, and Peter Bernstein. "NAACP, NBC Reach Pact ABC Expected to Follow Suit." *Variety*, 1. Jan. 6, 2000.

Schneider, Michael. "Diversity Directive: Touchstone, ABC, DGA Tout Hiring Effort." *Variety*, Mar. 30, 2004.

———."Skein Scene Hinges on a New CW Net's Exec Promise to Maintain Penchant for Diversity." *Variety*, Feb. 23, 2006.

Scott, Janny. "Who Gets to Tell a Black Story: Forum." *New York Times*, 1, 22. June 11, 2000.

Stam, Robert, and Ella Shohat. "Contested histories: Eurocentrism, multiculturalism, and the media," In *Multiculturalism: A Critical Reader*, ed. David Theo Goldberg. Cambridge: Blackwell, 1994.

Stengold, James "A Racial Divide Widens on Network TV." *New York Times*. Dec. 29, 1998.

Thompson, Robert J., and Gary Burns. *Making Television: Authorship and the Production Process*. New York: Praeger, 1990.

Times, Correspondents of the *New York Times. How Race Is Lived in America: Pulling Together, Pulling Apart.* 2nd reprint ed. New York: Times Books, 2002.

Turow, Joseph. *Learning to Portray Power: The Socialization of Creators in Mass Media Organizations*. Beverly Hills, CA: Sage, 1985.

Wallace, Marcia. "Modernism, postmodernism and the problem of the visual in Afro-American culture." In *Out There: Marginalization and Contemporary Cultures*, eds. Russell Ferguson, Trinh T. Minh-Ha, and Martha Gever. New York: The New Museum of Contemporary Art, 1990, 19–36.

Weinraub, Bernard. "Stung by Criticism of Fall Shows TV Networks Add Minority Roles." *New York Times*, 1, 14. 1. Sep. 20, 1999.

West, Cornell. "The new cultural politics of difference," In *Out There: Marginalization and Contemporary Cultures*, eds. Russell Ferguson, Trinh T. Minh-Ha, and Martha Gever. New York: The New Museum of Contemporary Art, 1990, 27.

Wild, David. *The Showrunners*. New York: Harper Collins, 1999.

Wyatt, Edward. "No Smooth Ride on TV Networks' Road to Diversity." *New York*

Times, 1. Mar. 17, 2009.

Zook, Kristal Brent. *Color by Fox: The Fox Network and the Revolution in Black Television.* New York: Oxford University Press, 1999.

Index of Television Shows

Index